D0903628

A Mountain Too Far

A Father's Search for Meaning
In the Climbing Death of His Son

Karl H. Purnell

New Horizon Press
Far Hills, New Jersey

Requests for permission should be addressed to:
New Horizon Press
P.O. Box 669
Far Hills, NJ 07931

Purnell, Karl H.
A Mountain Too Far: A Father's Search for Meaning in the Climbing Death of His Son

Interior Design: Susan M. Sanderson

Library of Congress Control Number: 00-132565

ISBN: 0-88282-204-7
New Horizon Press

Manufactured in the U.S.A.

2005 2004 2003 2002 2001 / 5 4 3 2 1

Dedication

This book is dedicated to Justin, my son, Alexandra, my daughter, and to Melanie Bell without whose constant encouragement and understanding this book could not have been written.

Author's Note

This story is based on my actual experiences and reflects my perception of the past, present and future. The personalities, events, actions and conversations portrayed within the story have been reconstructed from my memory and the memories of participants. I have changed the names of two individuals in an effort to safeguard their privacy.

Table of Contents

Acknowledgments

There are so many persons who have helped in the formation of this book that it's impossible to list each contributor. Yet, several friends who have played important roles in suggesting ideas, reading early manuscripts and being supportive of this project need to be mentioned.

One of the problems I constantly faced was both denial of the accident and the collateral emotions that go with the loss of a son. Often, I would simply avoid writing about certain details of what happened or omit my emotional reactions to some of the dramatic events that occurred during the journey. To do this was unfair to the eventual readers. Consequently, help from friends was needed to stay on course.

As we flew over the Himalayas in a small plane, Danielle Perron asked if she could read what I was writing. Since I had no printouts, I handed my laptop to her and she scrolled through an early and incomplete draft. Her enthusiasm and encouragement at that point was truly helpful and when she read the first full draft and made excellent suggestions several months later, I got a sense of what still remained to be done.

Tennis friends have always been a mainstay of my life. My sometimes doubles partner and a literary agent, Jacques de Spoelberch, was both encouraging and firm about what needed to be done to make this book a viable project. While playing in California, I met Carey McLehran who was running the tennis pro shop. She offered to do a reading and consequently made a series of suggestions which forced me to look carefully at my own emotions.

My long-time friend from Vietnam correspondent days, Jurate Kazickas was not only consistently supportive of the entire project, but insisted I climb and hike in the Tetons while staying as a guest at the Jackson Hole ranch owned by her and her husband, Roger Altman. While I was there, another houseguest, Ellen Levine, editor-in-chief of *Good Housekeeping,* made excellent suggestions about the placement of certain material which I followed to the letter.

Others, like Dr. Harry Garvin, former chairman of the Bucknell University Department of English, and his colleague, Dr. John Murphy, were tough but helpful in making suggestions. Wendy Cook's enthusiasm and editorial comments were a consistent inspiration. I'm also thankful for the help of Christopher's mother and my former wife, Janey Zietlow, who generously supplied letters, advice and background information needed for this book.

An invitation from Dr. Mary Cablx to join her in Yosemite for several days of climbing in the valley was a critical step in my understanding of the commitment which motivates those who seek satisfaction on a big wall or a high altitude mountain.

In her usual "how dare you use incorrect English" tone which I have endured for many decades, my ninety-seven-year-old mother, Marie, pointed out mistakes which all of us had missed after we thought the book had achieved grammatical perfection.

There were many others and to each of those people around the world who contributed so generously to the completion of this project, I extend my deepest appreciation.

Introduction

The Sherpa guide Teng Zing (Norgay) who climbed with Sir Edmund Hillary on the first ascent of Mt. Everest wrote in his memoirs that "A book is, I think, the story of a man's life. Here is my story. Here is myself." I have found his words to be true. Writing, for me, has always been a form of therapy and when I decided to retrace the life of my son Christopher, who had died in a mountain-climbing accident, in order to find out more about his life and understand him better, it was only natural that I would write about the experience as a way of dealing with the grief of such a catastrophic loss. Originally, I planned to retrace the climbs which Chris felt gave his life both purpose and passion and to tell the story of what it was like to bring Chris up and how our relationship developed over the years. As the book began to evolve and take form, however, it became apparent that his own story, as he himself wrote it, which I took along on my journey was almost like having a part of Chris with me. Along the way his own insights were added to mine and I found his more interesting. In the long report written about his year spent in Nepal studying Buddhist monasteries, in a detailed chronicle of his solo climb of Yosemite's El Capitan, in an opinionated article recommending a boycott of Chinese goods and in his diaries, I discovered the written testimony of someone who had lived with fervor and commitment.

During a year of sorrow, joy and discovery in which I tried to learn more about the life and adventures which Chris had undertaken, from climbing the French Alps to

Yosemite National Park in California and the Himalayas of Nepal, I was determined to be realistic and to avoid, at all costs, any idealization or exaggeration of who he really was or what he accomplished. After all, though I loved him mightily, Chris was not an easy person to live with and he had been a difficult child to raise. Furthermore, he would be the first to disparage a description portraying him as anything but an average young man searching for definition and purpose in life. I would have to be careful about glorifying someone whose own self-expressed modesty was uncompromising. As he wrote in his diary, which I found in his truck:

> Who is Chris Purnell? You're probably wondering what rad walls has he done? Well, I'm just one more wall climber, of which there seem to be so many these days. An average wall climber, bonded with a growing number of folks who have found adventure, terror, hard work and eventual reward, in short, purpose from the captivating pastime of climbing walls. That purpose so frequently lacking from real life, school, jobs and the like defines wall climbing. It's what separates it from the more traditional sports.

Yet in trying to find out who he was, I discovered by the end of my journey, not just a son I hardly knew, but a young man who lived his life to the fullest in a variety of ways. Chris, I learned, was unwilling to accept what nineteenth century philosopher and nature lover, Henry David Thoreau, called "a life of quiet desperation."

For Chris's obituary published in *Climbing Magazine*, a former climbing partner submitted these words:

Christopher Purnell, 28, on December 31 in Kicking Horse Canyon, Kootona National Park, British Columbia. Chris fell 1,000 feet when an ice column he was standing near collapsed. He was on the last day of a four-month road trip during which his climbs included The South Seas (A5) start to the Pacific Ocean Wall on El Capitan and the Sea of Vapors (WI7) in Banff.

A native of State College, Pennsylvania, Chris had traveled the world, living in Botswana and France and spending a year researching a book on architecture and language in Nepal. He earned a master's degree in geography from Oregon State University and worked as a vegetation modeler for the U.S. Forest Service.

Chris had climbed widely, but was especially fond of Yosemite. He spent two summers working for Search and Rescue and climbed El Capitan seven times, including solos of increasing difficulty on Zodiac (A3) and Zenyatta Mountain (A5). The former was his second big wall, the latter was one of the fastest solos.

Chris was also an avid mountain biker. After I struggled to keep up with him on a grueling training ride in the Oregon Coast Range, he told me, "All that's holding you back is pain and pain is bullshit." It was how he lived his life.

Tom Broxon

In addition to my efforts to comprehend the life path Chris was on, an unexpected development took place. While trying to discover who my son was, I found myself becoming more and more engaged in a journey to find out who I was. The answer to this most difficult of all questions began to surface only after I spent a considerable amount of time in the weeks following Chris's death asking the wrong questions and succumbing to unproductive emotions such as anger and guilt. Eventually, after a year of traveling, searching and learning to climb mountains he had conquered, an understanding of what really happened began to take place. I finally achieved a certain peace of mind as well as an appreciation for the son to whom I now felt so close. For this, I am eternally grateful to my son whose life, though short, has enabled his father to realize the importance of seeking meaning and understanding in his own life which has already passed the halfway mark. Thus, if this is Chris's book and the story of his journey, I suppose it is also mine. Even more, it's our story, the story of a father and son who have taught each other transcendent lessons about creating meaningful lives.

1

chapter

To the Woods, To the Mountains

For the thing which I greatly feared is come upon me and that which I was afraid of is come to me.

Job 3:25

A cold wind is blowing across the Connecticut shoreline on this rainy New Year's Day. As drops of water splatter against the windows of my study and trickle slowly down the glistening panes, I lean back in my leather reading chair and watch the dim light of late afternoon disappear against the dark waters of Long Island Sound.

I wonder if it's raining in Portland. Chris should be there by now. I assume that he's finished with a holiday ice climbing expedition in Banff National Park, and that he's even completed the long drive from Canada to Oregon in time to start his new job, which was slated to begin right after New Year's Day, January 2, 1997.

Throughout the holidays, I tried not to think about him and what he was doing. A trip to North Carolina, where I spent Christmas with his younger brother, Justin, had helped to distract me from the worry which always consumed me when I knew Chris was mountain climbing. Now I'm home again and relieved to think that my twenty-eight-year-old son is safely back in his new apartment and getting ready for work as a computer specialist analyzing satellite data for the United States Forestry Department.

He has lobbied long and hard for special conditions at this new job and I know that he intends it to be a stepping stone to the kind of life he is determined to live. During a phone conversation I had with him before Christmas, he said that they would be allowing him to work several months in succession and then take a few months off. He plans to use these breaks for climbing and also to explore alternative career possibilities. The importance of leading a meaningful existence is critical to him. It is no accident that Chris often refers to Henry David Thoreau's words:

> I went to the woods because I wished to live deliberately, to front only the essential facts of life, and see if I could not learn what it had to teach and not, when I come to die, discover that I had not lived.

I suspect that Chris has turned to climbing mountains for the same reason Thoreau went to the woods, although this is an issue we rarely discuss. I never like to be reminded of his climbing exploits which I fear, so we talk about other things, like his work, his girlfriend, the confusion he is feeling about his career and his determination to somehow balance the contradiction of having a successful job while living a simple and harmonious existence devoid of unnecessary possessions.

Like any close friends, we also discuss what I'm doing, how I feel about life and what my own aspirations are. Chris is a perceptive and sympathetic listener. He knows me better than anyone I have ever met.

So now, with darkness closing in and the rain still drumming against the roof, I'm wishing that I had his new phone number so I could call and talk to him. However, I don't know if he has a phone yet or even where he's living. He might be staying with friends. I realize the only way I can talk to him this afternoon is if he calls me.

His Christmas letter is somewhere on my desk. I shuffle through some papers and begin to read it again:

> I have to go back to work soon. My new job will start around Jan. 6. I think I'm looking forward to it, at least to the change of scenery that Portland will provide. But my climbing isn't over just yet. In several days, I'm going up to Banff National Park in the Canadian Rockies by Lake Louise. There, friends and I will split a motel room or something and then spend two weeks climbing the ice of the plentiful frozen waterfalls in the area. I'm psyched and scared.
>
> One of the shortcomings of living as I have been is the infrequent contact with family and old friends. I think about you all often and hope life is treating you well. I miss you all. Peace, love, regards. Happy Holidays. Chris

Suddenly, my reading is interrupted by the shrill clatter of the white phone sitting on my book-cluttered desk. I pick up the receiver hoping that it's Chris calling me.

It isn't.

Christopher's mother is calling from her home in North Carolina. Instantly, I'm wary. Our divorce took place more than two decades ago. Only the most serious emergency could bring a telephone call from my former wife, and mother of my three children. It's the dreaded message that threatens all parents from the moment their child is born.

"Something terrible has happened," Janey announces. Then she says the word "Christopher" and instantly I know she's calling with bad news. The human brain is still superior to the fastest microchip and in that split second between hearing my son's name and the rest of the sentence, my decade-long fear of his love for climbing mountains flashes through my consciousness.

The blunt announcement that would instantly change my life and forever justify years of worry and concern for his safety filters through the phone.

"Christopher is dead!" she exclaims.

"No!" I scream into the phone. "No!"

"The park police called from Banff where he was ice climbing," Janey says. "There was an accident."

"No! He phoned me before Christmas and said he would be back at his new job by now," I interrupt in a desperate effort to stanch the bad news by silencing the messenger. Then the fateful words "avalanche," "hospital," "three hours of emergency surgery" sear through my brain. Again, I shout, "No!"

As Janey continues, a slim thread of denial, even hope, suddenly creeps through my dazed thoughts. She has to be wrong. This could not have happened to our twenty-eight-year-old son. Chris is a superbly conditioned athlete who climbs with care and intelligence as well as courage. He has already spent a year in the Himalayas and a year in the French Alps while he was still in school. He has reached the summit of America's highest and most difficult mountains, including Mt. McKinley and Yosemite's El Capitan.

Janey's voice intrudes upon my stubborn refusal to accept her announcement. "He's been taken to a funeral home in British Columbia."

The words "funeral home" ricochet through my mind. Janey is describing an event that really did happen. There's no mistake. Chris is gone forever.

Instead of receiving a New Year's phone call from my fun-loving, adventurous son and enjoying a long conversation with him this afternoon, I would now have to make plane reservations for a trip to Canada in order to undertake the grim job of packing up his belongings, disposing of his small pickup truck, making arrangements for a cremation and deciding with his mother how we should conduct a memorial service.

After assuring Janey that I will call her back in the morning, I put down the phone and gaze at the dreary downpour outside the window. "Chris, why did you have to do this to me?" I shout angrily. Then, stung by the selfishness of this thought, I open the door and step outside into the freezing rain as if the cold wetness will shock not only my body, but my precept of reality.

As the icy drops of water mix with the warm tears on my face, I realize the enormity of my mistake in thinking this would never happen. In recent months, I had come to accept the false premise that Chris would be protected from a climbing catastrophe, because fatal accidents happen only to other people. Tragedies, I assumed, strike only those unfortunate or unskilled climbers one sees on television or reads about in the newspapers. Hope, plus the absence of any other comforting choice, had convinced me that avalanches, storms or falling rocks bring death to unknown and distant men and women who simply run out of luck. I gradually had come to believe in a personal immunity from the kinds of disasters and losses that happen so unexpectedly and undeservingly to other fathers and mothers. This, of course, I know now was a huge mistake. Now, I am thrust face to face with the reality that no parent is immune from this kind of loss.

Returning to the warmth of the house, I'm startled by the phone ringing again. Hope is rekindled. Perhaps it is all a mistake and Janey is calling back to say that it wasn't Chris but someone else who died in the avalanche. Maybe an error in identification has been made. I pick up the receiver and respond to the sympathetic and consoling voice of a good friend who has already heard what happened. It's the first of many calls I'll receive during the next few days. They're difficult for me as well as the callers. And yet they help...a little bit although I don't know exactly how to react.

There are so many important events in our lives for which we have no preparation, no training, no knowledge. How does one choose a lifetime career? What kind of man or woman makes the best husband or wife? How do we know if we've fallen in love for the right reasons or if we're in love at all? Which are the best rules for bringing up children? Make a mistake on any one of these and your whole life can be changed, perhaps even ruined. Yet, no required curriculum, no 101 survey courses ever covered those topics during my days in college and I don't think they do now. Psychologists and social researchers know a lot about these issues, but rarely are they taught either in school or at home. We're pretty much left on our own to figure out the solutions as best we can to some of the most basic problems of life. Now the question arises: what does a man like me do about the sudden loss of a child? Suddenly, I'm faced with Chris's fatal fall from the side of a mountain and I have no idea what to think or what to do. I was never taught how to deal with the early and unexpected death of a child. Should I be angry or bitter? Who's to blame for this? Is it my fault? If so, what did I do wrong? These kinds of questions gather momentum, but no answers follow. After all, this wasn't supposed to happen.

It occurs to me that I do not know how to grieve for my son. I retreat to the solitude of my study and spend the rest of the long night wishing it would all go away, wishing that I could awaken from this nightmare.

The following two days pass slowly in a painful daze of tears, denial, anger and guilt as I make plans for the trip to Canada where Chris made his last climb.

Still numb, I take the train to New York and catch a bus to Kennedy Airport where I've booked a flight to Calgary, Alberta. There I'll meet my former wife and we'll rent a car for the one hour drive to Banff National Park. Fortunately, our second son, Justin, will also join us.

Soon I'm on the plane, filled with dread toward this unwanted mission. Yet, as the aircraft gains altitude and starts to drone across the country, I begin to find some comfort in recalling what it was like to spend time with Chris when he was a small child and how proud I was of him as he grew older and developed into someone I admired and loved so completely.

There was no doubt that he made unusual choices. His contrarian tendencies were evident at an early age.

Once, when he was six years old, I took Chris ice skating at Rockefeller Center in New York City. He was a pretty good skater by then and he could hardly wait for me to lace up his skates that cold December afternoon. As he pushed out onto the ice, I retreated to a small restaurant next to the rink. However, I had no more taken a seat when I looked out the window and saw Chris skating clockwise directly into the oncoming crowd, almost knocking down several people who failed to get out of his way. Quickly, I raced outside and stepped onto the ice.

Before I could say a word, he glided up to me and shouted: "Papa, these people are all skating the wrong way."

The incident became a long-playing joke with us and through the years, whenever Chris complained unjustifiably about the actions of other people, I would remind him of the incident at Rockefeller Center: "Well, Chris, they must all be skating the wrong way." My thoughts turn to how he liked to race mountain bikes on the weekends and go on climbing expeditions with his old Nissan pickup truck whenever he could get time off from his job. How he wanted to live with a minimum of material possessions.

We are landing at Salt Lake City. There I board a connecting flight to Calgary. On the flight I'm seated next to a plump, middle-aged woman in jeans with short curls of gray hair covering her head like a thick wool hat. She immediately begins chatting about her planned visit to a newly married daughter in Canada.

She goes on to say her daughter lives in this small town outside of Calgary where her husband claims to be looking for work. "But they've been there for almost two years and he still doesn't have a job," she observes with obvious disdain for her son-in-law. I listen for a while as she continues talking, not sure whether to feel sorry for her or for the poor guy who would have to suffer this woman's presence during the next two weeks.

Suddenly, she turns to me. "What brings you to Canada? Business or pleasure?"

The question is like a sharp slap across the face. For the first time since hearing about the accident, I'm faced with the prospect of explaining to a stranger what happened to Chris. I find I'm not ready for that. Denial runs deep. The words "killed" or "died" are impossible for me to say. I put off answering.

"Neither one really. I...ah...I...have to meet some people in Calgary," I stammer.

"Oh, a big secret, huh?" she asks in a tone that suggests I must be on some kind of illicit mission.

"No. Not that. It's...ah...," I begin again, trying to determine if I should say I'm on a skiing trip and be done with it.

"Nobody goes all the way to Calgary in the middle of the winter unless they have a pretty good reason," she interrupts in an authoritative, no-disagreement tone of voice that convinces me to pity the son-in-law who is going to have to endure her visit.

I hit on an answer that is not a lie. "I have to meet with my ex-wife," I say.

She nods with understanding. "Oh, one of them meetings, huh?"

Fortunately, the stewardess arrives with an offer of various drinks and because my answers are so curt the woman figures I'm not worth any more conversation. She orders a Coke, gulps it down and then leans back against the headrest and goes to sleep. I know she must think I'm rude, but I haven't the energy for courtesy. All I can think of is my son. At last I'm free to escape into the sea of memories which is awaiting me. Waves of conversation fill my head, particularly the ones about the dangers of climbing Chris and I had when he was still in college.

One took place at the end of a cold spring day in early March after Chris finally persuaded me to take a rock climbing lesson when he was a sophomore at Penn State University.

On that windy, freezing morning, I climbed the steps to his disheveled dormitory room where I helped him pack his climbing gear and carry it to my car. Soon we were driving through the bleak central Pennsylvania countryside to a nearby stone quarry, laughing and joking about my inability to believe anyone could enjoy hanging from a limestone wall on such a miserable day.

"I've been looking forward to this for a long time. This is really going to be a lot of fun," I joked sarcastically as we unloaded his equipment from the car.

Chris laughed. "Now just be patient. You'll like this once we're there and you get the feeling of what rock climbing is all about," he promised.

"Maybe I can stay overnight in your room, if you can clear a space for me and we can come back tomorrow," I answered.

Chris parried my thrust at the condition of his room by taking a shot at my age. "That would be great, Papa, if you're not too tired and sore from getting a little exercise."

The score was even. By the time we reached the bottom of the quarry wall, we were both talking and laughing in an easy camaraderie that only the closest of friends can achieve.

After fitting me with a waist harness, Chris quickly climbed to the summit of the seventy-five-foot wall and anchored the rope around a tree growing on the top. Then he threw the rope over the cliff and rappelled down the wall with the prideful skill of a son showing off to a father who, despite a reluctance to admit it, could not avoid being impressed.

"Now, tighten this waist harness and I'll hook you up to the belay. Then you can start up and even if you slip, I can brake the rope and keep you from falling," he instructed.

I did what I was told and soon I was edging my way up the cold limestone as the wind howled along the top of the cliff. After a few minutes of total discomfort during which I managed to scrape a leg and almost dislocate two fingers while pulling myself upwards on a small protrusion of stone, I called to Chris who was holding the rope at the bottom: "Hey, Chris, this is really terrific. How come you never told me how much fun rock climbing can be?"

I could hear him forcing a laugh, although I suspect that he was also shaking his head in disapproval of a father who could not get "psyched" over the thrills of crawling up a jagged limestone cliff on a cold, blustery day.

We climbed for several hours and when it was finally time to gather up the equipment and head for home I invited Chris to dinner at The Tavern, a nice restaurant in downtown State College where we could have some wine, a hearty meal and get warm. "Chris, I want to have a serious talk with you," I said after we ordered dinner.

He knew what was coming. "About climbing?" he asked.

"Yes. I know you're good at it and I realize you try to climb safely, but it's still dangerous. One small quirk of fate like a falling rock, a wrong step or even a sudden storm can be fatal. Almost any little mistake that happens in a situation like that can lead to disaster. There are so many ways you can be hurt," I said.

"Everything is dangerous. It's dangerous to drive a car," he replied.

"Yes, but we need to do that. We don't need to climb mountains," I answered.

"Do you know how much climbing means to me?" he asked.

"Do you know how much you mean to me?" I persisted.

"But it's my life," he said.

I tried to convince him it was also mine and everyone else's who loved him. He would not agree and I soon realized there was nothing I could say that would make him quit climbing mountains. I tried to move the conversation into a lighter vein by telling him I didn't want to spend the rest of my life wheeling him in and out of men's rooms or feeding him baby food from a jar. We both laughed and by the time the soup arrived we had switched the conversation to his plans for spending his junior year abroad.

I flash to the present moment thinking now the price is being exacted for merely holding such a prideful conversation. As the plane drones on toward Canada, guilt washes over me and I wish I had done more than just talk that evening. The problem is, I think, *I don't know what more I could have done, what could have been*. And then as the past once again pushes the present aside I return to my memories.

2

chapter

Indestructible Bonds

No man can possibly know what life means, what the world means, what anything means, until he has a child and loves it. And then, the whole universe changes and nothing will ever again seem exactly as it seemed before.

Lafacadio Hearn

Chris once said that Yosemite National Park, where he spent so much time rock climbing, was a metaphor for his life.

During the past two million years, the rock walls of Yosemite have been created by the harsh grinding of giant icebergs, the slashing power of rivers and the thundering landslides that could reshape the entire valley in a few minutes. Perhaps Chris saw himself as molded by a similar domestic turbulence and upheaval during his own youth.

I suspect that he compared his own development and upbringing with that of the valley.

He was born in August, 1968 in Lewisburg, a small town in central Pennsylvania where his paternal grandfather had been a well-known country doctor and his maternal grandfather was an eminent psychologist and vice president of Pennsylvania State University in nearby State College. By the time Chris was born and joined his sister, Alexandra, at our home near the Bucknell University campus, I was the former editor and owner of the local weekly newspaper, had already served four years as an elected representative in the Pennsylvania Legislature and worked for two years in Vietnam as a war correspondent. His mother had worked for the Council of Voluntary Agencies during a year when we both lived in Saigon.

To all appearances, Chris was born into a stable, middle-class family where a wonderful childhood among adoring parents and an extended family of many relatives would be followed by good schools and a fine career. Like his older sister, Alexandra, and his younger brother, Justin, Chris should have enjoyed a supportive and secure upbringing.

However, this promise of a happy family life never materialized. It could be argued that any American child born in the late 1960s was destined for a difficult upbringing. Not only was the Vietnam War tearing the country apart, it was putting huge pressures on men and women like Janey and me. We felt compelled to reject the traditional values of American culture and government of which we had been such an integral part. In our case, the conflict was even more intense since we had been part of the electoral process within the Republican Party and also subject to the realities of war in Vietnam.

By the time Chris was a year old, his mother and I were finding it difficult to settle down to the traditional life of Lewisburg which we had enjoyed prior to living in

Vietnam. Although I was offered the Republican Party's nomination for a return to the state legislature without the necessity of a hard campaign, the idea of serving in a government in which the lies of the Vietnam War were being perpetrated seemed to me totally immoral and unacceptable.

We purchased a beautiful stone farmhouse near our previous residence and moved to the countryside where, like so many other disillusioned members of our generation, we tried to find meaning and happiness through farming. When Chris was a year old, we even made a return trip to Nepal where we had visited two years earlier.

From the day he was born, Chris was never an easy child to deal with and he proved himself to be demanding and cranky on this trip. Yet, his enthusiasm, energy and love of laughter would always make up for the hard times, even as a one-year-old. One of his friends would later write: "I'll never forget his smile and his gentle laughter. He had a passion for the outdoors that few of us will ever be able to match."

Traveling in a country like Nepal where few modern amenities exist, camping in native huts and handling sightseeing all day with two small children offers ample opportunity for fathers and mothers to get to know their offspring. Though Chris's temper was short because of the strange places and food, we all got along well, and if Chris was not old enough to remember this first foray into the foothills of the Himalayas, he would hear enough about it in future years to think of Nepal as a familiar land. Twenty years later, in fact, he would return there to complete his junior year abroad. It was there he developed a love for high altitude mountain climbing.

We returned from Nepal, via a quick visit to Cambodia to an America that was falling apart over the continued escalation of the Vietnam War. Another son, Justin, arrived that spring and six months later, Janey announced that she wanted out of the marriage because irreconcilable differences had arisen between us. She soon formed a new relationship with a man whom she eventually married. Together, they moved to North Carolina.

I suspect that my own frustration over the derailment of a successful career in politics and journalism, plus the inability to focus on an acceptable alternative for supporting a large family, created tensions that were obviously difficult for any wife to deal with. The war took its toll on all of us and, like so many others, we paid a heavy price for our involvement in those revolutionary times.

Despite what I thought was our original agreement that the two older children would stay with me, a bitter custody battle eventually took place in which the judge automatically awarded custody to the children's mother. Unwilling to accept this verdict, I picked the children up during a school day, drove them to Philadelphia and threatened to take all of them to Canada unless we worked out a plan in which I could continue to play a meaningful role as the father in my children's lives. A compromise was worked out in which Chris and Alexandra would stay with me and Justin would stay with his mother. This arrangement was flexible, however, particularly during the period when Chris and I lived in New York City, and during a two-year period when all three children joined Janey and her husband in Africa.

The heaviest burden of all this chaos seemed to fall hardest on Chris and for the rest of his life he was torn by the divisiveness of his family situation. Even on his last Christmas, he decided to go ice climbing in Canada rather than face the turmoil of having to spend the holidays jockeying between two families living three hundred miles apart. Two-turkey-dinner Thanksgivings became our children's birthright and the stability of a happy, intact family would constitute a world they would never know.

If it's difficult to be a single father, it's got to be even harder to be the child of one. While attitudes are changing today, at that time fathers were not highly thought of in our society. In fact, their reputations were usually negative ones. While my children were growing up, fathers were rarely treated positively in American fiction or drama and were of little concern to those writing about family relationships. Library shelves still are filled with books on mother-daughter relationships, but only a handful of writers have made the effort to examine the role of fathers and sons. Even worse, the literature on family relationships frequently focuses on the absent father, the drunken father or the philandering father. This stereotype is so pervasive that I suspect it actually provides a negative role model which encourages aberrant behavior on the part of some fathers. "Oh well...that's the way dads are" becomes an excuse for opting out of the fathering responsibility with the consequence that one of life's great experiences is lost.

When Chris was six years old, I ran into this idea of father as the bad guy and it was a devastating experience. In the fall of 1974, he and I went to live in a small, one-bedroom apartment in New York on Ninety-first Street and Third Avenue while Alexandra and Justin remained with their mother who had relocated to Washington, D.C. Chris and I moved in on a rainy Saturday morning, both of us lifting boxes and hauling mattresses up the three flights of stairs. It was fun and Chris was very excited about the two of us sharing an apartment in this high-energy city. He could hardly wait to go off to the park and then, on Monday morning, begin his first day in a school three blocks uptown at Ninety-fourth Street.

An attractive young woman with carefully coifed blonde hair, who introduced herself as Barbara, was leaving as we moved in. She had taken a loft downtown and we helped her carry a few remaining boxes to a car she had rented for the day. I suggested that perhaps she might like to have a cup of coffee before going to her loft.

Barbara shook her head with disapproval. "I don't like what you're doing here," she said bluntly.

Surprised, I asked why.

"That young boy should be with his mother," she replied with unconcealed outrage. It was plain that in her opinion, only a woman could really bring up a child properly.

I merely nodded and helped her into the car, thinking that if I were Chris's mother just moving into this apartment, Barbara would be congratulating me on my courageous decision to care for the young boy alone.

For Chris and me, the day-to-day reality of living together was a stimulating situation and I turned to my new role as a single parent with the enthusiasm of the newly converted. Not only was I determined to perform the functions of a caretaker, I would attempt to accomplish what so many mothers do. I would make parenting a major obligation. Being the father of a small boy would become the focus of my daily life, my *raison d'être*.

Bringing up a six-year-old boy as a single parent in New York City produced a series of wonderful adventures. One of the first places we went to visit after moving into the apartment was the Guggenheim Museum on Fifth Avenue with its winding ramp. As we started to walk up and view the pictures, I suggested to Chris that he should bring roller skates next time, so he could coast down the spiral ramp and look at the paintings on the wall at the same time. The idea enchanted him. From then on he loved going to the Guggenheim. During this time, he became fascinated with the work of M.C. Escher and spent hours trying to figure out how the famous architect and artist had drawn his angles.

The natural props for imaginative play situations are unlimited in the Big Apple. Among our favorites were the cement trucks decorated with blue, white and purple circles that looked like balloons. Often we would see one of these trucks on Ninetieth street. Then, after a ten minute subway ride downtown, we would see another one in Greenwich Village.

"Look Chris, there's that truck. How did it get downtown so quickly?" I asked. It never occurred to him that there was a fleet of those trucks. Instead we tried to figure out how a truck could be so fast. Did it fly? Did it burrow underground and race us downtown? We spent hours imagining how that truck could be so speedy.

Another favorite game we loved to play was Director of Fire Trucks. It seems as though there is always a conflagration taking place somewhere in New York City, with fire trucks wailing their way around the crowded streets like screaming monsters. One morning as we were walking to Central Park, I heard a fire truck coming up Madison Avenue. I also saw smoke coming from a building in the middle of a side street.

"Chris! Look...there's the fire!" I called. He saw the smoke and quickly asked what we should do. "Go to the corner and signal the fire truck to turn," I replied.

Chris immediately ran to the corner and as the gleaming red fire truck approached with sirens wailing, he shouted and signaled for it to turn. Sure enough, the huge fire truck turned sharply onto the side street in accordance with his directions and raced toward the fire.

"Chris, you did it. You made the fire truck turn. You probably saved all those people," I shouted. Unaware that the driver already knew the address of the fire, Chris was thrilled that he had directed the truck to the fire. After that, whenever he heard a fire truck, he considered it his responsibility to help the engine arrive at the right address.

A critic might suggest that I was teaching deception to my son or that I was making a fool of him. On the other hand, I felt that we were playing creative games in which his opinion and his contributions were important. Later, as he learned what was really happening, he saw the humor in it all and it became something we laughed and joked about for years. In fact, there were many other incidents that happened that year which became personal jokes between us.

We indulged in a lot of imaginative games and creative play which helped us to learn a great deal about each other. They also allowed Chris to develop an engaging sense of humor that would make laughter an integral part of his personality.

In our small household we had a rule that reading a book was a sacred ritual which nothing could disturb. If he was reading, I never asked him to do anything else. The dishes could go unwashed, his bed unmade and all appointments postponed in favor of reading. One evening when I wanted him to help me carry some laundry downstairs to the laundromat, he quickly ran to the bookshelf and picked up a book by Dr. Seuss. "I can't, I'm reading," he said.

"Oh sorry," I apologized. "I'll take care of the laundry. I wouldn't think of bothering you."

Never again did he purposely use the reading excuse to get out of work.

Although he was energetic and prone to laughter, Chris also possessed a difficult side to his personality that could be trying to the people around him. After I went to a great deal of trouble to arrange cello lessons for him when he was eight, I had to stop them because he verbally abused the teacher whenever the notes were too difficult. A kindly doctor who was giving him shots suddenly found himself being kicked on the shins and attacked by his nine-year-old patient who wanted no part of his needles.

When he was in his late twenties, Chris became furious with a friend who insisted on sending him to the hospital when Chris was sick. As another friend, Dan Whaley, later recalled in his diary of their days together in Nepal, Chris had a way of annoying acquaintances and losing some friends through his stubbornness: "A lot of the people here have problems with him to some extent because he can be kind of insensitive and callous even to the point of being amazingly rude...he has a hard time mellowing out and rapping with people, so sometimes he can create a tension in a room that turns others off. Through some stroke of luck I managed to realize that underneath he is a really fine person and I hope our friendship stays off the rocks."

One of Chris's favorite pastimes as a young boy was to listen to me tell him stories. Among these was the morality tale of a man who went looking for mushrooms. It was a story my mother had told me and her parents had told her: All night long, the mushroom hunter searched the hills and valleys looking for mushrooms. When dawn finally arrived, he returned tired and discouraged to his small cottage next to the woods and there, growing in his back yard, were dozens of mushrooms.

Another plot with many variations he liked was one I made up. It was the story of a young boy named Chris who wanted to compete against the famous stuntman, Evel Kneivel, in a jump-off at the Grand Canyon. The story would usually end with the small boy overcoming difficult odds to win the event as the crowd clapped and cheered,

"Hurrah for Chris!" In the autumn of the year we lived in New York, Kneivel actually did jump his motorcycle across the Snake River. Chris was fascinated with the entire event. On the Saturday morning of the great jump it rained in New York and as we walked down the sidewalk, Chris leaped over every puddle of water we came to, calling out to anyone who would listen: "Look at me! I'm Evel Kneivel jumping the Grand Canyon!"

After school, I always picked him up following my own day of writing magazine articles and working on a novel in the apartment. Together we roamed the streets of New York, sometimes stopping at Central Park, sometimes going to museums or occasionally attending movies. His energy and that of the city were equally matched.

Looking back, I realize that many of the lessons I was trying to teach him were never fully articulated or planned out in my mind. Rather, my parenting was guided by subconscious, somewhat fuzzy, feelings and inclinations. In retrospect, perhaps I should have done it all differently. Or maybe not.

Developing a vision of what to expect and what to ask from a young child is undoubtedly one of the hardest tasks of being a parent. Fathers are often uncertain about how they want their children to behave because of an increasing confusion about their own lives and how those lives should be lived in such a drastically changing society. This vision of what fathers should be like is particularly difficult for men whose ideas and expectations about life and people were radically altered in the social tumult of the 1970s.

I often felt that by the time Chris was old enough to learn what I had to teach, I was no longer sure of the lesson. Too many things had gone wrong. The American dream, promised to men of my generation, had turned into the American nightmare. Confused and uncertain about what I should do or think, I could hardly pass on a positive cohesive message of assurance to my son.

The writer Robert Bly wrote about this in *Iron John: A Book About Men*: "The Fifties man was supposed to be like football, be aggressive, stick up for the United States, never cry, and always provide. The Fifties male had a clear vision of what a man was, and what male responsibilities were, but the isolation and one-sidedness of his vision were dangerous."

I was a fifties male. Most of my youthful leisure time had been spent playing sports in prep school and college where the values of the locker room were clear and unequivocal. In that world, a man perceived a woman as important for her looks and her homemaking potential. Later, when he selected a woman for a wife, she would assume significance for her ability as a household manager, cook and mother of the children. That is how it was.

By the end of the sixties, however, all that changed. Men were no longer sure they wanted to be strong silent warriors. The Vietnam War in which I was a correspondent had changed all that. In addition, with the rise of the feminist movement men of my age were forced to re-think and re-interpret their attitudes toward women, how we spoke to them, how we treated them. Perhaps, more importantly, fathers needed to adjust their actions and outlooks concerning women in order to teach their sons how to get along with females and form healthy relationships. We had to learn to see wives as friends and equals whose needs and aspirations merited our attention and concern. We had to overcome our ingrained attitudes that viewed women as unequal partners. To pass on to our sons the male chauvinist shibboleths acquired from a previous era would be cruel and wrong. It would only impede them from having happy marital relationships in the future.

After almost a year in New York, Chris and I moved back to our beautiful stone farmhouse in Pennsylvania which his mother and I had restored several years earlier and where we had all lived for a short time as an intact family. His sister, Alexandra, who loved riding horses, soon left Washington D.C. to join us at this farm located near the small town of Mifflinburg where I had grown up. Together we formed a happy and busy trio, although I soon found that watching the television show *Hee Haw* on Saturday nights with two young children would have to substitute for the culture of New York to which I had become accustomed.

The relentless chores such as feeding animals, cleaning stalls, planting wheat, baling hay and harvesting corn were important lessons on the necessity for hard work in achieving one's goals. The death of a small calf or the birth of a new colt were incomparable learning experiences in the joys and sorrows of the life-death cycle. Despite the hardships, however, the benefits were overwhelming. The rhythm of farm life, with its heavy reliance on the cooperation of each person to complete the day's work, taught us the strength and importance of the family unit.

During this period, both Chris and Alexandra were able to develop senses of their own worth and ability by observing the results of their contribution toward the successful operation of the farm. When they hitched the hay baler to the tractor, they could witness the value of their effort as I drove off to gather hay with the proper equipment secured to the hitch. Finding eggs in the barn, after they had been laid in obscure nests of grass by our secretive chickens, meant we could have an omelet for breakfast. Feeding the pigs on time would prevent these highly intelligent animals from sniffing their way up to the house for food, though they often did that anyway. When Chris fell asleep in my arms to the monotonous drone of the tractor as we plowed the fields, he was content and confident, knowing that the result of our work would result in green shoots springing from the earth after the winter snows had melted.

As he grew older, Chris developed a love for racing BMX bikes. The experience of spending endless and boring days taking a young child to a race or competition, waiting hours until the event is finished and then driving the tired young athlete home is familiar to many parents. With Chris it was doubly hard. Watching him pedal his bike up and down hills with other young boys when I really wanted to enter him in a junior tennis tournament, or even better, stay home and work with me on the farm, was, as I saw it, simply one more sacrifice to be made on the altar of parenthood. His doing *his* thing rather than mine was never easy for me to accept but I tried.

Eventually, I married again in a desperate attempt to find a substitute mother for my children. It was not a good reason for the formation of a permanent relationship and after several years we divorced.

Throughout all of our time living together, Chris spent long and regular visits with his mother who had also remarried. His times with her were happy ones and the close relationship he maintained with his mother was always a positive and meaningful part of his existence. In fact, when Janey's new husband found a job in Botswana which would allow Chris and Alexandra to attend a fine private school and benefit from living abroad, they were thrilled to be allowed to accompany their mother, her husband and Justin to Africa. It turned out to be a wonderful experience for them all. After Chris and Alexandra returned from their two years in Botswana, our truncated family was together again. However, when Janey eventually moved to North Carolina, taking Justin with her, visits were often restricted to the summer months.

Although bringing up a son can be a constant challenge to any father, the responsibility of raising a daughter was pure fun for me. Determined that Alexandra would grow up to be an intelligent woman who was also interested in competitive sports, I encouraged her to accept every challenge that came along. She rarely backed off. If she fell off a horse and ended up with a bloody nose, she was always ready to jump back on and continue riding. I also encouraged her to play ice hockey at a young age and she continued to do so on the men's intramural team at Penn State. I sometimes had to look the other way as my beautiful, 115 pound daughter skated into the boards with a 160 pound defenseman bearing down on her, but she was a scrapper and seemed not to understand the meaning of fear.

An avid reader with an impressive memory, she won the first prize in a school sponsored poetry reading by reciting all thirty minutes of "The Highwayman" at the age of sixteen. A year later, I drove her around a small resort town near our home and waited in the car while she interviewed a series of people for a newspaper article. The freelance piece was published as a full page story in the Harrisburg Patriot Sunday section and provided her with a clip that would eventually get her started in a newspaper and television reporting career, one that she continues to pursue while raising two young daughters.

During the hectic days of growing up during the 1970s with a single father, Alexandra and Chris developed a close bond. The loss of Chris has been a difficult burden for her, as it has been for Justin who was always in such awe of his older brother.

Looking back now, I realize that life as a single

father was a lonely and difficult experience. There were times when I became unreasonably depressed over the conflicting need to be a sympathetic and attentive parent while attempting to pursue a meaningful career of my own. Yet the close and trusting relationship Chris and I eventually developed can undoubtedly be attributed to those years we spent together in which we were dependent on each other for so much companionship.

By the time Chris reached the age of sixteen, he and I started to engage in the kinds of conflicts parents so often experience with their teenage children. He began acting differently from my expectations and I became the father who could do nothing right.

During that period, for example, Chris could see no merit in my involvement with the construction of houses on a tract of land I owned in Lewisburg. What had started out as a simple investment in some land had escalated into a major commitment as a real estate developer and builder of unoriginal homes. It was an occupation I despised and hated, although I was not above enjoying the relatively painless income it provided and the time it allowed me to spend writing. Aware of the uneasiness I felt about my occupation, Chris began to taunt me with remarks like: "Why are you wasting your time building these stupid houses?"

It was a trap without an exit. If I agreed that I was building "stupid" houses, he complained about the immorality of my occupation. If I protested on the grounds that I had to earn money for our household, I then became a despicable, profit-seeking capitalist who thought only of material gain. No matter what my answer, I was the wrong-headed father. Though it strained our relationship in the moment, nevertheless, the bond between us remained strong. As Chris wrote in a letter he sent to his girlfriend while he was in college: "My dad is crazy as hell but I love him dearly."

More than once as Chris grew to manhood, I had to remind myself of the words of Mark Twain to maintain my self-esteem. Twain wrote: "When I was a boy of fourteen, my father was so ignorant, I could hardly stand to have the Old Man around. But when I got to be twenty-one, I was astonished at how much he learned in seven years."

If the times Chris and I spent together during those years were often filled with frustration and disharmony, as well as fun and learning, they also eventually formed a foundation of a relationship characterized by an understanding and love which, like the mountains themselves, seemed indestructible.

3

chapter

Howl with the Wolves

I know the purity of pure despair
My shadow pinned against a sweating wall
That place among the rocks–is it a cave
Or winding path? The edge is what I have.

Theodore Roetke, *In a Dark Time*

The plane flies north toward Canada until it finally bumps down on the frozen, snow-lined runway of the Calgary International Airport. I pick up my luggage, clear customs and locate the information desk. A polite and solicitous young woman who has read about the accident in the local newspaper directs me to a hospitality suite where my ex-wife Janey and son Justin, who have already arrived, are now meeting with the two climbers who were with Chris on the day of the accident.

When I enter the room, Janey approaches and we politely embrace each other like old friends. Her hair is white now, but the passing years have not dulled the sparkling luster of her blue eyes. I'm still confused by this woman whom I can never evade or forget, because of the irrevocable fact that we are the parents of a daughter and two sons.

Fortunately, Justin is here with Janey. I look at my younger son with pride. Frustrated throughout his earlier years by a mild form of dyslexia, his struggles with book learning and getting through college were not easy, although he stayed the course and received his degree from Appalachia State University in Boone, North Carolina. Charming and handsome, he's great with kids, a skill he puts to good use as a teacher and Activities Director at the Christ School in Asheville, North Carolina. He and I shake hands and hug each other with an affection now emphasized by our shared loss. I'm relieved that he's here to offset the shock of suddenly being in the company of my former wife after all these years.

My regret is that our daughter, Alexandra, already the mother of a three-year-old girl and expecting again, couldn't leave Honolulu to join us, since her husband is unable to get a break from his duties as a submarine officer with the Navy.

Janey introduces me to Wally Barker and Susan Lilly who were with Chris on the holiday ice climbing expedition. Wally, thirty-nine, has the good looks and physique often pictured on the cover of slick climbing magazines. Tall and lean with long, muscular arms and legs that can undoubtedly stretch four or five feet to hook onto a distant rock ledge, his physical appearance easily suggests the conviction he shared with Chris that climbing mountains is the only worthwhile activity in life. When he says to me, "I've been wanting to meet you. Chris said you were really cool," I have to turn away and stare at the wall in order to hold back my tears.

Petite and pretty, with waif-like features and a ready smile, Susan, twenty-six, is also an experienced climber. She and Wally had been conducting an on-again, off-again relationship for several years and the holiday trip to Canada was apparently an attempt to bring permanence to their romantic involvement. Their decision to wait several days in Calgary for us to arrive so they could explain Chris's accident was obviously an expensive and inconvenient thing to do, since they both had to be back at their jobs in Southern California. When I thank them for staying until we arrived, Susan replies simply: "We want to be here for you." It occurs to me that Chris spent his last days with some very good people.

As Wally begins to describe how the accident happened, I walk to the corner of the hospitality room for a few moments to avoid hearing the devastating details of the ice avalanche that swept Chris off the side of the mountain, narrowly missing Wally in its path of death. I am not ready to hear the dreadful details of the accident. But I feel compelled to have my questions answered and return to his side.

By the time we finish talking, darkness has settled around the airport. We plan to rent a car and drive to Banff, where we can find a hotel for the night, while Wally and Susan need to start their drive back to California without further delay. Janey suggests that a memorial service might be scheduled in Yosemite National Park later in the spring near Chris's beloved rock wall, El Capitan. We talk some more and then we all hug each other and say goodbye.

The air in Calgary is so cold this evening it's hard to breathe as we walk from the airport to the rental car. The agent shows us how to work the battery generator which needs to be plugged into an electrical outlet at night during the sub-zero weather. Then we pack our bags in the trunk and Justin gets behind the wheel, while I sit in the front and Janey takes the back seat. To a casual observer, we probably look like a nice American couple taking their son on a winter vacation.

The truth, of course, is far from the appearance. As we start down the frozen, snow-covered highway, I try to let go of the bitter memories of the past twenty years and those painful days when Janey and I were battling in court over who should have the legal right to bring up our three children. For the next four days, I tell myself, I will have to put these bitter thoughts aside. The past cannot be discussed. Having too much to say, I say nothing.

After an hour's drive we arrive in Banff, where Justin and I enter the lobby of a hotel in search of a room.

"We should get one room for all of us," I say.

"That's a good idea," Justin agrees.

"Don't worry about a thing, Justin. I lost my marital privileges a long time ago," I add with a smile.

Justin laughs and shakes his head. "This must seem pretty weird for you and Mom," he says.

"Weird? Try unbelievable," I respond.

After we've registered, Janey enters the lobby and asks if she can stay with us. "I'd hate to be in a room by myself," she explains.

"Justin and I talked about that and we all agree. None of us should be alone tonight. Justin and I will share a bed," I answer.

After taking our bags to the room, we stop at the hotel bar where we order pre-dinner drinks and sit at a table near a large fireplace where comforting flames cast red and gold shafts of light across the room. One might suppose that our conversation would be muted with sorrow this evening, but, on the contrary, we're soon sharing happy memories of Chris.

Janey tells us about a week during the previous

summer when she visited Chris at Yosemite. "The first night I was there, Chris fixed a pasta dinner which we ate on one of the picnic tables at Camp Four. We talked for a long time and then, since it was getting late, he tossed me a headlamp and told me to bring my sleeping bag and follow him. We climbed to a rock ledge above the camp and, just as I arrived at a huge boulder, I saw Christopher standing in a circle of stones in the soft light of the moon. His arms were outstretched and his body was framed by the huge monolith known as the Sentinel which loomed behind him. I was really touched by the beauty of the scene and by his joy in sharing this sacred place with me. I laughed and told him he was a Druid priest."

A waitress appears with our drinks and informs us that the dining room will be closing shortly.

Janey continues: "We slept out on a nearby rock ledge that night where he had been staying for the past two months. I expected the rock to be hard and uncomfortable, but it was strangely yielding. As we lay in our sleeping bags, watching the stars, Christopher spoke of his love for the rock walls. He talked about their textures, their moods and their personalities and he told me about his increasing sensitivity to them."

As Janey finishes her story, we all sit silently for a few minutes staring into the fireplace where the flames have burned out and the crimson embers now stare at us like the eyes of secretive animals on a dark night. It occurs to me that our loss is a greater catastrophe than any human being should have to bear.

After finding a table in the dining room and placing our order, we discuss our plans for the next day when we'll have to find Chris's truck, pack all his belongings and ship them back to the States. I suspect it's a relief for all of us when we finish eating and retire to the hotel room where we can shelter our tormented minds with sleep. My own last thoughts of the day dwell on the sad truth that it has taken Chris's death to bring us together again. This is the first time Justin has ever been together with his mother and father since Janey's announcement twenty-two years ago that she was leaving the marriage. Divorce is an ugly experience, made more so when there are children to be raised and protected.

The following morning, we have breakfast in the hotel dining room. Although we attempt to create pleasant conversation, the burden of the day's agenda weighs heavily on our minds. As we look out the dining room window where a snow-covered mountain peak glistens in the early morning sun, we all realize we're about to experience the worst day of our lives.

After breakfast, we pack our luggage in the car and soon we're driving west through a valley in the Canadian Rockies where a spectacular display of snow-capped mountains appears on each side of the road. Suddenly, on a ridge just above the road, I see a wolf trotting between several trees.

"Look! A wolf!" I call out.

It's difficult to see because the animal's gray coat blends in with the shadowed background snow. However, I'm positive of the sighting. Justin stops the car. He also catches a glimpse of the animal before it disappears behind a stand of pine trees.

"Where? Where is it?" Janey calls from the back of the car.

The wolf has disappeared, so Justin drives the car out onto the road again. Janey is disappointed and a bit suspicious. "Did you really see a wolf?" she asks.

"Absolutely," I reply.

Justin backs me up: "I saw it too."

"Didn't you see the two naked women running with the wolf?" I ask, the words popping out before I have time to consider them.

Justin laughs, but Janey only snickers.

She doesn't know I'm aware that *Women Who Run with the Wolves* is a book whose title she found compelling. Yet, I suspect Janey understands I'm being sarcastic. She probably can guess that I consider the book to be a feminist bible mostly because of the titillating title rather than what I consider the mismatch of female myths it describes. Even so, I wish I hadn't given her the slight. Indirectly, by the use of pseudo-humor, I've just been critical of her literary tastes and she knows it.

The incident reminds me that divorced couples may stop seeing each other for long periods of time, but the subtle ways of communicating learned during the marriage live on. Janey and I can still read each other's body language and subconscious use of words. That means we've got to be doubly careful about everything we say if we're going to avoid conflict. After all, the chances of fooling each other for even a second are slim. As Penelope says of her long-departed husband who has suddenly returned from his long voyage: "If really he is Odysseus, truly home beyond all doubt we shall know each other better than you or anyone. There are secret signs we know, we two."

After an hour's drive, we stop at Kicking Horse Pass, a gap in the mountains where the road and the Canadian Pacific railroad tracks follow a small stream that cuts through a high, rocky ridge. The accident occurred here on the ice-covered cliff looming above us less than a week ago.

We leave the car and step across the road. It's almost noon and a few streaks of sun have broken through the gray skies to light up the snow-covered mountainside.

Halfway up the steep slope, at approximately 1,000 feet from the road, we can see a frozen waterfall glittering in the morning sunlight. Like an evil monster with half its teeth knocked out, the middle of the ice wall is sheered off, a grim reminder of what happened on that snowy afternoon on the last day of the year.

My mind conjures up horrifying images of the day Chris died. So many small things had gone wrong that day. A sudden warming of the weather, after two weeks of sub-zero temperatures, had made Wally and Chris cautious. They were planning to climb elsewhere, but came here with the belief that there was less chance of melting ice breaking apart. Because of the heavy snow, the road from Kicking Horse Pass back to Banff was closed, which meant that Wally could not flag down a passing motorist and send for help immediately after the accident.

"Only the gods could have created the combination of small details needed to make this awful thing happen," I say to Janey. Then I kick a piece of ice across the road and go back to the car. Soon Janey and Justin join me. It relieves the frustration we all feel.

We drive into Golden, Alberta, where Chris's Nissan pickup was towed on New Year's Day. The back of the truck is filled with climbing gear, a mountain bike and camping equipment. The sides are stuffed with pieces of insulation which protected Chris from the cold, since he often slept in his truck even in sub-zero weather. There is a plastic crate filled with books. I pick up *Surfing the Himalayas,* a book about Buddhism which I bought for him several months earlier. The pages are earmarked. Within the limited space of his truck, Chris had stored almost everything he owned. He took unmitigated pride in how few material goods he possessed.

"I don't want to own a lot of stuff," he often said when we talked about where he might live when he moved to Portland.

It is difficult to stand, but we pack all his belongings in several large cardboard boxes which we mail to Janey's home in North Carolina from a nearby United Parcel Service center. Then we return to our car and drive two hours west to Salmon Arms, British Columbia. We arrive at the funeral home there by six o'clock that evening.

The owner's daughter, a tall, young woman with a quiet voice, ushers us into a room where we sit for several minutes waiting for the director to appear. The terrible realization now sweeps through my mind that Chris's body is lying in the morgue just a few feet away. I could stand up, take several steps, go through a door and there he would be. I want so much to see him again, perhaps to hold his hand or to embrace him one last time. Yet, there is also the deeply felt desire to avoid seeing him lying there motionless, without the breath of life. I want to retain my memory of Chris as the happy, energetic and alive young man I loved so much.

We had, in fact, decided earlier that we would not ask for a viewing. Janey apparently feels the same as I do about wanting to preserve a memory of our son in life rather than death. In a few minutes, however, the funeral director arrives and begins filling out papers. Then he looks up at us through heavy glasses that reflect the neon ceiling lights. "Would you like to see your son?" he asks in the same quietly solemn voice of his daughter.

Janey hesitates and then begins to cry. I know that, like me, she wants to see Chris once more. We both want him back so fiercely and yet our only option is to view his lifeless body. I remind her as gently as I can that when we discussed this in the car, she had decided against a viewing. She nods and we both agree, along with Justin, that we will forego a final farewell.

When the official forms are filled out and the expenses paid, the funeral director suggests that a cremation be performed that night. He tells us, "You can pick up the urn containing the ashes in the morning." I feel a burning in my throat at his words. It's all so efficient, so well-arranged, as if we had just ordered a new cabinet for the kitchen which the carpenter can make by the next day. But I suppose it has to be that way. As the funeral director blandly states while we're waiting to leave for the hotel: "With all the skiing and mountain climbing going on around here, this is a busy season for us." I stare at him for a few minutes, but don't reply.

That evening, Janey and I sit on a couch in the hotel lobby to discuss what kind of memorial service we want to have for Chris. She feels the service should be held at the Quaker Meeting in State College, Pennsylvania. "'People can sit in silence or rise to speak if they care to," she says.

My immediate preference is for a more traditional service with readings and music to be held at a church in the small town of Mifflinburg, Pennsylvania, where both Chris and I were brought up and where my own father is buried. Since Janey is a practicing Buddhist and I'm a Unitarian, our options are not limited by any special theology. Nevertheless, my sense of tradition prompts me to suggest that the service should be held in the town of Chris's grandfather and father, in a church where there could be music and some readings.

"Perhaps we could combine the two concepts by having some poetry reading, some music and also include the Quaker tradition of silence," Janey suggests.

That sounds to me like a reasonable solution. Since

I have a brother who lives not far from the Meeting House, I suggest that we could have a reception for guests at his home after the service. The compromise is agreed upon. We go back to the hotel room where Justin has been phoning family members who want to know what is going on. Finally we turn in for the night.

The next morning, after picking up the small container containing Chris's ashes, we drive back to the Calgary airport. Justin and I are planning to fly to New York, while Janey will stay in Canada for another few days with some nearby relatives. We say goodbye to Janey and then move on to the security gates.

As we board the plane, I turn to Justin. "I wish Alexandra could have been here."

"Maybe it's just as well. This has been a hard three days," he replies.

While we're in our seats flying back to New York, I remind Justin of the conversation Chris and I had only a few months earlier about the dangers of mountain climbing. "I told him this could happen, but he just wouldn't quit," I say.

"He was doing what he loved to do," Justin replies in defense of his departed brother.

"There are lots of things we all love to do, but we give them up for one reason or another. Here we are, Justin, me without my son, you without your brother, all because he 'loved' to go mountain climbing. Is that fair?" I ask.

"We just have to learn to be accepting. After all, it was his life," he replies.

I press the issue: "But no one has the right to an activity which can cause so much suffering and pain to others just so they can do something that is fun."

"You have to stop thinking that way," he answers, a tone of concern in his voice.

Justin is undoubtedly right, yet I still cannot dismiss my feelings of resentment at this so-called 'sport' which causes such damage to so many people. We land in Salt Lake City and then board a second flight to Kennedy Airport. I turn to Justin again. Like a dog with a bone, I cannot stop.

"What is it that drives people to climb a mountain? Why would anyone take such risks and undergo so much pain just to get to the top of a pile of rocks?" I ask him. My voice sounds distant, haunted.

Justin turns his blue eyes toward me. "Maybe you should try it and find out," he says.

Astounded, I look at him to see if he's joking. He isn't.

"You mean I should become a climber?" I ask.

"Remember what you always told us about the wolves?"

"If you want to know about the wolves, you have to howl with the wolves," I recite.

"So if you think climbing is dumb, then go try it out. You may be surprised at what you find. After all, Chris was not a stupid person," Justin says.

I turn my head toward the window and, looking out over the sea of clouds far below, I reflect on just what kind of sons I have brought up. The only response they seem to know to just about anything is: *Go for it!* Once, when Chris was eleven and we were having dinner in a restaurant, we struck up a conversation with an older couple at the table next to us. As we rose to leave, the woman said: "You've left your mark on him." She meant that as a compliment, but I was never sure what that mark was. Lately, however, I'm beginning to get the picture.

I nudge Justin's shoulder. "Are you telling me I should go somewhere and climb a mountain just to find out what Chris was doing on that ice column last week?"

"I'm not saying you should do it. Of course not. But if you're going to stay all bent out of shape about why Chris was drawn toward climbing, maybe you better find out about it instead of being critical of something you don't understand."

As the two grow older, there's a transition in the relationship between a father and son where a power shift occurs and the son begins to assume a kind of squatter's right to equal authority. If the father can accept this change and listen, which is not easy after so many years of unquestioned autonomy, a real friendship can begin. It happened with Chris and me a couple of years ago. I even began looking to him for advice. Now I sense it's happening with Justin and me. He's telling me what to do. Instead of rejecting his opinion because he's my young son, I listen carefully, recognizing a certain rationality in what he is saying.

"If I do this, don't start telling me I'm turning into a damned fool," I say after a long silent period during which I try to wrap my mind around the idea.

He leans back in the seat and smiles. "Maybe you already are," he whispers.

Outside the window there's a break in the clouds exposing a series of snow-covered mountain peaks far below. The plane shudders a few times and the pilot tells us to buckle our seats. I look at Justin and nod.

Maybe he's right.

Perhaps learning to climb is the only way I'm ever going to achieve any understanding of Chris's death. Without understanding, I'm afraid my anger will solidify into bitterness. There are so many reasons why Chris should not have been on the ice-covered slope at that precise moment, but I'm not sure I know what they are.

Yale professor Nicholas Wolterstorff, in *Lament for a Son,* his book about the climbing death of his son, wrote:

"But why did he climb at all? What was it about the mountains that drew him? I suspect that only those who themselves climb can really know. I can only imagine."

However, imagining is not going to work for me. I need an answer that I can kick and feel and smell. Like the Greek hero, Prometheus, I want not just theoretical answers from the gods but the secret to fire itself. Yes, I decide, I need to howl with the wolves.

Unfortunately, there are several good reasons why I shouldn't accept this challenge, why it's too late. First there is the titanium ball inserted into my left hip several years earlier to replace a worn-out joint that was clicking out of place each time I sat down. This replacement hip has worked well, but I can no longer stretch my left leg more than a foot off the ground. Even worse, an orthopedic surgeon recently told me that it's time for a replacement of my right hip which has become increasingly bothersome during the past year. All of this means that a simple walk across the street can be a painful ordeal. Distance running is out of the question. A hike in the afternoon leaves me stiff and sore the next morning.

Secondly, I've just turned sixty-five years of age and no matter how much I might like to deny the effects of the passing years, the inevitable has happened. Arthritic fingers and joints are beginning to appear on schedule. My speed at doing anything is diminished. Fatigue sets in quickly. Thirdly, even though I've spent a lifetime as an athlete from football and ice hockey to boxing for the United States Army, I've learned about the hardship and pain that comes with the kind of physical conditioning needed to get into top shape. Nevertheless, despite my artificial hip, I've maintained my tournament tennis ranking in the top ten of my age group in New England and so I'm in better physical shape than many men my age.

Mountaineering, however, is another matter. Only the toughest, best-conditioned men and women in the world are climbers. Survival on rock walls thousands of feet above valley floors requires leg and arm muscles trained to stretch and pull for long hours. Years of experience and the strength to endure unexpected disaster are the *sine qua non* of those who would ascend high altitude mountains.

So why should I think I can do this? What kind of person am I to even consider climbing at my stage in life?

My mind spins back to an early lesson I learned on the necessity of experiencing things for one's self in order to understand them. During a creative writing course when I was a freshman at Harvard, our instructor, the famous poet and novelist, May Sarton, asked us to write a short piece of fiction each week. One of my first submissions was a short story about a young man who went to a whorehouse in Boston's old Scully Square. A week after the story was given to Miss Sarton, she called out my name at the beginning of a class. Confidently, I stood up to identify myself, hoping that she was planning to commend me in front of the entire class of both Radcliffe and Harvard students for such a fine piece of writing.

"Did you write this story?" she asked, holding up my paper.

"Yes," I replied proudly, thinking that perhaps I would be accorded the special honor of reading part of it to the class.

Then, her narrow lips protruding with indignation, May Sarton asked: "Mr. Purnell, have you ever been in a whorehouse?"

My face turned crimson and several of the "Cliffies" began to giggle. After years of living within the confines of strict boys' prep schools, my sexual history could have been recorded on a postage stamp. "No, I have not," I responded weakly.

May Sarton placed my short story on her desk and then, to my great embarrassment, proceeded to castigate me and all other writers who would even think of committing the unforgivable sin of writing about unfamiliar topics. "Until you have actually participated in an experience, you know nothing about it," she announced to the class.

Now, as I reflect on the lesson she taught me so many years ago, I wonder if that's really the only way to discover the meaning of what has happened. In order to truly understand what it's like to gasp for breath in the thin, cold air at 19,000 feet, to feel the deep pain of freezing and exhausted limbs, to sense the fear of near death on a storm-swept glacier or discover the thrill and satisfaction climbers experience after such an adventure, do I need to climb a mountain? Is that the only way I'll understand Chris, his motivations and his death? If May Sarton was right, to understand mountains, whorehouses or any other subject, one must participate in the experience, one must, as Chris said: "Go for it." Were they both right? And if so, in a sense do I have a choice–if I really want to understand this loss?

4
chapter

Fatal Premonition

I climb because it makes me feel real, and you're never as real as when you might die.

Stevie Halston, X Games athlete

As the cold winter months slowly pass and then the wind and rain of early spring begin to blow across Connecticut from Long Island Sound, the reality of what has happened begins to sink in. Denial no longer works. The dark hole of loss is omnipresent. Sorrow and tears kick in at the sight of an old photograph, a remembered joke or a hastily scrawled letter accidentally discovered at the bottom of a desk drawer.

There are so many people lost when a son dies. There's the infant boy smiling and wriggling in your arms whose laughter or tears rule most of your day. Then comes the demanding yet affectionate young lad of five or six who needs to know the answer to a thousand questions. He's followed by the rebellious teenager who realizes how wrong his parents are and how much he knows about everything. Finally the loyal and affectionate young man appears, your best friend. Each stage is unique and all have different personalities and when the last one ends, it is over.

As time passes, I feel compelled to discover the meaning of what has happened, however difficult or painful this may be.

In fact, the first step may be the hardest. I've got to find out exactly what happened on that fatal December afternoon in Canada. I wasn't ready to hear it in the days following Chris's death. Now I am. I've decided to talk first with Susan Lilly, Chris's climbing companion, who lives in Joshua Tree, California. By early summer, I book a flight to Los Angeles and rent a minivan.

The distance from Los Angeles to Joshua Tree is only 150 miles. Yet the drive to this moon-like vista with its huge rock monoliths sprouting up from the desert floor on a warm afternoon seems to take forever. I'd like to cancel this trip, I think glumly, and avoid the conversation about to take place.

The sun is casting shadows from the nearby cactus-covered hills when I arrive at a cement block house a short distance from Joshua Tree National Park. The door opens and Susan Lilly, whom I met briefly in Banff, steps into the sunlight. She knows why I'm here and with the understanding of someone who has also experienced sorrow, she embraces me in her strong arms.

"I know this is difficult, but I'm glad you're here," Susan says. She ushers me into the small house from which several excited dogs are immediately pushed out the back door into a fenced-in area next to a stable where her horse is quietly munching hay. Then Susan brings two mugs of tea from the kitchen and we sit on a comfortable couch in front of a small wood-burning stove.

"At the Calgary airport," I remind her, "I moved across the room to avoid listening to you and Wally Barker describe the details of the fatal accident. Now I need to find out why Chris was so intent on climbing," I explain. Then I ask the questions that have dominated my thoughts for the past five months. Why was he on that particular ledge when an ice wall broke loose and swept him down the side of a frozen cliff? Was this accident the inevitable result of an activity which can bring death to anyone who takes up climbing, or was it just a freak circumstance of nature?

"Maybe it will help to hear my recollection of the accident," Susan says, as she hands me a photograph taken in a restaurant during their ice climbing expedition. It's a picture of Wally leaning against her shoulder while Chris is engaged in one of his favorite activities: laughing. The unexpected sight of my son's familiar blue eyes, sandy blond hair and wide-mouthed grin immediately stirs memories of happier days. I look again, recognizing the blue button-down Brooks Brothers shirt I gave him a year earlier for Christmas. After several years of climbing and mountain bike racing, his six-foot, 185-pound frame was rock solid and superbly conditioned. It's difficult to look at this picture of my son, so filled with life, for even an instant without being struck by the enormity of the loss which all of us who knew Chris are now undergoing.

"We asked a waiter to take this picture one evening," Susan says. "We were all having such a great time that night, laughing and enjoying a buffet dinner after a day of climbing."

As she speaks, Susan suddenly picks up the photograph and looks at it longingly. I realize it represents a doubly painful memory for her. Not only is Chris gone, but in the past month, she and Wally have broken up. His determination to make climbing his main commitment in life has finally been too much for both of them and the resulting separation is terribly difficult for Susan. I place my arm around her shoulder in a sign of sympathy.

In preparation for my visit, Susan has thought carefully about what she would tell me. There are certain details, she says, which I will have to get from Wally since only he was on the mountain when the ice column collapsed. However, she does warn me that something happened on the climbing expedition that I did not know about, a premonition of disaster she had experienced which I might find upsetting.

"Do you really want to hear this?" she asks.

"It's okay. I need to know," I tell her.

"All right then. I'll start from the very first morning we arrived in Canada, just two days before Christmas," she says.

The ice climbing expedition had been planned earlier that fall when Chris and Wally met while climbing the rock walls of Yosemite National Park, Susan tells me. Although they didn't know each other that well, Wally told Chris he was planning to go ice climbing in Canada with Susan over the holidays and wanted to know if Chris would like to join them. Chris was ecstatic at the prospect and immediately accepted.

By the time Wally and Susan joined him in Utah to form a two-car caravan to Canada for Christmas, Chris was ending a long sojourn of living out of his pickup truck while climbing in places like Yosemite, Joshua Tree and Zion National Park where the rock formations are well-known Meccas to the climbing community. This was all ending by December and he was planning to start his new job at the beginning of the new year. First, however, he was determined to have a final and happy climbing trip with his new friends.

"Chris was ecstatic that first morning when we arrived in Banff National Park," Susan says. "We had been driving for two straight days under difficult conditions because Wally's car broke down right after we crossed the Canadian border and all three of us had to jam ourselves into the front seat of Chris' old Nissan pickup for the rest of the trip.

"We never thought of turning back. We just cramped ourselves together for the long drive and talked a lot. Since neither Wally nor I were that well acquainted with Chris, it was a chance to find out what an interesting person he was. Chris had this capacity for listening to people. He didn't just hear what you said, he seemed to understand what you meant. He would listen to you here," she says, pointing to her heart.

As the trip continued, Susan came to feel a close sense of friendship with Chris, and their conversation spanned a wide range of topics. In particular, she speaks of a conversation they had about the year he spent in Nepal. It started when she noticed a small medallion of the Dalai Lama hanging from the mirror of the pickup while they were driving to Canada.

Chris explained that while he was still in college, he had spent his junior year in the Himalayas studying the architecture of Buddhist monasteries in several rural Tibetan villages of northwestern Nepal. One day, while he was trekking near the border of Mustang, he noticed a small boy wearing the medallion. When Chris asked the boy about the glass-covered picture of the famous exiled leader of the Tibetan people, the boy took it off and gave it to him.

"The picture and how he acquired it was a symbol of the sharing and giving nature of Buddhism to Chris. Yet, when I asked him if he were a Buddhist, he told me that he believed in their principles, but he also read the Bible and belonged to a Quaker Meeting. That was typical of him. He placed a lot of value on anything that was good whether it was his particular philosophy or not," Susan says.

Although Susan soon learned how enthusiastic Chris was about everything he did, she was nevertheless surprised at what happened when they finally reached a frozen waterfall at Canmoor Mountain, about thirty miles from Banff. The weather was incredibly cold with the thermometer dropping to thirty-five degrees below zero. Without hesitating, Chris wanted to start climbing immediately. He gathered his gear together that morning at a frozen waterfall called the "Junkyard" and started to climb alone and unroped.

"I was pretty shocked that he would just go at it like that without taking a day or so to get acclimatized," Susan tells me.

Then, suddenly, the incident happened which would plague Susan for the rest of the week and become a premonition that eventually turned into a fatal reality.

"While I was watching Chris move slowly up the ice column, I suddenly had a vision of him falling. It was incredibly real. He just kept tumbling down the side of the ice. In all my years of rock climbing, I never experienced anything like that before and it really scared me," she says.

Although she later informed Wally of her vision, she tried to put the incident out of her mind, since they were all having such a good time. For Wally, the *de facto* leader of the trip, Susan's frightening image constituted one more reason for climbing safely and with caution during the following week.

As Susan continues to talk, the sun is casting its last light of day across the distant hills in a brilliant array of pinks, reds, browns and a dozen other unique colors created by this centuries old combination of sun and desert. Glancing out the window at the dark shadows falling across the barren landscape, I realize that something much more troubling than I anticipated had happened on the fatal ice climbing expedition.

After two days spent on the frozen waterfalls near Banff, the three climbers decided to phone their families and relax on Christmas day. Chris called me that afternoon in North Carolina where I was visiting Justin.

"Papa, I wish you could be here, this place is just fantastic," he said with his customary enthusiasm. "I'm having a great time ice climbing with my friends and Banff is incredibly beautiful at this time of year." After informing me that he would be leaving Canada in a few days for his new job in Portland, Oregon, Chris assured me that he would be coming to the East Coast to visit by early spring. "This job is set up so I can work a couple of months and then take time off," he said.

I knew that although his new job would afford him time to travel and continue climbing, he was still feeling unsure about himself, still trying to understand who he was and what kind of life he wanted to lead.

Like so many young men of his generation, Chris wasn't sure what he really wanted for a long-time career. Sometimes he would talk about going to law school. The next week he was thinking of becoming a stockbroker. A few days later, he was fantasizing about traveling the world as a climber and writer. Through all of this, his search for purpose and fulfillment and his determination to lead a meaningful life was relentless.

In fact, several months earlier we had discussed the

importance of seeking a meaningful existence and I remember summarizing my own conviction. "There are two main challenges in life. The first is to find out what your real passion is and the second is to let go of everything else and do it," I said to Chris, hardly aware of the degree to which he would eventually follow this advice.

Susan, Wally and Chris spent the next few days climbing in Banff during the day, locating buffet dinners where they could eat all they wanted in the evenings and then sharing a single room in a hostel each night because it was too cold for Chris to sleep in his pickup truck. By the end of the week and just before New Year's, however, the cold spell came to an end. Although Wally and Chris were wary of the sudden change in weather that could quickly begin a melting process on the frozen waterfalls in the area, they were determined to keep climbing.

On Saturday, Susan decided to stay in the hostel. During most of the other climbs on the ten-day expedition, she struggled gamely to keep up with the two stronger and more experienced men. Only when she felt the frozen waterfalls would require more technical skill or strength than she possessed did she stay back and avoid climbing. Yet, this was not the case that day. Despite her years of experience at rock climbing in California and her recent success on the ice walls of Canada, Susan stayed back at the hostel. She had a different and far more compelling motive for remaining there that morning.

Despite all the laughter and fun, she was unable to forget the frightening vision she had seen on their first day of climbing at Canmoor Mountain. This was the reason she decided not to go with her companions. Instead, she planned to join them for a New Year's celebration that evening.

"I know this will sound strange, but I feared that

something might go wrong that day so I decided to remain in bed where it was warm and safe," she says. Consequently, she told Wally and Chris to go ahead and that she would stay at the hostel to get some sleep and write some letters while the two men went climbing.

Night is falling across the desert by now and I realize that Susan is reluctant to go much further in a detailed discussion of the accident.

"I think you need to talk with Wally about that since I wasn't there," she says.

I agree and we switch topics. Susan tells me about a trip to Europe she's planning for the summer. However, as an opaque darkness sets in around the house, my need to return to nearby Palm Springs becomes apparent. After a promise to return a few days later when Susan will show me the climbing area of Joshua Tree, I'm on the road again heading west to a motel where I'll stay overnight before returning to Los Angeles for a meeting with Wally.

Soon, I'm driving through the star-filled night with the strange desert canyons and rocky craters of western California basking in the gray light of a half moon. I wonder once again what might have happened if Susan had told Chris about her premonition and her consequent fear of an accident. Would such a warning have kept him from climbing that day of misfortune? It seemed unfair to ask Susan, yet I've come to understand that the soul-searching debate about when to retreat and when to press on to the top gets to the very heart of what climbing is all about.

I wonder if Wally Barker, Chris's climbing companion, shared Susan's premonition. In two more days, I'll find out when we get together in Los Angeles. He and I have agreed to meet at the entrance to Sears department store at the South Coast Plaza, south of Los Angeles, in the late afternoon. He's under contract as a professional accountant for a large corporation until summer when he can finally go climbing again for several months.

Two days pass and finally, the day of our meeting comes.

While waiting for Wally to appear at the appointed hour, I'm filled with anxiety. Listening to the details of how Chris's tragedy occurred will not be easy.

Wally arrives at the mall just after three P.M. and together we decide to escape the heat, drink iced tea and talk in the relative quiet of a nearby restaurant.

After we order, Wally begins.

"The first thing I should tell you is how much fun we were all having," Wally says as we take a seat next to the window overlooking the mall. "Chris had Susan and me laughing all the time. For example, one afternoon, after we had been climbing all day in some terribly cold weather, we decided to have dinner at the Lake Louise Chateau. We were so hungry, we went straight to dinner without changing or taking a shower. We started laughing as soon as we walked into the formal dining room. Everyone was dressed for dinner and some of the men even wore tuxedos. We still had on our smelly climbing clothes and our hair was matted and wild after having been frozen during the day. The other diners stared at us in horror, but we just marched in and took our seats.

"Several days earlier, Chris had been telling us about his family, including an uncle named Rudi, who was both funny and sophisticated. Apparently, he once gave Chris a cigar and told him it was a particularly good cigar, because it had been hand-rolled on the bare thighs of Cuban virgins. It was a preposterous story, but it made us laugh. After dinner on this particular evening at the hotel, a waiter approached with a humidor and asked us if we would like to purchase a cigar. Without hesitating, Chris gave him this condescending look and in a very authoritarian way, announced that he wanted to buy a cigar which had been hand-rolled on the thighs of Cuban virgins. The waiter's face went blank and we cracked up. For the rest of the trip, whenever any one of us mentioned Cuban cigars we all started laughing."

After the waiter delivers two glasses of iced tea, Wally leans forward and moves quickly to the subject we have come here to discuss. "On the last day of the year, it was still snowing when Chris and I left the Lake Louise International Hostel to go climbing. The weather had turned warmer and that can melt ice on the waterfalls, so we were feeling pretty wary.

"During breakfast, I said to Chris that we should be careful where we climb since the temperature was up to almost twenty-five degrees. Chris suggested we look for a small waterfall in the western section of the park where it's safer than some of the bigger routes."

Wally explains that despite the warming spell, they were both anxious to climb somewhere that day. The trip was almost over and in another twenty-four hours they would have to begin the long journey back to the States where jobs and the responsibilities of earning a living awaited them.

Perhaps they were feeling overconfident. After all, on one particularly cold day some time before, Wally and Chris had decided to climb the Sea of Vapors, one of the most challenging frozen waterfalls in North America. After starting at four in the morning, they managed to reach the top of this 600-foot climb without incident and be back in the hotel that night for dinner. They were both proud of this unique accomplishment, because the thin ice on several pitches and the overall rating of W-17 have given this ice wall a worldwide reputation as a hard and dangerous climb.

That fatal morning, after traveling along the snow-covered roads for almost an hour, they came to the approach of a waterfall that had looked good on the map. However, heavy snows blocked the logging trail leading to the base so the proposed climb was aborted. By now, it was noon and although they knew they couldn't do much that day, they still wanted to climb something. So they continued west to Kicking Horse Pass near the small town of Golden where the side of a mountain rises above the trans-Canadian railroad and where underground springs had created several frozen waterfalls.

Parking the pickup truck at a spot along the highway where the railroad crosses the road, they shouldered their heavily loaded packs and walked approximately fifty yards along the tracks toward a short gully which would lead to the base of the mountain. Just then, however, they heard a whistle and immediately realized a train was approaching through the falling snow.

Shouting and waving his arms, Chris stood on the tracks as the train drew nearer and Wally took his picture. Like two small boys, they laughed at their fake bravado, realizing the picture would show the train much closer than it really was. After moving to the side of the tracks, they watched the train roar by and disappear into the white void as it continued toward Vancouver. Then they turned to the mountainside. It was time to begin climbing the frozen waterfalls above.

"It was early in the afternoon and we knew that conditions were different from the morning," Wally says. "The snowfall was getting heavier and I've been near enough avalanches to know that that is not the way I want to die. I was feeling really cautious so I chose a path up to the waterfall that wouldn't expose us to any sudden shifts in the ice columns. That meant staying on the ridges and avoiding any gullies."

Chris was wearing a well-insulated red parka and inside his blue Northface pack he kept his camera, extra cold weather gloves and even a book of poetry he often packed in case of a long wait or even an overnight stay on the mountain. After putting on his crampons, he volunteered to lead the first pitch.

"Chris climbed a short twenty-foot vertical section, then a sixty-degree ramp for another thirty feet which led to the main waterfalls. He went up first, unroped, to the base of the falls. It really isn't too smart to climb without protection, but you do it every so often. And you have to understand that when you do it, you just can't screw up. It was only a twenty-foot section and I knew Chris could move through it pretty quickly without getting tired. That's when bad things happen, when you get tired," Wally explains.

By approximately two in the afternoon, Chris had climbed the two sections of snow-covered rock to the base of the ice falls. Wally waited for him to complete this section since he had long ago acquired a strong aversion to climbing beneath someone else, knowing from experience how easily a climber above can loosen a rock or piece of ice and send it crashing down on the head of the climber below. After a sufficient wait, he got ready to climb the twenty-foot section that Chris had ascended a few minutes earlier. He pulled his ice ax from his holster and started up.

"Suddenly," Wally says, "I heard this rumbling noise. I had heard a sound like that only once before in my life and I can tell you it's not a good noise to hear. I knew something bad was happening, but I didn't even look up because I knew that whatever hit me would take me away. So I jumped," Wally says.

Six to eight feet away, there was a large rock with a little wall above it. Wally speaks slowly: "Just as I reached this spot, tons of ice came roaring by. Half of the waterfall had just sheered off, and even though I was behind this rock shelter, I was getting hit by pieces of ice. I kept saying to myself, 'I'm alive. I'm alive. Focus! Stay conscious. Don't let go.'"

As the huge chunks of ice roared past him, Wally realized that Chris was being carried down the mountain with the avalanche.

"Oh my God! I'd climbed for twenty years without ever losing a climbing partner and now Chris would just die. In my mind, I could not imagine that anyone could survive this avalanche. The ice would carry him straight down over two cliffs and then five hundred feet down the mountain," Wally states.

When the avalanche finally stopped, Wally pulled a rope and ice screw from his backpack, drove the anchor into the rock and then rappelled down the side of the mountain. He found the spot where Chris was lying. He was not dead but badly injured.

"What happened?" Chris mumbled.

"You fell, but I'm going for help," Wally answered, amazed that his climbing companion could still be alive.

After making Chris as comfortable as possible, Wally raced down the rest of the mountainside to the railroad tracks where he found several workers coming by in a small truck. He told them to report the accident and then went back up to be with Chris.

When Wally got back to Chris, he seemed worse. Wally waited impatiently for help.

Finally, a rescue team arrived and after they checked Chris, a helicopter was summoned to lift Chris out. He was taken to a hospital in nearby Golden.

"After the helicopter left, I hitched a ride back to the hostel at Banff to tell Susan what happened. Later that evening, we called the hospital and found out that Chris was unable to survive despite three hours of emergency surgery," Wally says.

Chris died six hours after the roar of the avalanche cracked the silence of the quiet, happy afternoon doing what he loved best.

As Wally finishes recounting the details of the fatal climb at Kicking Horse Pass, he sits back and stares out the window. I suspect that it has been almost as hard for him to relive the experience as it has been for me to hear about it.

Yet, though I hated to hear them, I had to. With the details of the accident out, I realize that this was not a mishap that occurred because of carelessness or lack of preparation. An ice wall had collapsed at just the moment Chris happened to be there. He would not have been saved by a belay rope, anchors or any other safety device.

Dazed and practically incapable of speaking, I try to remember the questions I've been thinking about since I learned of Chris's death.

"I heard about Susan's premonition of an accident—and Chris even wrote that he was scared of the ice climbing trip. Do you think he might have been talked out of climbing with you that day?"

Wally shakes his head. "We all have times like that when we just can't quit," he says. Wally pauses and looks out the window for a few moments. Then, he speaks slowly, choosing his words carefully: "Climbing is a dangerous activity and those of us who undertake it know we can be killed at any moment. We are always aware of that and we live with that possibility. In fact, Chris and I talked about it and he told me he had even discussed it with you. So we accept the fact that death can happen at any time."

This prompts me to ask Wally another question I've thought about for a long time. "What about us, the parents, the wives, sometimes little children, who have to suffer from such losses for the rest of our lives? Don't you people ever think about that?" I ask with a hint of the old anger still influencing my thoughts

Wally shakes his head. "Everyone has to live his own life," he replies.

"Maybe you're right," I respond. "But there's still another question I want to ask you."

"Go ahead," he says.

"You may consider this foolish, but do you think there was any chance that Chris would have stopped climbing if I had asked him to quit? If I had pleaded with him to give up doing it out of respect for the people he loved, would he have stayed away from the mountains? In short, do you think I could have done more to prevent his death?" I ask.

His answer doesn't surprise me and yet I'm shocked by the speed and certainty of his response.

"Nothing would have stopped Chris from climbing," Wally says bluntly. "It was his life."

The vision of Chris tumbling down the mountain in the midst of an ice avalanche, plus Wally's frank assessment of my son's intense desire to climb numbs my ability to think. I sit back for a few moments then finish the glass of iced tea.

Then I turn to Wally. "I'm leaving for Yosemite National Park this afternoon," I say softly. "I don't think I'll ever understand why people like you and Chris become so infatuated with climbing unless I actually try it," I say.

Wally smiles. "That's a good idea. You might even get to like it."

"I doubt that, but at least I'll have an idea what it's all about," I somberly reply.

"I think Chris would approve," he says.

"Probably," I answer, "but I'm doing this for myself. I need to know all of this."

"It's not going to be easy," Wally warns. "Nevertheless, there are people who have to try new challenges. They're not satisfied with the way things are. Chris was like that and I suspect he got it from you."

"Me!" I exclaim defensively. "Hey, Wally, I would never do this without a very good reason. The very idea of climbing scares me to death."

"But you're going to do it and that's what counts," he replies. Wally pushes his chair back and stands up. "I hope you don't mind my saying that about your similarity to Chris."

"No. Of course not," I answer. Then we shake hands and in a few minutes I'm standing there watching as he saunters across the parking lot. As I watch him go, I cannot help thinking that the last person to be with my son as he lay dying on an ice cliff in Canada is disappearing among the rows of shimmering cars in the late afternoon sun.

5

chapter

The Valley of Eden

If at times I hate the place, it is probably because I love it so. It is a strange, passionate love that I feel for this valley. More than just a climbing area, it is a way of life.

Yvon Chouinard

A brilliant mixture of orange and yellow sunlight rises steadily behind the jagged edges of the distant Sierras as the rental minivan climbs quickly from the flat plains of California's San Joaquin Valley towards the soaring cliffs of Yosemite National Park. Finally, I'm making the long awaited trip to the stunning rock walls and Eden-like valley where Chris had sought to learn so much about climbing and even, I believe, about the workings of his own inner self.

At the entrance gate, a friendly young woman wearing the familiar stiff yellow hat and green uniform of a park ranger takes my admittance fee and smiles. Then my minivan passes through the famous rock arch and I step down on the gas. The van picks up speed toward the valley. For a few minutes, I drive along the twisting road, next to the clear waters of the Merced River, until suddenly, like the opening crash of a Beethoven symphony, the great rock walls of Yosemite appear above the trees.

Stopping the car at a small roadside parking area, I step into the warm, pine-scented air. On each side of the valley, towering rock walls are basking in the morning sun. To the east, above the dense, muted green fir trees, the shining rock face of El Capitan is silhouetted against a cloudless blue sky. The Cathedrals, looking doleful and sad, with gray and orange-splotched faces, loom against the southern sky with all the dignity of a cathedral like Notre Dame or St. John the Divine.

No matter how much one hears about Yosemite or how many pictures one sees of these granite towers rising straight up from the valley floor, the impact of actually viewing such spectacular rock cliffs is a mind-altering experience. It's the stuff that epiphanies are made of. Immediately, the first seeds of understanding are planted in my mind as to why Chris loved it here. Looking around, I see that the Yosemite valley is truly one of the most beautiful spots on earth.

Before I can adjust to the splendor of these silent granite giants hovering against the horizon, a bus filled with German tourists pulls up behind me. Quickly, they cluster along the road and begin pointing at the distant face of El Capitan, where climbers are slowly making their way to the top. *"Die Idioten! Sie sind verrückt!"* ("The fools! They're crazy!") they mutter to each other as they pull out their Leicas and Nikons and focus on the ant-like creatures slowly crawling to the top of the rock wall.

Suddenly, one of the men, a small, owlish-looking fellow with blue eyes, walks up to me and asks: "Why zey do zat? Ist not dangerous?"

"I don't know. I really don't," I reply, consciously declining to explain that discovering the answer to his question is precisely why I've come here.

After clicking their cameras at the climbers for several minutes and shaking their heads in disbelief that any human being would do such a risky thing, the group heads back to the bus at the urging of an impatient tour leader anxious to move on to the next stop.

Returning to the minivan, I repeat to myself what the Germans were saying: *"Die Idioten! Sie sind verrückt!"* And then I wonder if that was true of Chris. Had he been crazy to spend his days climbing those distant rock walls or was there a huge gap of knowledge on my part and the parts of others like the busloads of German tourists who could never understand his devotion because we never attempted it? Might there be some distant mystical secret which climbers, as they work their way higher and higher, discover? Do they possess some metaphysical key to a particular wisdom which the rest of us don't know about? In his diary and in things he had said to me a year earlier, Chris suggested there was a spiritual element to climbing a mountain which he found irresistible. At the time, I didn't understand nor did I take his idea very seriously. "You don't have to climb a mountain to find God, Chris," I told him. He had shrugged his shoulders and moved on to another topic of discussion. Perhaps he understood that his father was not yet prepared for the enlightenment which the son had already embraced.

As I begin driving slowly along the river once again, a new and almost consoling sense of calm suddenly emerges from the realization that now, at last, it's time to find out. However late, the hour has arrived to discover why the rigorous and dangerous world of mountain climbing was so essential to my son who had so much to live for. I have made a decision. I will take Justin's advice. I'm going to howl with the wolves. The decision, made over the past few months, to climb here in Yosemite might be foolish, but at least it's a first step toward doing something to end the confusion and bitterness that have shrouded my days since Chris's fatal accident.

In a few minutes, I arrive at the visitors' center where the usual mundane and mind-numbing slide show, endemic to most national parks, is offered to arriving tourists. I make a cursory tour of some other attractions. I see a display of Native American artifacts in the park museum introduced by a wall-sized photograph of an Indian dancing in front of tourists in the 1950s. The dancer was apparently a grandson of a Yosemite Indian who survived the genocidal attacks by federal troops who drove the Indians from the valley in 1851 and forced them to give up their fertile land to white settlers. I can imagine Chris would have said of this embarrassing image: "Sick!"

By mid-afternoon, I stop the minivan in a parking lot next to the famous Camp 4 where Yosemite climbers have camped and congregated for the past forty years. Multi-colored, one and two-person tents are spread throughout this half acre of wood and rock-filled terrain where men and women from around the world sleep each night in their sleeping bags and depart, usually before dawn, to climb the nearby rock walls. At the western end of the campsite, several white tents are pitched on wooden platforms indicating the presence of the Search and Rescue Team, known locally as SAR. One of Chris's proudest moments occurred when he was hired by the Park Service to join these elite climbers who are sent out day and night to rescue stranded climbers, lost hikers and accident victims. My guess–my hope–is that some of the SAR people who knew and climbed with Chris will still be here.

My hunch proves correct when I find Eric Rasmussen, a dark-haired young man of twenty-eight with small goatee stubble on his chin, who informs me that he had climbed with Chris for several seasons and knew about his death. In fact, he points out, "Chris and I established a challenging first ascent on the Firefall Wall, the upper headwall of Glacier Point."

After I explain that I've come to Yosemite to learn more about climbing and why Chris had become so involved in what I consider to be a dangerous and senseless activity, Eric suggests we go to the base of the Firefall Wall and have a look at the climb he and Chris made a year earlier.

As we drive across the valley, Eric asks me, "Have you ever climbed before?"

"Only once. Chris gave me a lesson on a small cliff, but I don't understand how it all works out here," I tell him.

"It's the same on all walls. After you go up more than twenty or thirty feet, a fall can be fatal," Eric responds.

We cross the Merced River where a sign indicates Curry Village, a tenting and shopping area for tourists, is just ahead. I ask Eric one of the questions I have been anxious to direct at someone who could talk knowledgeably about the accident rate at Yosemite.

"Has SAR had a busy summer?"

"Yeah," Eric admits. "We get called out almost every day."

Like a chess master ready to call out "checkmate," I fire my next question at the young adventurer sitting in the passenger's seat. "How many people were killed here this year?" I ask.

Eric hesitates. "You mean climbing?"

"Yes. Climbing."

"Ah, well, I guess there was one guy. He didn't place his cams properly and when he weighted the gear, it pulled. He decked and smashed his head. He just wasn't careful and that can be fatal," Eric said.

Surprised and somewhat incredulous, I ask: "Only one?"

"Yeah." He nods. "There's usually one person killed while climbing here each year. Most of the people we rescue have heart attacks while hiking or they get lost. Stuff like that."

This is not what I expected to hear. Of all the thousands of men and women climbing Yosemite's rock walls, I was certain that far more than one would die each year. I knew that more than one hundred people are killed annually while climbing in the Alps, so it seemed to me there would be equivalent numbers here.

"That's hard to believe," I tell Eric, as we stop at the base of Glacier Point and step onto the parking lot. "I mean one fall up there and it would all be over."

"Not really," Eric responds. "You have to remember that when rock climbers fall, which is often, they rarely hit the ground. A climber wears a waist harness attached to a rope which is then secured to bolts, or pitons, fastened into crevices of the rock wall. This belay system stops the fall after ten or twenty feet."

"You're saying that since few people are seriously hurt then it's really not that dangerous," I exclaim, with a trace of disbelief still in my voice.

Eric tilts his head in agreement. "That's right. If you're careful and you always practice the right safety measures, there's not much chance of a fatal accident."

"But people come here and see you climbers up on those high walls and they think you're crazy," I protest.

"That's because they don't understand what kind of equipment we're using or what kind of training we have. They don't bother to find out how we're actually secured to the wall in case we slip. In fact, it was in Yosemite where techniques and equipment were first developed for climbing these rock walls without a lot of people getting killed," he says.

"How did that happen?" I ask.

"Back in the nineteen fifties and sixties, a lot of people came up here and started making special pitons that could be hammered into the cracks of the rock. One of the first to revolutionize climbing techniques was a man named John Salathe. He was a blacksmith who figured out how to make pitons from carbon steel mixed with vanadium. This alloy steel could be pounded into the small cracks of the wall and was strong enough to hold the weight of a human being. These same pitons could be removed and reused through a system of release springs. With these kinds of bolts securing the ropes, a person could safely climb a vertical wall that no one ever thought possible," Eric says.

We move closer to the base of Firefall Wall and walk along its perimeter. I remind myself that Chris was here, climbing, only one short year ago.

"If no one is being seriously hurt, then it's really not that dangerous," I conclude.

Eric nods his head in agreement. Then pointing to the 3,000-foot wall in front of us, he offers a chilling description of how he and Chris climbed the Glacier Point headwall during a four-day assault.

Eric recalls: "On the last few pitches, Chris was having a great time, shouting and laughing. I was on a limited schedule so we had to climb late at night with head lamps. Some of the tourists saw us and reported to the SAR team that two guys were stuck or lost on the wall. We yelled down at them that we were okay and told them to leave us alone. Then we kept on climbing. We found a ledge and bivouacked around midnight. The next morning we topped out and a bunch of tourists were looking out over the cliff when we showed up. It really freaked them out."

Ironically, the two climbers named the new route Ashes to Ashes. "The Park Service used to light a big bonfire on top of the headwall and then push it off the cliff at night," Eric explains. "The glowing embers could be seen for miles as they tumbled down the wall and it was a big tourist attraction at the time. It also left a lot of ashes on the ledges below, which Chris and I had to push away during the climb. So we called the route Ashes to Ashes because of that and also because of the old European song about the plague which we thought was appropriate." In a soft voice, Eric intones:

"Ring Around the Rosie
A Pocket Full of Posies.
Ashes, Ashes we all fall down."

After explaining that the route will be listed in the next Yosemite climbing guidebook, Eric returns with me to the car. It occurs to me that I might ask him to be my climbing teacher. Yet it seems inappropriate to make such a request to a member of the Search and Rescue team whose job is to keep people like me off the mountain. I say nothing about my plans. It's getting late and by the time we arrive back at the SAR site, I'm anxious to have dinner and then go up to a ledge above the rows of tents where Chris had often camped for the night while climbing at Yosemite.

Darkness has fallen across the valley when I finally leave the minivan in the crowded Camp 4 parking lot. With the aid of a small flashlight, I scramble up through a tree line and over a series of boulders to a ledge. There, several carefully selected rocks have been stacked to form three granite seats on this level, finely-crushed stone platform. Sitting on these surprisingly comfortable rock chairs, one can watch each morning as the sun emerges from the distant Sierras and splashes the mountain peaks of Yosemite with a gold, orange and yellow veneer. As I look around now I think how typical it was of Chris to camp in a place like this, a rock ledge far above the noise and the presence of the other campers. He liked marching to his own drummer.

Yet, as I look out over the dark valley this evening, I wonder why Chris had to develop a passion for high-risk sports when other safer activities were available. Could he not have stayed with the mountain bike racing he loved so much? What is it about climbing mountains, rock walls and columns of ice that drive young men and women like Chris to take chances which could easily claim their lives? What strange siren call draws people to a rock ledge or a frozen field of snow thousands of feet above the safety and comfort of a valley floor? Is there a genetic pull that entices climbers from around the world to summit a Mont Blanc or an Everest? What perverse motivation inspires intelligent, loving and otherwise normal people to lust for the top of an El Capitan, a Sea of Vapors or an Eiger Wall? Is there some dreadful chromosome mutation or subconscious emotional damage that I and other parents pass on to our children which forces them to seek their dreams within a framework of danger and high risk sports? Where does it come from, this powerful drive to live on the edge and challenge the very gods of the mountains? Is it no more than the normal activity of a competitive person looking for a thrill, or is there an inherent flaw in the very idea of mountain climbing that challenges the laws of human nature and defies the more sensible way most of us live our lives?

Sitting here this evening, I suddenly realize that perhaps I have no business making judgments about a son who chose to climb mountains. After all, was it not me, his father, who taught him the thrill of taking chances? How many times had I galloped on a horse across a field at full speed while holding him in my arms when he was not yet a year old? How many times had we gone swimming at Thanksgiving just to prove we could take the cold? Chris had listened intently to a father who recounted exploits to his son about the racing motorcycles, skydiving or watching shells and mortar rounds explode overhead during a firefight in Vietnam.

In his book, *Iron John,* the psychologist and poet, Robert Bly, says that a physical exchange of cells takes place between a father and son in which the son learns from his father the rhythm and feeling of what it is to be a man. He calls it the dance of the male molecules.

Once, when Chris was eleven, I took him to Florida for a week of intensive tennis lessons. While there, I suggested that it might be fun to rent some scuba equipment and go diving. He loved the idea. Although I had a good deal of experience with scuba equipment and had once owned my own regulator and tank, I had no license.

"Come on, Chris, let's see if we can chat these people up and get some equipment without the license," I said as we jumped out of the car and headed for a scuba shop.

An attractive young woman in tight shorts, bleached blonde hair and a deep Florida tan looked us over as we entered the shop.

"Hi, I'm trying to get some equipment for a short dive," I said.

"Sure. No problem. Got your license so I can take down the number?" she asked.

"You won't believe this," I said. "But I've been diving for years and I never got around to...you know...taking the test."

Miss Florida Deep-tan rolled her eyes.

"I do believe it," she said.

I gave her my friendly laugh, the one that says, "Hey we're all in this together."

"Is that your son?" she asked.

"Right. I thought it might be good to give him an idea what this is all about. You know, a quick lesson in some real shallow water?"

"Yeah?" Miss Florida Deep-tan asked approvingly. A picture on the back wall indicated that she had kids at home. I wondered if her kids had a dad who would take them out scuba diving.

"I'm not supposed to do this...but no deep stuff, eh? An' be back in two hours."

Within the hour, Chris and I were in the water with our tanks and regulators on. I showed him how to breathe, how to blow out air to clear his mouthpiece, how to flutter his fins slowly back and forth to control his underwater swimming.

"Have you got it now?" I asked, after we had gone through most of the procedures.

"I think so," he said with a confident grin.

We started out into the clear, still water. Slowly we started to descend and in a few minutes we were swimming along the bottom at a depth of perhaps ten feet. A few fish appeared and I felt pressure from his small fingers. Some tall sea grass floated back and forth in front of us. Again Chris squeezed my hand, a signal of concern. We kept moving slowly along the bottom. After a while, the bubbles coming up from his regulator grew steadier. He was relaxing, becoming confident.

Suddenly, we came to a sharp drop-off where the bottom of a canyon could barely be seen far below. Chris panicked. Despite our buoyancy, he was sure we would fall off the edge of the cliff to the murky depths below. He squeezed hard on my hand.

Through my mask, I could see his eyes open wide with fear. Immediately, I squeezed back and with a free hand made a circle with my thumb and forefinger indicating that everything was okay. Almost immediately, I could see him smile. He signaled back that he understood and was no longer afraid. It was an instant reflex of confidence, a reaction as old as civilization itself, a learning experience signifying that in time of danger, the son can trust the father. We had danced the dance of the male molecules. The father-son team of hunters had bonded. The body-on healing had taken place under the sea on a warm Florida afternoon.

After placing my sleeping bag at the foot of the stone chairs, I lean back and drink in the beauty of the distant mountains profiled against the star-bejeweled night sky. The thought occurs to me that finally I'm coming to Chris's home. Here on this granite stone is where he sat. On the level section of the ledge, where my own sleeping bag now lies, is where he slept. At last I've come to visit so that we can be together in what has often been described as the greatest event in a man's life: the reconciliation and bonding of father and son.

I realize this trip has been put off for much too long. For years, I avoided visiting Chris at Yosemite and requested of him that we even refrain from discussing what he did here. My tactic had been a refusal to sanction his interest in climbing by boycotting this place and eliminating any talk about it so that he wouldn't do it any more. I had given Chris my phone credit number so he could call me at no cost, providing of course that we didn't bring up the one subject he loved most.

Now as I sit here alone on this stone ledge, looking out over the dark dome of sky above the valley, I realize the foolishness of such a strategy. Where had this desire for ignorance on my part come from? Since when did avoidance, boycotts or rejection help anyone do anything, let alone send a message to one's own son?

Clearly, I had relied on the traditional role of parental authority in order to be influential. Not only was this strategy flawed, but now the price being exacted for my mistake, the chance of a potential reunion between father and son, was lost. Only the father was left.

Even so, I decide that I must go on. In the morning, I'll find someone who can teach me how to climb so I can try to discover what it was that motivated Chris's love for these huge rock walls standing sentry high above the valley. But, instead of the ruggedly handsome young man with the blue eyes and constant smile whose mantra for just about everything was "Go for it," I'll have to find a stranger for a teacher. My instructor will not be the child I had argued and fought with and loved as he struggled through his teenage years. Nor will it be the twenty-eight-year old son with whom I had finally established a bond of humor, understanding and unquestioned trust. The instructor will be good and experienced, but the climbing lessons will never be combined with the comforting mixture of masculine love and faith which only a father and child can achieve.

A breeze picks up across the valley and the lure of my warm sleeping bag becomes irresistible. In a few minutes, I'm squirming around trying to find a comfortable spot between the small stones of the ledge. Then, finally, sleep overcomes the endless contradictions, the painful memories and the frustrating attempts to comprehend or find answers for the questions which seem to have no answers.

6

chapter

Basic Lessons

There is nothing so dangerous as the absence of all enemies.

Ignatius Loyola, Jesuit Founder

In the dim light of early morning, I wake on the stone ledge at the foot of the mountain and slowly crawl from my warm sleeping bag. The air is still cool but the emerging glow of sun against the horizon promises to heat up the valley in a few more hours. This could be a perfect day to begin learning about rock climbing if I can find a teacher. How I wish it could be Chris.

After taking a seat on the stone bench above the ledge where the night has passed so quickly, I watch for several minutes as the red and yellow hues of light filter slowly through the gray dawn. Finally, I stuff the sleeping bag into Chris's old backpack which I now use with unabashed pleasure and descend to the parking lot at Camp 4.

Several climbers with tanned, weathered faces are sitting next to an old, rust-covered pickup truck organizing their climbing gear before heading out for a day on one of the nearby granite walls. They're lean and young with muscular legs that display scars from collisions with rock and stone. They're sorting out chalks, carabiners, camming devices, pitons, daisy chains and other climbing equipment I've never seen before. They're talking in a lingo I find incomprehensible. "So I'm leading this five nine pitch and just as I finished placing this bomber Friend, my belayer takes a whipper," one of the young men says. He could be talking Swahili or Farsi as far as I'm concerned. It occurs to me that confiding my plans to climb one of the nearby rock walls would make them laugh. Perhaps I should get in the minivan and leave the valley immediately. No one would know.

Just then, a middle-aged man riding a bicycle and wearing a worn baseball cap wheels up to me. His neck and back are bent forward in what appears to be a fairly advanced state of scoliosis.

"Hi," he says with a friendly smile. Dismounting from his bike, he introduces himself as Tim Noonan. I soon learn that he climbs here several times a week and sleeps each night in a nearby station wagon. Tim comes to Yosemite every year in April and stays until the cold weather arrives in late September. He supports this minimalist lifestyle by working each evening as the house manager of the park theater where live performers enact various personalities and events associated with Yosemite Valley's history. He knows most of the men and women who have climbed at Yosemite over the past decade and he remembers Chris. He knows about the accident.

"Chris did some pretty amazing climbs when he was here," he says.

Tim is also an expert climber and it occurs to me as we talk that perhaps he can be helpful to the cause which has brought me here.

When I explain that I just came down from the talus line where I spent the night, he replies: "Excellent. Excellent." Then he asks: "Are you here for a visit?"

"More than that. I want to learn how to climb one of those," I reply, lifting my eyes upwards at the distant face of the Sentinel.

Tim conceals his surprise by turning his head toward the parking lot for a second. Then he looks back at me through heavy-rimmed glasses. "That's a pretty big order. You ever climbed before?"

"Just once. Chris gave me a lesson, but I didn't learn much," I respond.

Tim nods slowly. "I'm headed to the cafeteria for some coffee. You wanna come along and we can talk?"

I agree and in a few minutes, Tim has locked his bike to the back of the station wagon and we're on the way.

The cafeteria is located fifty yards down the road in the middle of a large motel complex run by the Curry Company, which has owned a monopoly on Yosemite since the 1930s. Food is served throughout the day to the crowds of tourists who come to observe the astounding natural wonders which have made the park famous. The cafeteria is also the unofficial coffee house for the climbing community of Camp 4.

After we take a seat at one of the tables, I ask Tim: "So what do you think? Is it possible for someone like me who's never even seen a big wall before to climb here in Yosemite?"

Tim chuckles and takes a sip of coffee. Then he asks: "Why do you want to do that?"

"To find out what climbing is all about. You know, learn by doing it," I reply.

"So you can understand why Chris was so intent on climbing?"

"Exactly," I reply, nodding my head.

Tim sips his coffee for a moment. Then he leans forward in his chair. "What did you think of Chris's involvement in all of this?" he asks.

Shocked at the sudden poignancy his question induces in me, I nevertheless answer candidly: "I was opposed to it. What father wouldn't be? In fact, I talked to him about it several times. We even joked about it. I told him I didn't want to have to spend the rest of my life wheeling him into a men's room or feeding him baby food because he broke his back climbing."

"So you think climbers are crazy?" he asks.

"Of course," I answer.

"Then why not accept it at that? Why come here?" he asks.

"Maybe I'm wrong. Maybe there is something to be learned by risking your life two thousand feet up on a rock wall and since climbing was Chris's passion, I want to know," I respond. Then I tell Tim about having met Eric Rasmussen the previous day and how surprised I was to find out that rock climbing here in Yosemite was relatively safe if proper precautions are taken.

"Yeah. Eric's a good climber. He knows what he's doing," Tim says.

I pursue the issue at hand: "So you think I'm on a mission impossible?"

Tim avoids the question. Instead, he moves the topic into deeper territory. "You know, climbing is like a lot of other things in life. What you see isn't necessarily what you get. When you look up on those walls and watch people climbing, you can't tell what they're doing, what they're thinking or even why they're up there. People climb for different reasons. It's not like there's a brass ring at the summit which everyone wants and once you climb up you get it."

"Are you saying that I won't learn much by trying one of these walls?" I ask.

He looks at me closely for a moment then goes on. "I don't know. What you're going to learn is up to you."

"Me?" I ask.

Tim nods. "What you find on a mountain depends on what you take with you," he says.

I laugh uneasily. "You sound like some New Age guru. You know, 'the journey is the destination'...'the wheel must come full circle.'"

He smiles as a few climbers pass by. "Hey, Prez, how's it going?" they call out. Tim is obviously a legend in this place. Some call him the "President of Camp Four."

Ignoring my comment, he turns back to me. "One of the things you learn when you climb a big wall is to get focused. You have to concentrate on what you're doing. Each move is important because your safety depends on it and because sometimes it's very difficult. Some athletes call this getting into the zone. A guy like Wayne Gretzky probably enters the zone the moment he skates out on the ice. Michael Jordan can obviously switch into the zone when he grabs a basketball. It's a sort of mental leap into total concentration and not everyone can do it. It means there's nothing else in your head but the particular move you're making at that time," Tim says.

"So learning to focus is what climbing is about?" I ask.

"An important part. And it takes time. It takes training and discipline. Remember, you're going to get tired up there because it's punishing physical work to constantly stretch and pull yourself up a vertical rock wall. Not all climbers can do that. They can't push themselves that hard or stay concentrated that long. It can be painful and most of us like to stay comfortable. We like to do what's easy. Have a nice climb and come back to Camp Four for a beer. Hang out. Talk to friends. That's okay, but it's not what true climbing is all about. To find the real meaning you must learn how to focus. If you can get yourself into the zone, as Chris did, then a whole lot of other things start happening. Experiences take place that can really change your life."

I lean back and glance around the room. The sun is beginning to shine through the windows now. The senior citizens who are staying at the lodge are filtering into the cafeteria in their colorful track suits, Nike shoes and ubiquitous eyeglasses. I pass no judgment on the apparel of my silver-haired contemporaries. When you live in a glass house, you don't throw stones.

"So, Tim, are you saying I'm not going to learn much by making just a few climbs, because I can't learn to focus without years of training and experience?" I ask.

"I can't answer that," he responds, shaking his head. "Maybe you already know how. Maybe, for you, it's just a matter of learning some techniques and getting into shape. That's why I said it depends on what you take with you. It's impossible to predict. What I do suggest is that we go out this afternoon and give it a try."

We finish our coffee and retreat to the parking lot. Tim sends me off to buy a pair of climbing shoes at the outdoor sports store located close to the cafeteria. He suggests that when I return, we take the minivan and go to a small cliff not too far down the valley. "It's big enough to give you a feel for what it's like, but not too threatening," he says.

As I drive to the store, the sun is directly overhead, casting its warmth through the trees, stirring birds, butterflies, grasshoppers and a variety of bugs into their daily rounds throughout the Tuolumne Meadows. The Merced River, winding at random along the valley floor, reflects the blue sky through its glistening stone bottom. It's not surprising that the Native Americans who first lived here had to be driven away at gunpoint before giving up their camps in this abundant, beautiful valley where fish and game were once so plentiful.

I find the store and select a pair of lightweight, tight-fitting climbing shoes. The black sole is made of soft rubber that sticks to a stone surface when pressed down by one's body weight. I throw them into the back seat and return to Camp 4 where Tim is waiting with a pile of gear he has either borrowed or retrieved from the back of his station wagon.

A half hour later, we park along the road several miles to the west and carry a rucksack filled with gear across a field and through some fir trees to a small cliff approximately one hundred feet high. Numerous cracks and small ledges line the face of the rock, ideal for foot and finger holds.

"If you look carefully, you'll see some bolts sticking out from the face of the rock," Tim says. "They've been placed there by other climbers. We'll tie into them so that taking a fall won't be dangerous."

After looking closely, I see the small protrusions of steel shining all along the face of the rock. I ask Tim the same question I had inquired of Eric Rasmussen the previous afternoon: "Isn't that cheating? I read somewhere that if you have bolts in the rock, you're climbing a ladder rather than a rock wall."

"It's a controversial topic. A lot of people would agree with that idea and a couple of national parks have even outlawed the placement of any bolts or pitons in rocks. On the other hand, we only use them for breaking a fall so you have to decide whether it's wrong to keep a climber from getting injured or killed simply because it's not as sporting to place some steel bolts in the wall," he explains.

It sounds like an argument that has no perfect answer, so we turn to the immediate task of learning about the equipment Tim is now pulling out of his haul bag.

"This is a carabiner," Tim says, handing me a D-shaped aluminum ring. "There are several kinds and you need to know how to use them all."

Some of the "beeners," as climbers call these lightweight devices, open simply by pressing down on the gate while others are spring-loaded and need to be twisted in order to open. As I soon learn, each piece of equipment has been constructed with a fail-safe design. If properly used, there is practically no possibility of an operational failure. We also check out chock slings, fifi hooks, chains and spring-loaded camming devices. The number and variety of pieces of equipment used for securing a climber to the wall seem infinite.

"The first and most important step in climbing is learning how to tie into your gear so that if you do fall, your rope will hold," Tim explains as he shows me how to tie a figure-eight follow-through knot securely to my harness. Then comes a lesson on how to belay by feeding out rope to the lead climber, yet always being ready to brake the rope in case the person above slips. Each move made on the wall is almost always covered with protective countermeasures to avoid a serious fall. Even the language used in climbing is precise and designed to avoid confusion; "on belay," "tension," "rope on" are all specific directions which climbing partners give to each other before moving in any direction. If followed, these directions should eliminate the possibility of an accident caused by poor communication.

After my mind has absorbed as much new information as possible, Tim decides it's time to start climbing.

Together, we walk up the backside of the cliff and secure the top rope to several bolts. Then, after throwing the rope over the side of the rock wall, we hike down and prepare to climb. I hook my waist harness to the belay rope which is now secured at the top of the cliff. Tim can play out this safety rope or draw it tight, thus preventing my rapid descent in case of a fall.

The first few feet go easily enough. As I move up the craggy side of the rock wall, Tim calls out instructions: "You want to push off your legs, not pull up with your fingers or arms." A small ledge at waist level appears. Slowly, carefully, I lift my foot up and place weight on the protrusion. A good leg push moves me several feet upwards. I look for the next foothold. A smaller crack appears on the left. I jam my toe into this fissure and move up again. Then I get stuck. I look around, feeling a bit of trepidation. There's nothing to grab or step on that's within reach.

"What now?" I call down to Tim.

"Come down a step and then move up to your left," he advises. "You'll find a better foothold over there."

Gingerly, I begin to step down, but Tim calls out: "Swing out and sit down on your harness." I take a deep breath. That requires more faith in the rope than I can manage. I push back slowly and then quickly shift my weight back to both feet.

"Don't worry. It's going to hold. You have to trust it," Tim calls out.

Tentatively, I try sitting in the harness and breathe a sigh of relief. It holds. I'm swinging free of the rock and feeling surprised I'm not crashing to the ground. The important lesson of trusting one's gear has been learned. Next, Tim shows me how to shove the rope through a small steel cylinder called an ATC (Air Traffic Control) which allows me to brake the rope at any time or lower myself down the wall by playing the rope slowly through this rappelling device.

"Okay, now climb up again," Tim says.

Once more, I reach up for a crack in the rock and place my feet in the nearest foothold. For several minutes, I move up nicely and then suddenly, like an ebbing tide, all strength seems to flow out of my arms and legs. Breathing becomes difficult. The rock becomes slightly blurred. I can no longer move. I remember getting this awful feeling while playing hockey in college. We called it the "shakes." One's whole body seems about to give out. The only remedy is to sit down and rest.

"Tim, I'm tired. I'm coming down," I call out.

"Okay. Rope up," he says as he plays out slack which allows me to retreat.

I descend until I'm on the ground. "I need a few minutes," I whisper as I find a nearby rock for support.

After about ten minutes, I'm feeling better, although still a bit dazed and weak.

"You've been exercising a lot of muscles that aren't accustomed to being used. It will take time to get in shape for serious climbing. Why don't we call it a day," Tim suggests.

Like a schoolboy being released for recess, I quickly agree.

As we gather up the equipment, it occurs to me that this is harder than I thought it would be. No one, not me or even some young hotshot athlete is going to walk up to Yosemite's big walls and climb to the top without a lot of physical and mental training. My plans for climbing have undergone a preliminary reality check.

"Well, I guess that's it." I shake my head. "If I can't go up forty feet without becoming sick and exhausted during the first hour how can I ever climb two or three consecutive days to reach three thousand feet," I say to Tim as we fold the belay rope into the haul bag.

"Don't be so quick to give up. Keep in mind why you're here," Tim replies.

"I know why I'm here," I answer testily.

"Maybe you don't have to climb a big wall to find what you're looking for," he suggests, glaring at my weary state. "Maybe you can do something else."

"Like what? Talk to other climbers?" I ask in an edgy tone I can't suppress.

Tim hears the sarcasm in my voice and shrugs his shoulders: "I can't tell you. You'll have to find that out for yourself. In the meantime, we'll go out again tomorrow and give it another try."

We return to Camp 4, but a few minutes after arriving at the parking lot, I decide to head for the cocktail lounge of the Ahwahnee Hotel for a libation strong enough to eradicate the memory of the day's failure and some dinner.

Afterward, I'm ready to retire. I go to my campsite and climb into my sleeping bag. Exhausted, sleep overcomes me quickly. Right before I sink into the the ether though, I see Chris's face and he is smiling.

The next day, Tim suggests we go to the foot of El Cap where there are some small cliffs on which we can again practice some more basic climbing techniques. This time, we are going to spend the entire afternoon moving up several easy pitches where Tim coaches me on each move while keeping me carefully on belay. Each time I move up, he calls out: "Use your legs. Don't pull yourself up with your arms. You'll never last." At the end of one pitch, I put my knee on a ledge and begin to move slowly forward. "Don't use your knees. Get your foot on the ledge and stand up," he calls.

These basic lessons take time, but as the afternoon

sun slides across the valley casting long shadows along the rock from nearby trees, I'm slowly learning to follow Tim's advice. At times, I call out, "This move is impossible!" Tim calls back: "You can do it. Reach your leg up to that next small crack and step up." Each time, I hesitate for several minutes and then lift my leg up. Suddenly, miraculously, I'm several feet higher. I feel exhilarated at my progress. Yet, by the time Tim climbs quickly up the wall to unhook the top rope, I'm glad to be finished. It is hard work. "I can't even imagine how a climber can spend several consecutive days climbing on the huge walls above," I tell Tim.

"Don't worry about it for now. Just do your best. Take one step at a time and see what happens," Tim says.

We return to the car and drive back to Camp 4. As I maneuver the minivan into the parking lot, Tim suggests I attend the theater that night where he works. "There's a program about John Muir you might like. He's the famous naturalist who first climbed and wrote about Yosemite," Tim says.

"Sounds good," I reply.

7

chapter

The Inner Voice

Be like a lion, going forth with slow, gentle and firm steps. Only with this kind of vigilance can you experience total awakening.

Thich Nhat Hanh

The small theater located next to the Yosemite Park museum is an effective venue for one or two person presentations. An adequate lighting system and bench seats for approximately one hundred people enables the audience to watch the performers move about on a small stage where they offer interpretations of interesting local residents. While waiting to attend the evening performance, Tim introduces me to a Yosemite rock climbing legend who is also standing outside the theater.

Slim and handsome, with neatly combed white hair, Tom Frost is one of the early Yosemite climbers who revolutionized the art of rock climbing during the 1960s. Possessed with a quick sense of humor and a wealth of life experiences, he's constantly stopped by admiring climbers who ask for autographs or who just wish to shake the hand of this modest yet fascinating icon of the climbing world. Now in his early sixties and retired from his partnership as a designer and manufacturer of climbing gear with another famous valley climber, Yvon Chouinard, Tom was on the first team ever to climb El Capitan in one continuous ascent without fixed ropes.

In his book on the history of Yosemite climbing, Steve Roper wrote:

> Tom Frost was the quietest and most modest person to inhabit Camp 4 during those early years. Only much later did I learn that he had been a champion sailboat racer in his early twenties. Bright and super clean both in looks and language, he preferred to stay out of the limelight, rarely arguing, rarely writing about his exploits. Robbin (Royal) later described Frost as one of those spirits I cite to illustrate that the quality of people in climbing is one of the reasons I love the sport. Tom, besides being an outstanding climber, is a walking emanation of good will.

After Tim introduces us and tells Tom why I have decided to climb El Capitan, Tom is immediately interested. "What you're trying is courageous. Don't get discouraged. The small walls can be just as tough as the big ones," he says. As we enter the theater, I sense that here is someone who probably understands what I'm looking for.

During the next few days, Tom and I see one another every morning after we've spent our nights in sleeping bags at Camp 4. He has a tent, while I normally go up the ledge or sometimes just sleep on the ground near the parking lot. However, since we both rise at daybreak, we start the day with a breakfast of cold cereal and bananas which we store in the back of our vehicles.

During one long conversation, I mention that Chris once told his mother that he could feel the rocks and understand their mood when he climbed. A devout Mormon from Boulder, Colorado, Tom nods knowingly and whispers the word, "awesome."

After these morning breakfast sessions, I sometimes wander over to the Ahwahnee Hotel and spend a few hours reading or writing. The magnificent hotel, built at the turn of the century to serve wealthy overnight visitors to the park, offers free coffee to their guests throughout the morning. In the main lobby I easily mingle with the guests for coffee and a reading of the morning newspapers from San Francisco. When this leisurely ritual is completed, I take a seat in the huge sitting room with its gigantic fireplace and timbered ceiling where I can spend the morning clicking away on my laptop while always trying to appear like an elite and wealthy guest enjoying the amenities of the hotel rather than a nomadic writer looking for free coffee and a place to work. The days pass quickly and happily except when I think about Chris and how much I wish he were here with me in this valley he loved so much.

The evenings are usually spent sitting next to Tim Noonan's station wagon in the parking lot of Camp 4 after he comes back from the theater. We listen to the young climbers who come to the "Prez" with their aspirations and problems. Climbing stories are frequently mixed with confessions of love affairs gone awry and boastings about big walls, of which the confident climbers repeat to each other: "I'm gonna send it tomorrow, man." Pretty girls with college degrees, strong arms and muscular legs talk about how hard it is to get any commitment from their adventuresome boyfriends, whose only serious attachments are to the dark stone walls looming high above us in the starlit night. The young men complain about their lonely lives: "No women around. You take up climbing, man, you give up women." These macho, frustrated young men are talking about more than women. They want connection, identity, a sense of belonging and so they've turned to the ready-made, tightly-knit community of climbers. They've discovered that, for now, "sending" a big wall can buy a paid-up membership in the club. It might not last long, but for the present it works. And if the price is exorbitant, so be it. No one complains that it's excessive. The need is too intense. Always my mind turns to Chris.

One evening, while some climbers are sitting around Tim's station wagon talking, a young male voice emerges from somewhere in the darkness and claims that the only people he can trust are climbers.

"My parents, like, they just don't get it. My dad's a stockbroker. Wants me to work for him selling that kinda shit," the voice says disdainfully.

"What is it you want to do?" I call through the dark.

"I don't know. I've got a degree in computer science, but I can't stand watching that screen all day. You know, not talkin' to anybody, workin' ten, twelve hours a day. What for? So I can join the country club, play golf and own a big house in some suburban development? No way, man. No way. I'll stick to climbing."

Later, after the climbers have left and I'm ready to go up to the ledge for the night, I ask Tim who the voice was.

"Larry. He's been here two months now. He's a pretty smart guy. Owns that Nissan sports utility vehicle at the end of the parking lot. His dad bought it for him."

"Is he a good climber?" I ask.

"For sure. He's done most of the big walls here, some of them solo. I guess he'd be good at just about anything he tried," Tim adds.

"So why has he turned to climbing?" I ask.

Tim is silent for a moment. Then, through the dark, warm air I hear him sigh. "Probably the same reason as Chris."

In the afternoons, Tim and I slip back to a rock wall somewhere in the valley and take turns climbing and going on belay for each other. Each time it gets a little better. A new kind of strength and enthusiasm begins to seep into my arms and legs. A feeling of worthiness in accomplishing a hard task is offering welcome mental satisfaction. Yet, despite the progress, I often look up at the towers of rock high above the valley and realize that I'll never gain the strength and stamina needed to climb a 3,000-foot wall. I'm beginning to think that the secret of El Capitan's summit will forever remain a mystery. I suppose Chris understood that.

And then one morning, Tom Frost seeks me out and makes a suggestion that changes everything. "You know it's possible to hike up the back side of El Capitan. It's about ten miles and if you want, I'll go with you this weekend. We could camp overnight on top and then walk down the next day."

"I'd love to," I respond without a moment's hesitation.

The prospect of hiking with someone who knows so much about climbing and with whom I've been able to laugh and share so many similar experiences from the past forty years is irresistible. I can hardly wait for the next two days to pass so we can start our hike.

When Saturday morning finally arrives, the word

has spread around Camp 4 that Tom is going to take me to the top of El Cap. As we pack our gear in the back of the minivan, a number of young climbers come by to wish us well. I feel like a celebrity, even if it is Tom's autograph they request when the pencils and paper come out. Nevertheless, the mood is upbeat when we finally start the car and drive several miles to a logging road where the hike will start. I have a strong premonition that the next twenty-four hours are going to be important steps in my journey.

It's noon when we finally get underway. Three ridges and ten miles to the east, a bright sun glistens against the rock summit of El Capitan, which we had planned to reach by early evening. However, with this late start, the likelihood of arriving before nightfall is growing slim. I'm not worried. After all, I'm in the hands of one of the most experienced climbers in the world.

For the first mile, we shuffle past burned out trees and blackened patches of ground where a forest fire had raged a year earlier. I explain to Tom that Chris's job often required him to assess whether a forest should be allowed to burn after he had evaluated its condition via satellite imagery.

"That's right," he exclaims. "Chris had a real understanding of the trees."

For a moment, I hesitate, surprised that he would describe what Chris was like without ever meeting him. "You mean because of his ability with the computer to make studies of the environment?" I ask.

"No...not that. You said the other day that Chris told his mother he could feel the rock and even sense its mood when he was climbing. That tells me a lot about him. Very few people can do that," Tom explains.

For a few minutes, we walk in silence as I reflect on

what Tom has said. When you lose someone as close to you as a son, most people avoid mentioning him. Even relatives and friends feel it's best not to bring up the sensitive subject of your grief. However well-intentioned, they're wrong. Grieving people need to be with friends who will converse about the sorrow and recall memories of the person who is gone. The fact that Tom feels free to bring up Chris as if he is part of this trip is an unexpected and welcome addition to my search.

After climbing the slope for almost an hour, we begin to descend into a valley where a small stream flows from a fissure in the mountain and large boulders are exposed in the creek. By next spring, they'll be covered with rushing torrents of water.

I decide to confront Tom with my feelings of anger about the mountain climbing which caused my son's death which, I suspect, will be a little like telling the home run slugger, Mark McGwire, why you don't like baseball.

"Have you ever talked to someone who believes climbing is a dangerous con game where a lot of people are tricked into thinking they're doing something terrific, when actually they're only wasting time and making fools of themselves?" I ask.

Tom senses my meaning. He suggests we take a break and points to several fallen trees where we can sit and talk for a few minutes.

"For a lot of people, that may be true," he says, unslinging his pack and pulling out a plastic water bottle. "On the other hand, it can be...well, a spiritual experience...a way of learning about life, getting to know who you are and how you need to live."

"Oh come on, Tom, if that were true, we'd all become climbers," I protest. "There are a lot of people who would give anything to solve their life problems. These things can't be solved simply by putting on a pair of rubber shoes and climbing a rock wall."

Tom smiles and slowly begins to slide his knapsack across his shoulders, signaling that it's time to move on. "Let me explain to you what climbing is all about," he says as we return to the trail. "And perhaps you'll understand Chris's love of it." The meadow soon leads to a steep, rocky slope where Tom continues to speak in a steady and easily audible voice.

"There are three stages of rock climbing and each one is important," he says. "The first is to know yourself and what you're capable of doing. We have to learn what our limits are. There are a lot of people who come up here to climb for the wrong reasons. They want to show off to their girlfriend or prove they're not scared of anything...all kinds of foolishness. With little or no training, they try to climb these walls and inevitably they get hurt. Just this summer, some guy who had never climbed before tried to rappel without securing his belaying rope. He fell and the belay failed so he took a whipper and broke his back. If he had been aware of his limitations, he would have been more careful."

"I've met that type already," I reply without breaking stride. "It seems there are a lot of very insecure people who turn to climbing because they don't really have to train or develop real skills. It's a quick, easy way of convincing themselves or their friends that they're brave when really they're only fools."

"Maybe you're right. But they don't last long here. The walls of Yosemite are too big, too tough for ego trips. People like that take one or two falls and then they quit. If they're properly secured, they don't get killed, but a good tumble can discourage a person pretty quickly."

For a few minutes we hike in silence as Tom gives me time to process his words. Then he continues: "The second rule is to know what you're up against. We have to know about the mountain before we start climbing in order to understand what kind of technique we're going to use. That means studying the rock and becoming familiar with as many characteristics of the wall as possible. We need to learn about the cracks, the holds, even the texture of the rock so we can sense how we're going to climb.

"Finally, when we go up on a mountain, we have a certain sense about it. There are a lot of signs out there and we have to be aware of them. You might say that we have to listen to our 'inner voice.' A climber must have a double level of awareness. If we have a feeling that we shouldn't make a certain move or that we should not even climb that day, we need to heed that advice. If, on the other hand, our inner voice tells us to move forward, to go up the next pitch, then we must listen to that as well."

As Tom finishes his analysis of what climbing is all about, we slowly traverse a stone-filled slope that leads us into a flat valley filled with giant fir trees whose thick bark wraps around the massive trunks like heavy wool scarves. He gazes up among the trees where shafts of sunlight filter through the green branches.

"Chris knew all this," he says.

Again, Tom refers to Chris as if he knew him well.

"How do you know that?" I ask.

"Because of his sensitivity to the environment and the climbs he did. Chris was on another level," Tom answers casually and with such confidence that I can only remain silent while remembering the words which Clare Booth Luce once wrote: "There are those who can always hear, beneath the rumble of the traffic, the stars singing."

Was Chris one of these people? Was he really someone who had learned, through climbing, the secret to living on another level so that he could feel and understand a rock as a living thing?

"Preposterous," I say to myself. Even he would laugh at such a proposition. Perhaps Tom Frost is some kind of fanatic who talks about people he's never known as if they were his oldest friends. I remind myself that I did not come to Yosemite to glorify or idealize Chris, nor did I come here to be victimized by the kind of mystical beliefs about the mountains that has snared so many thousands of other climbers. In his diary, written a few months before the accident, even Chris had described himself in the most humble of terms:

> Who is Chris Purnell? You're probably wondering what rad walls has he done? Well, I'm just one more wall climber, of which there seem to be so many these days. An average wall climber, bonded with a growing number of folks who have found adventure, terror, hard work and eventual reward, in short, purpose from the captivating pastime of climbing walls. That purpose so frequently lacking from real life, school, jobs and the like, defines wall climbing. It's what separates it from more traditional sports.

Still, as we prepare to leave this cathedral-like valley of giant trees basking silently in the warm afternoon air, I find myself placing more and more trust in my climbing companion. His understanding of both the mountains and the people who climb them is contagious. I know now Chris was saying the same thing as Tom when he confessed to finding "purpose" here that he found nowhere else.

It occurs to me that perhaps Tom would understand an event which has been challenging my long-held belief that mystical experiences in which the dead come back to visit the living are nothing but figments of a tortured imagination. I decide to tell him what happened on a hot Monday morning a few weeks earlier.

It took place during a tennis match which I was playing at the National Men's 60s Grass Court Tennis Tournament on Long Island, not far from the location of the United States Open. Many of the finest senior tennis players in the world who are sixty years old or over come there each year to compete against their peers on the well-groomed grass courts of the Rockaway Hunting Club. This was my third year of playing the tournament, although I never did particularly well mainly because of an inability to adjust my game to a grass surface.

As we begin moving up the trail again with Tom in the front, I begin to tell him about my experience that day and explain that when playing on grass, it's important to serve well and get to the net quickly where a good volley can usually win the point. During the first match of the day, I was playing against a smart, aggressive opponent who constantly anticipated where my service was going. Late in the first set, with the score even, I tried twice to hit the serve wide to his backhand, thus pulling him off the court and creating an opportunity for me to come to the net and volley for an easy winner. Both times, my opponent anticipated this strategy by moving to his left as I was serving and hitting a winning backhand service return.

For the third time, I prepared to serve wide to his backhand hoping he would never expect me to use the same tactic again. As I tossed the ball into the air, I noticed a white cloud passing against the clear sky above and suddenly the age-old belief that departed loved ones can look down and observe those left behind, filled my thoughts. I wondered if Chris was watching. As my arm started its upward arc toward the ball, his voice suddenly resonated clearly through my mind.

"Of course I'm watching...and I think you should jam that guy down the middle instead of hitting wide where he's been returning perfectly on the last two points."

Chris was right. If I went for the wide backhand again, my opponent would slide sideways and nail the ball for a crosscourt winner just as he did before. Again, I heard Chris' voice: "Jam him, Papa. Jam him."

Heeding his advice just before my racquet struck the ball, I shifted my arm an inch to the left and hit the ball directly at the receiver who had once more started his move sideways. It worked. He was caught with the ball coming straight at his chest. He tried to reverse direction and wiggle backwards, but it was too late. He stumbled off balance and knocked the ball into the net. I glanced up at the cloud again. "Thanks, Chris," I whispered.

As I finish the story, Tom stops in the middle of the trail and our eyes meet. A slight smile tugs at the edge of his mouth. "You see, Chris isn't gone. He's still here taking care of you."

Shifting my pack, I look at the trees above. Sensitive to the tears forming in my eyes, Tom turns and starts up the trail again without another word and for the next few hours, we move rapidly, silently along the trail. The sun is beginning to drop across a distant rim of rock walls, but we're determined to reach the top of El Cap before darkness sets in.

An enthusiastic young climber, Scottie Burke, who is attempting to do a free climb of a difficult route called the Nose, has been camping all summer at the top while he studies the wall and practices on several of the more difficult pitches. At this point, a woman, Lynn Hill, has been the only person to "free the Nose," so Scottie is trying to be the first man to accomplish this climb. We expect to find him and share his campsite that night.

As we approach the summit of El Capitan, I recall Tom's definition of climbing, particularly the last point about listening to one's inner voice. Through my mind pass several similar ideas: George Fox, founder of the Quaker religion, admonished his followers: "To follow our inner light and walk happily on this earth." "Everyone who is of the truth hears my voice," Jesus told Pilate, during an inquisition which ended in the Crucifixion. "Be still and know," the Buddha says.

Is it possible that some climbers learn to hear their inner voices and use them to climb and, even, to live on "another level," as Tom Frost suggested? Is there a zone, a point of concentration which human beings can achieve, as Tim Noonan said, where experiences take place that are not available to the average person?

Scottie Burke, whom we hoped to find, is not here and darkness has settled over the top of El Capitan. With the sure-footed confidence of a mountain goat, however, Tom reconnoiters the area and soon finds a suitable campsite. The bivouac area is nothing more than a flat ledge between two boulders, but it's all we need. As we begin pulling our sleeping bags from the packs, we suddenly hear voices coming from the edge of the 3,000-foot cliff. Then, the forms of two young men appear against the starlit sky.

Realizing they're arriving on top of El Capitan after climbing a particularly difficult route, Tom calls through the night: "Hi, fellows. What route did you do?"

"The North American wall. We've been on it for five days. We didn't expect to see anyone here," one of the young men replies, obviously happy but surprised to hear a human voice.

Tom steps across a long slab of rock and introduces himself in the friendly manner endemic to most climbers: "Congratulations. I'm Tom Frost. Nice to see you. Great job."

From somewhere in the darkness, I hear a stunned voice reply: "THE Tom Frost?" At that point, I 'm convulsed with laughter at the thought of the first climber of that famous route running a Welcome Wagon program on top of the very cliff he climbed so long ago. When Tom returns to our campsite, I suggest that he go to work for the Park Service as the official greeter for those who climbed the mountain.

"You could have a little chair up here and perhaps give a gold star to each person who makes it to the top," I suggest.

He laughs good-humoredly.

Since we have no cookout for dinner, I retrieve some bread and cheese from my pack and quickly make sandwiches for both of us.

"Wonderful. This is great," Tom repeats several times as we sit quietly, munching on our simple but delicious meal. Sensing an opportunity to learn more from my master climber companion, I shift the conversation to the topic we had discussed earlier in the afternoon.

"You said that climbing consists of knowing your limitations, learning about the mountain and listening to your inner voice. Which is the most important?" I ask.

"They're all pretty much equal," Tom replies without hesitation. "Recognizing your own ability and what you can climb is just as important as learning about the mountain. I'm not just talking about muscle strength or ability to reach high up for a crack. It's like being an artist. A pianist doesn't try to play a concerto if he's still learning the scales. By picking a route equal to your ability, you assure yourself of a safe and satisfactory experience. It's the same with life. You have to live within the limitations of your talents and experience and then perform at your best level. It's an important principle for climbing and for living."

"But what about the inner voice? Suppose you don't hear it?" I ask.

For a few moments, Tom thinks about the question as a slight breeze begins to stir along the top of the cliff. "Then you're not listening," he finally responds. "Let me tell you a story about several people who died in the Himalaya mountains and several who lived because some listened to their inner voices and others didn't.

"Last year, I attended a lecture by a well-known climber named Todd Skinner who was speaking in Boulder, Colorado about his ascent of the Trango Tower in Pakistan. Todd and his three companions had been climbing for forty-three days and were getting close to the peak when suddenly they saw a black cloud approaching in the distance," Tom relates.

"They knew it was a bad storm and that they should probably rappel down the mountain to their base camp. On the other hand, they didn't want to give up their hard-won position on the mountain, a spot that would enable them to gain the summit when the weather cleared.

"Todd told the crowd at this lecture that he and his companions held a discussion about the weather and then decided to go down to the safety of their tents 1,000 feet below. It was a smart move. The storm lasted for nine days and they were able to survive. Twenty miles away on K-Two, the same storm hit and some climbers decided to keep climbing upwards. None of them survived. One of the climbers who died was Alison Hargreaves, the well-known English climber, who left two children at home. This extraordinary woman had summited Everest the year before, alone and without oxygen, but after almost two months of trying to reach the top of K-Two, she decided to continue climbing despite the oncoming storm. Peter Hillary, son of the first person to summit Everest, Sir Edmund Hillary, was climbing nearby, but turned back."

"Hillary later wrote in the New York Times: 'I was becoming progressively concerned about the bank of evil-looking clouds emanating from the north, from western China and, at midday in a cloud of falling snow, I decided to descend alone while the other seven continued on. None of them survived the one-hundred-mile-per-hour winds that blew them off the mountain.' As for Hargreaves, Hillary said he felt she was so anxious to summit and return home to her husband and two children that she put pressure on herself to keep going up, rather than descend."

Tom shifts his weight and pauses for a few moments. He's wearing a wool skullcap now and I can barely see him through the darkness as he continues. "My wife and I left the lecture, but when we got to the parking lot, I told her I wanted to go back and ask Todd Skinner an important question."

"What was the question?" I ask.

"I asked Todd what made him turn back and rappel down the mountain when he wanted so desperately to summit the Tower. Todd told me that his group had listened to their feelings, not to anything they knew about the upcoming storm. He said by doing that, they had survived."

It's getting late now and we decide to head for our sleeping bags. Arriving at the flat section of the ledge, I can see the outline of Tom's face looking out over the valley.

"It's tempting to make risky decisions when you get near the top," he says softly. "All of your ambition urges you on. But if you're motivated by ambition, you'll hear ambition. If you're climbing for the right reasons and you're ready to listen, you'll hear your inner voice. The one can cost you your life; the other can save you."

As I crawl into my sleeping bag, I wonder if Chris was listening to his inner voice when he started his fatal ice climb in the Canadian Rockies. "Psyched and scared," he wrote in a Christmas letter to our family, before arriving at the frozen waterfalls of Kicking Horse Pass. Did he sense a warning signal as Susan Lilly had? Did Chris dismiss the message of an inner feeling or was this an accident in which there were no premonitions of disaster? Fortunately, the dark mantle of sleep arrives for me and ends the koan-like questions and their still elusive answers.

8

chapter

Signs of the Zodiac

Oh ye Athenians, will you believe what danger I incur to merit your praise?

Alexander the Great

Before dawn begins to spread its pink patina across the tip of the valley walls on the second morning of hiking with Tom Frost, I wake on the top of El Cap in the warmth of the sleeping bag and realize that my right arm is thrown over a small granite boulder for comfort. I can imagine Chris laughing and calling out, "Hey, Papa, these rocks feel almost as good as a sexy woman."

He would be in a fine mood this morning if he were here on the slanted rock slab summit of the famous wall he tried so hard to climb six years earlier. I know a lot about this event, because Chris wrote an article about his amazing four-day solo ascent in the hope that it might launch a career in which he could finance his dreams of climbing around the world as a paid writer. He called the piece, "Signs of the Zodiac."

It was his first summer in Yosemite and he was eager to qualify as a big wall climber. You can sit around Camp 4 and do a lot of talking about "sending a wall," but in the end, the rock has got to be faced and the summit gained if you're going to establish a reputation in this Mecca of world-class climbers. No one was more aware of this than Chris. He needed a major accomplishment before the summer ended. By late July, the opportunity suddenly arrived so fast and unexpectedly that it came as a total surprise even to him.

In fact, he had not planned to go up alone. The climb on El Cap was intended as a two-man venture. However, at the last minute a would-be climbing companion backed out. Chris wrote that a situation like this: "Makes you angry, angry at your partner, angry at yourself, angry at the world around you. It also makes you even more driven."

Yet, the anger he felt that day extended to far more than disappointment with a friend. He was beginning to realize that life in the valley was not quite the dream world he often imagined and that Yosemite can easily evoke a love-hate relationship. His words reflect his disgust with the commercialization of the park:

> I drove down to "Zodiac Beach," the parking lot by the Merced River at the base of El Cap, where all the tourists gape up at the ominous South-East Wall and the Curry Company's 'Green Dragon' tour ride cashes in by pointing out climbers and exclaiming to the tourists how crazy they must be.
>
> I realized how sick I was getting of life on the valley floor. I was sick of the trashed-out, ranger-infested, ghetto atmosphere of Camp 4. I was sick of eating tortillas and

beans in the toxic parking lot dirt every night. I was sick of the Coney Island the National Park Service and the Curry Company had created.

This was vintage Chris in his early twenties. The disillusioned traveler suddenly discovering that sin exists in Paradise. The strokes of his brush were broad. Few were spared condemnation:

> Didn't these people see how their swimming pools, video stores and hamburger stands that overwhelm the valley floor are nothing short of a cancerous disease that is slowly infesting an otherwise healthy soul?

Yet, frustration alone is not sufficient. If the valley is being destroyed, the angry young man must do something. A disillusioned Hamlet can rail against his fate, but in the end he must take action. "The world is out of joint; oh cursed spite that I were born to set it right," Shakespeare's young Prince complained.

In Chris's case, it seemed that the only choice left to him on the warm California day in the middle of summer was to "go for it." He would do something, even if solo climbing a 3,000-foot rock wall without the proper experience or equipment was the only option! Standing on the hot valley road while studying the complex Zodiac Route winding its way to the top of El Capitan's distant summit, he made up his mind:

> Looking up at the Zodiac's spectacular granite crack systems, dihedrals and roofs from the baking asphalt, the motivation in me was burning fiercely now. "Go for it," I said to myself. "I'll solo it."

Once the decision was made, there was no turning back even if that meant going by himself. After all, others had done the same thing:

> Now let's get it straight–Zodiac is not that rad. Only sixteen pitches makes it short by El Cap standards. Rated A3+ in Meyer's and Reid's green guidebook ("the Bible") and probably A2 in reality. Basic nailing. Gets done a lot.

Despite his immediate frustration and long-term ambition to break into a higher level of climbing, Chris was not ready for something like this. His decision to go up the Zodiac solo without the necessary experience for climbing a big wall was a violation of the rules of safe climbing which Tom Frost had outlined to me the previous afternoon.

The first rule, which Chris had been ready to break is: "Know yourself and what you're capable of doing." Chris had never once inserted a steel piton into a rock wall, nor was he adept at tying the kinds of knots needed for this kind of effort. Both are basic skills needed for climbing a world class wall like El Capitan. It was a classic contradiction between a lack of preparation and the need to succeed immediately: a Catch 22 where he couldn't gain the required experience without experiencing it. Chris was aware of his transgression:

> But I had only one grade VI to my name, and I'd never hammered a piton into Yosemite granite in my life. And except for figuring out how clove hitch soloing works on the Lost Arrow the week before, I had never solo aid climbed in my life. I was in for a wild several days.

Had I, his father, been there at this point, I would have advised Chris to immediately return to Camp 4, buy a book, seek out some companions and sit out the weekend reading or talking to his friends. However, I wasn't there to give that kind of advice and I doubt that he would have followed my recommendations had they been offered. Instead, he proceeded to break Tom's rule number two: "We have to know about the mountain before we start climbing in order to understand what kind of technique we're going to use."

Chris had neither knowledge of what he would be climbing nor the technique and equipment necessary for doing so. Admittedly, this scared him:

> Amassing gear, route info and food back in Yosemite village, my emotions changed from anger to fear and uncertainty. Back at Camp 4 that afternoon, I spread all my stuff out on a tarp under the tree next to Werner's old Pontiac. The Search and Rescue guys kidded around with me, saying things like, "Yer gonna diiie!" I'd stare a confused hollow gaze at nothing in particular, digesting their predictions. My face would break into a smile of appreciation when I heard, "Naw, just kidding. You'll send it, dude." In fact, better climbers, many of whom were on the SAR team, genuinely encouraged me in spite of the obvious terror which overwhelmed me. They were getting pretty skinny by late July and the prospect of a big wall rescue was sounding good to them, since they get paid by the rescue. The other "resident" climbers were really generous. Mike lent me his bivy sack, shocked that I was planning to go without one. Brad lent me his lead rope when I discovered a big cut in my own. Pat lent me half his whole rucksack! The Camp 4 resident climbers' sense of fraternity is strong and generosity is the rule.

Now as I sit here on the summit of El Cap this morning, I'm disturbed at the disdain Chris displayed toward the basic rules of safe climbing. Yet the question which intrigues me most is why he violated Tom's third rule about climbers needing to listen with a double level of awareness. Tom's sage advice that we must heed our inner voice if it tells us to give up or go on seems so on target, so rational, so unquestionable.

With this rule in mind, it would appear from his own words, that Chris should not have climbed that day:

> I had a fitful night's sleep in the back of my truck, knowing that the next day would be "the day." I must have dreamed every horrible climax to the climb that I could imagine: sliced ropes, dropped racks, big falls. I woke up at five-thirty with the sheets tangled all around my legs from rolling around all night and went across the road to the Lodge cafeteria, drank too much coffee as usual and headed out.

"Fitful night's sleep," "dreams of big falls!" Surely, these are the characteristics of an inner voice screaming to abort a dangerous climb, I think at first. Then a new thought enters my mind. Or are these no more than the normal concerns of a young man about to solo one of the biggest rock walls in the world?

The Colorado mountaineer and writer, Pat Ament, in his book, *How To Be A Master Climber*, points out that experienced climbers advise against attempting a route that is frightening. Yet, Ament also admits: "I have been a bit scared on almost everything I have ever soloed." Other questions rise to my mind: Was Chris refusing to abide by a level of awareness that told him to stay off the wall or was he simply overcoming his fears and displaying the courage necessary for a challenging venture?

Before I can try to answer the imponderables, I suddenly see Tom in the early light of dawn standing next to his sleeping bag. "Is that THE Tom Frost?" I call out. Tom laughs and in a few minutes we've resumed our perch on some boulders near the narrow campsite. With no coffee or even matches for making a fire from some of Scottie Burke's leftover coals, we take several long drinks from our water bottles. Fortunately, I had also thrown a packet of dried apricots into my pack which we now attack with the enthusiasm of two hungry "gastronomiques" dining in a four-star restaurant. I tell Tom what I've been thinking about this morning. "It must be difficult to hear–and understand–the meaning of one's inner voice."

He nods.

"If you're scared when you're about to undertake a climb, does that mean you shouldn't do it?" I press.

Tom answers after a few moments of reflection. "Learning to distinguish between real danger and unrealistic fear is never an easy task," he says. "Yet we can't overestimate the importance of recognizing one from the other."

I reflect on his words as we finish our breakfast. Then Tom announces that he's going to rappel over the edge of El Cap to Scottie's favorite New Dawn ledge so he can take a few photos. "I'll be happy staying where I am in order to enjoy the spectacular view," I assure him. It's getting better by the moment as the sun rises. A few minutes later, I see Tom hook a small nylon belt with attached rope around his waist and clip it into a carabiner. Then he snaps it into a sling which had already been tied to one of the few trees growing on top of the mountain. Gear securely in place, he lowers himself over the edge of the wall and disappears, leaving me alone to think again about Chris's solo climb of the Zodiac.

I root around in my pack searching for an overlooked morsel of food and instead find a wrinkled copy of Chris's article. He wrote:

> The exposure was sick. I didn't have to look over my shoulder to see the ground. It was right between my legs...the road...the meadow...the sky. It wears off, though, like a soldier who finds himself in the middle of a battle zone for the first time, the apathy towards danger sets in quickly.

He found the first hour terrifying yet he also became acclimatized to the fear of falling. Chris's analogy to war is reminiscent of my own initial fears about death when I went to Vietnam many years earlier. I can easily relate to his analogy of El Cap to a battle zone. In fact, I suspect that climbing provided Chris with the same kind of coming of age experience I found as a reporter in Vietnam. Even my love-hate relationship toward the war was probably a lot like Chris's feelings toward Yosemite.

Sitting here on the top of the "Big Rock" as climbers like to call El Capitan, I recall that first month "in country" when I arrived at a small airfield north of Saigon in February of 1967.

A major military operation was underway. Called Operation Junction City, it was a combined effort of American and Vietnamese units to clear thirty square miles of jungle and rice fields north of the city from which the Viet Cong were staging major assaults.

After driving my motorcycle to the airfield, I waited all morning to get a lift on one of the many helicopters departing every few minutes with another load of men and supplies being poured into the thirty square mile attack zone known as the Iron Triangle. Flashing my official press card, which allowed reporters to ride on any military aircraft if space was available, I shouted to each of the grim-faced pilots as they revved up their engines: "You have any extra seats?"

Each one shook his head. Then each chopper would rise in a could of dust and disappear beyond the tree line toward the fighting. The helicopters were loaded with crates of ammunition, water and boxes of C rations. Some were jammed with squads of helmeted soldiers in flak jackets, clutching their M-16s and staring straight ahead to conceal the fear that pulled the tanned skin of their cheeks and jaws tight around their young faces.

Suddenly, the dispatch sergeant, who was attempting to direct air traffic from a small wooden shack next to the landing zone, called to me: "There's a ship getting ready over there. He might give you a ride."

I could see a single Huey starting his engine fifty yards away. "Thanks," I shouted at the sergeant. Then, clutching my two cameras against my chest, I ran toward the chopper. It was filled with boxes. I had no idea what they contained but it didn't really matter. Like Chris wanting to climb El Cap even if he had to go solo, I was desperate to take any space available. After all, the biggest story of my journalistic career was probably taking place just a few miles to the north.

"Can I get a ride?" I shouted to the pilot who had been watching me sprint across the landing zone.

He nodded and called through an open window, "If you can climb on top of the ice cream."

I stepped back to the side of the chopper where the side gunner grabbed my hand and helped me to climb up on top of the boxes. Immediately, the engine shuddered with full power and we lifted off. In a few moments, we were streaking northwards at treetop level towards the fighting.

I took a seat on the top row of boxes. They were cold. I looked down at the labels where the words *Vanilla Ice Cream* were clearly stenciled in black letters. Then I remembered what the pilot had told me about the load he was ferrying into the war zone.

I looked at the side gunner who was aiming his door-mounted, M-60 machine gun toward the jungle below. Pointing to the boxes, I called out, "What's this?"

He pushed the small microphone attached to his helmet away from his mouth and leaned toward my ear. "Colonel wants ice cream for his guys. Says they fight better that way," he shouted above the roar of the engine and the cracking of the helicopter blades against the still air.

I rolled my eyes and shook my head in disbelief. The gunner shrugged, swinging his mike back into position.

In a few minutes, we rose to an altitude of approximately 2,000 feet. Below, billows of brilliant red and orange exploded against the lush greenery of the jungle as jet pilots released canisters of napalm on suspected enemy positions. As I looked at the scenery passing below, I began asking myself the usual question that came to my mind whenever I approached a danger zone: *Why am I stupid enough to get into this situation?* My thoughts were interrupted by our descent to tree level once again, then a bumpy landing in a small clearing. Several soldiers in green, sweat-stained fatigues began grabbing the boxes of ice cream and loading them onto a small, gasoline driven flatcar called a Mule. The ice cream, only slightly melted, would be served at the battalion mess that evening and, presumably, the men would fight more fiercely during the following days.

When I first told Chris, who was twelve, that story I remember him saying, "Ice cream? No way!" But then, I suspect that in reading about his climb up the Zodiac, I'm also prompted to say, "Climb solo? No way!"

That night in the Iron Triangle, I managed to find a place to sleep on a cot in the small infirmary which had been set up near a battalion headquarters. The next morning, however, the press officer asked me if I wanted to go on a patrol with a small company of Army "grunts." I jumped at the chance and before the sun had begun to heat up, we started out through the triple-canopy jungle.

At first, I walked as carefully as possible. After all, only a week earlier I had joined Mary McCarthy, the writer, and Bernard Fall, the renowned French historian who had written extensively about Vietnam's history, for lunch at the Danang Press Center. As Mary McCarthy nodded in agreement, Fall had predicted that the Americans would delay but never prevent the North Vietnamese from winning. Several days after our discussion, Fall was cut in half and killed by a "Bouncing Betty" land mine after he accidentally kicked an unseen trip wire while walking through the jungle with a company of United States Marines.

With this memory fresh in my mind, I carefully lifted each foot high in the air and examined my surroundings with every step. After an hour of this, however, I lost interest in being so careful. It also became apparent that I wasn't keeping up with the other men so I began shuffling through the heavy brush with abandon, feeling that if it was time to die, there was nothing I could do to prevent it. The only choice available was to rely on fate, the same option which Chris was forced to select as he started up the Zodiac.

Yet, fate was not so generous to several members of our patrol that day. As the heat increased and the morning wore on, we could hear the firing of rifles, machine guns and the detonation of high explosive bombs snapping and crackling in the distance. The company commander, a young Lieutenant named Henry, had been ordered to search the perimeter of a small firebase near a village called Cu Chi. He placed me at the rear of the patrol, next to the last man, thinking that would be the safest spot.

By noon, we had tramped through the jungle and investigated burned-out huts for five hours without seeing a living creature. The men sweated and cursed as they moved slowly along a dusty path toward a series of rice fields.

"For Chrissake, Lieutenant, there's nobody out here. A goddamned robot couldn't survive all the bombing that's been going on around here," Ellison, a young private, grumbled.

When Henry called battalion headquarters to request a return to base, the Commanding Officer's voice crackled over the radio. "Keep looking, Lieutenant. If there's one little Commie bastard out there, we're gonna fry his ass before this is over with."

The company continued and when we finally stopped for a lunch break, not a single person had been spotted. The men broke out some C rations and filled their canteens with water from the rice fields. Then they started out again, slinging their M-16s carelessly over their shoulders and cursing the bad luck that had delivered them into this burned out hellhole that even the enemy appeared to have abandoned.

After a half hour of trudging along a dusty road that seemed to lead nowhere, Henry called up to the point man, a tall, skinny kid from Nebraska who had been in country only three days. "Hey Amos, if we don't have any contact in an hour, I'll call headquarters and tell them we're coming in."

"About fuggin' time," I heard Amos grumble.

A few minutes later, we arrived at a narrow dirt path separating two fields of green rice. To the left, a series of palm trees ringed the paddy, standing listlessly in the sun. Straight ahead, a deserted village stood at the end of the path.

"Okay guys, heads up and stay thirty feet apart," Henry called to his men.

Amos started across the narrow berm. The others began to follow.

The patrol was half way across the paddy field when the Chinese made, 30 caliber machine gun opened fire from somewhere in the village. Amos toppled forward and splashed into the knee high water of the paddy field. Two others fell across the path as the rest of the company began yelling and jumping into the rice field. I dived into the water, trying to hold my cameras above my head.

"They're in the village! Call a goddamned strike, Lieutenant!" The company radio operator screamed as he backed toward Henry to allow him to grab the phone.

As the men tried to organize and return fire with their M-16s, Henry grabbed the green phone from the radio pack and shouted into the speaker. "Bravo Five, Bravo Five. This is Charley Six. We've been hit! Position, two, zero, niner. Request air strike, artillery, anything! They've got us pinned down in the middle of a goddamned rice paddy."

Before he could finish, two mortars suddenly exploded into the middle of the company.

"The bastards! They've got us bracketed!" Ellison shouted.

The water was turning red with blood as the men still alive splashed around trying to get a position on the berm and return fire. For several minutes, the men emptied their M-16s into the village and the tree line, trying desperately to suppress the mortars and machine gun fire that were quickly decimating the company. I tried to snap pictures but the camera lenses were wet.

Then, suddenly, two jets appeared in the distance and made a quick pass over the ambush site. Immediately, the mortars and machine guns stopped. Henry radioed his position to the pilots and the jets returned low over the paddy field. Silver canisters of napalm rained down and exploded on the tree line in a huge ball of orange and red. The jets rose up, arced against the sky and then came in over the village, releasing another deadly storm of napalm.

Silence. For several moments, the men watched in wonder as the jets disappeared into the sky and made their way back to Saigon. Fires burned at the tree line. The village was now a smoking stack of burning timbers and blackened cinder blocks.

Henry glanced at the wounded men lying and sitting in the bloody, mud churned water. He took the field phone and called battalion headquarters again. "Request emergency Dustoff. Have a couple kias and at least four wias," Henry intoned. When he hung up the phone, he called out, "Get these guys up to dry ground next to the village. We'll have a Dustoff here in a couple of minutes."

The men looked through the smoking village and tree line, but found no bodies, no weapons. The Viet Cong gunners were gone.

When the olive green Dustoff helicopter with a red cross painted on its sides appeared ten minutes later, Amos and two others had been stretched out on the ground next to the paddy field. Tarps covered their motionless bodies. Four men, badly wounded, were quickly helped into the chopper, and then the three bodies were loaded.

"You wanna go back or you wanna stay?" Henry asked me. Fortunately, I had a good excuse.

"I'd like to get back to Saigon to file my pictures," I answered. Then I climbed into the helicopter and took a seat next to the wounded men. The Huey rose up in a cloud of dust, tilted its nose forward and the village of Cu Chi quickly disappeared behind us. Twelve minutes later, we landed at an Army hospital near Saigon. From there, I hitched a ride back to the small airstrip where my motorcycle was parked.

As I headed to the office where I would file my photographs, I reflected on the strange disappearance of the enemy gunners. They seemed to have just vanish. Now, of course, I know that they had not disappeared into thin air, but had gone down into the bowels of the earth, into the tunnels they had dug around Cu Chi. They survived to fight and, perhaps, to be killed another day. Amos, on his third day in country, had run out of luck, along with two other members of the company.

The experience in the Iron Triangle, along with other events in Vietnam, were compelling lessons on how we're all dependent on fate. Certainly, Chris's continued ascent up the granite wall of El Cap was also heavily reliant on good fortune.

I muse on this thought for several minutes as I sit at the top of El Cap. The only choice available, I decide, is a reliance on good fortune, the same option which Chris was forced to select as he started up the Zodiac.

After several hours of climbing, he reached a difficult position on the wall where he needed to depend on a small piton, called a Lost Arrow, which he had placed in a crack. Before putting his trust on this questionable piton, Chris tried to make sure it would hold his weight. However, the piton was off to one side and that made it difficult to test. He began climbing anyway without making sure the piece would remain in place when subjected to the pressure of his 170 pounds.

> Pieces are hard to test when they're off to the side; it's difficult to pre-weight them to see if they'll hold body weight. No matter, this was only my second wall and I was blissfully naive about the importance of rigorously shock testing the gear.

Then Chris heard the sudden snapping noise that all climbers fear crack through the warm midday air. The Lost Arrow slipped out of the wall crack.

"I eased onto the piece, and 'POP!' Out it came," Chris wrote.

The safety rope tied to his waist harness went slack. Chris lost his balance. He began falling headfirst toward the valley below. Then the slack rope pulled tight. Another Lost Arrow, placed ten feet below the start of his fall, held as his full weight jerked against the placement. The fall was broken, but Chris had toppled about ten feet upside down.

In my mind I see Chris hanging by his waist harness with his feet in the air, head pointed at the valley below. His climbing gear, consisting of carabiners, pitons, fifi hooks, etc., which had been "racked" together around his waist were suspended in his face. The piton continued to hold. The knot which secured his waist harness to the safety rope remained secure.

> The rack was dangling in my face. A very marginal Lost Arrow held me and the clove hitch on the double locked carabiners at my waist welded tight.

There have been many reports on the thoughts of climbers who have fallen to what should have been their deaths. What they were thinking during these supposed final seconds is not terribly dramatic. It seems that the human brain can accept death with surprising calm, a sort of "Oh shucks, I'm gonna die" attitude. Because Chris fell only ten feet, he felt somewhat unconcerned and apparently had no hesitation about continuing. He was determined to summit El Cap. Once again, I think of what my advice to him would have been at this point. The fact that I wasn't there to speak these warnings weighs heavily on me. I feel almost angry that he continued to climb under such risky conditions.

Just then a slight breeze stirs across the top of El Capitan and Tom appears, pulling himself off the edge of the wall and drawing his weight toward the tree where he had top roped earlier. He's so casual about walking around the edge of the cliff that I can't watch. His easy acceptance of danger once again brings thoughts of my son.

"I've been thinking about Chris and his first solo when he was twenty-three. It was crazy what he did," I call out to Tom.

"Young climbers often take chances that they avoid later on. It's part of the learning experience," Tom answers.

Tom is too understanding. I want him to say that Chris was foolish for trying to solo El Capitan at that early stage of his climbing career and that I, his father, should be pretty disgusted with a son who would try a stunt like that. But Tom won't play my game. Instead, he moves off to take more photos and I'm once again left alone to contemplate the past and Chris's daring solo climb on the Zodiac.

After falling ten feet, he regained his position on the wall, pulled up his haul bag and began to climb once more. He was wide awake and fully focused for the next section of the wall. Tim Noonan might suggest that at this point, Chris was in the zone.

Now I was fully amping from the sudden flood of adrenaline that released into my bloodstream after the fall and the rest of the pitch went quickly.

Then hard times came again in the form of the infamous Zorro Roofs where the climber must proceed along the bottom of overhanging, horizontal rock formations. This procedure is accomplished easily by flies, spiders and cockroaches. For humans, however, walking on the bottom of a flat rock is more complicated. Rock climbers must tie their safety rope to a series of special pitons, called "angles," which can be wedged into cracks on the horizontal wall above. The length of these specially constructed metal "stakes" are bent at right angles for additional strength. The climber then propels himself forward while hanging from a harness (attached to the angles) or by stepping on a sling (also called "aiders") created from nylon straps.

I was now perched directly below the Zorro Roofs, a series of three roofs ending in a long overhanging section of ancient frayed copperheads.

The problem is that it's almost impossible to climb through the Zorro Roofs without angles. Chris couldn't find them on his rack, so he concluded they had been left in his truck.

I started up into the first roof. It was time to use the angles but I couldn't find them. "Where the hell are those angles?" I asked myself as I sifted through all the iron and aluminum hardware that draped off my waist and shoulders. Did I leave them in the truck? I had a

> vivid image in my head of all the angles sitting on the passenger seat down in my truck, which I could just make out through the trees, two thousand feet below.

This was trouble and he knew it. There was no way of proceeding without the angles. He picked out a smaller piton called an "HB." It wasn't what he really needed, but there was no other alternative so he shoved it into a crack in the stone that was too large for the piton. Nevertheless, it seemed to work.

> Sweat was beginning to saturate the bandanna tied around my head. Oh man! Okay number three HB, about the size of a pencil eraser. The pin scar flared more than the HB, so only the narrow edges, several millimeters of brass, were in contact with the rock. Clip into it with my daisy chain, test it...gently...it shifts to a funky angle, but it works. I stand up into the lowest step of the aiders and the piece still holds.

Climbers' hands probably get dirtier than in any other sporting activity except for mud wrestling. In addition to grappling in dirt and sometimes dusty rock for a finger hold, chalk is also used regularly to prevent fingers from slipping off rock. Add to this various kinds of grease used on the gear and you hardly have hands ready for ballroom dancing. "My hands feel slimy from the greasy gray paste of the black aluminum oxide from the carabiners mixed with sweat," Chris wrote.

Chris was now connected to the small piton with a fifi hook, an aluminum hook secured to a short sling made of nylon webbing. He prepared to move up again by slowly stepping on the sling. Then he shifted his full weight onto this step in order to reach a small crack where someone had placed and then removed a piton (pin scar) during a previous climb on that route.

Then terror struck again! He heard the dreaded popping sound that, a few hours earlier, signaled a failure of his piton and that a fall was about to take place:

> I move up into the second step and lean back on a fifi hook connected from my harness to the HB. POP! Like getting electrocuted, every muscle in my body tenses up as I prepare to get dropped.

Perhaps waiting to fall is worse than falling. Chris was certain that the sound of the fifi hook snapping into place in the carabiner meant that his piton had slipped from its precarious placement in the wall crack. However, instead of another tumble down the face of the wall, it remained in place. The HB was holding.

> No. It was just the fifi hook shifting its seat in the carabiner. I can see a nice pin scar up higher. I reach as high as I can...no, second step wouldn't cut it. I had to top step.

The placement remained and he moved up again, but still could not reach the pin scar. His fingers squeezed on a small protrusion of granite (a flake) which provided some balance and kept him in an upright position. He placed all his weight on the aiders, reached as high as he could and then desperately looked for some kind of replacement for the sorely needed angle.

> Up, up, up, gritting my teeth, praying that the HB holds. There–I'm precariously perched in the toe step

of my aiders, pinching a little flake for balance...now, find something that'll fit, since all the angles are in my truck.

The TCU (a camming device which spreads out against the crack when its spring is released) he selected for a placement was too small for the crack. Nevertheless, he clipped his carabiner into its small connecting ring. Slowly he eased his weight onto the step fashioned from his aiders or "atrier." For several moments the TCU held. Gently, he placed all his weight onto the piece. Then the sound of the camming device slipping out of its place in the rock gave him an instant warning of what was coming next. Pop! Once again, the belay rope went slack. There was nothing holding him to the wall. The steps sewn into the nylon webbing of his aiders were no longer secured to anything but the warm air of a July afternoon in central California. The law of gravity kicked in swiftly and without mercy. At two thousand feet above the valley floor, he began another downward fall along the face of the rock wall.

Once again, however, the belay rope went taut. His waist harness tightened around his hips and lower torso. The small HB which he had placed ten feet below absorbed the shock of his sudden weight. Once again, after ten feet of falling downwards, Chris was jerked to a halt. The fall was broken and for the second time Chris was dangling from the wall of El Capitan at the end of a 1½ inch nylon rope. Now, terror replaced ambition. This time, Chris was seriously frightened at what was going on.

Amazingly, that marginal HB held the fall. But this time, the second fall of the day, I was freaked. There I was, feeling very alone, hanging off a very sketchy micro-nut, at the start of a pitch of basically unretreatable and

> severely overhanging rock. I couldn't do without the angles that were down in my truck. The first fall that day was cool, but this wasn't so cool. I was perplexed, frustrated and scared.

With no options left, he decided to quit climbing for the day, get some sleep and hope that a miracle would happen the next morning.

> I finished the pitch in the dark and pulled up onto the sloping twenty-inch-wide ledge, which was home for the night. Rap, clean, haul and the day was over. I equalized the rusty quarter-inch belay bolts by headlamp and set up my portaledge. It was a flimsy, homemade canvas ledge, a version of which most wall climbers endure through their first few routes. Climbing into it was novel, as it shifted and swung back and forth on the anchor. The pole running along the side was cracked and the jagged metal end tore through the canvas and protruded into my ribs as I slept.

I'm not sure how anyone can sleep in a small hammock dangling two thousand feet above ground, secured only by a few bolts, but I suspect that eventually exhaustion overcomes fear and finally one can no longer stay awake. Chris not only got some sleep that night, but when he awoke, the miracle he desperately needed appeared.

> When I woke up the next morning, the sun was already fully illuminating the appropriately named "Wall of the Early Morning Light." I groped around in the bottom of the haul bag for breakfast–a can of fruit cocktail. Down at the very bottom, in between the duct-taped two liter bottles of water, I felt the familiar cold

steel, the heavy, rounded metal edges, the fine grained rusty texture. The angles! They hung up on things and clanked reassuringly as I tugged them out. As I sifted them through my blackened, gobied hands, a nice three-quarter-inch Chouinard sawed-off stood out: it was just the right one for the pin scar that spit out the three cam unit. With new found enthusiasm, I cruised back up to my high point, fired in the angle (or at least an inch of it), jumped on it and climbed through.

And so he made it! Not only did Chris reach the top of El Capitan, he learned some important lessons from the experience.

Honestly, there was probably a good dose of ego ingrained in my plan to solo Zodiac at first. I had a chance to tell my friends the stories of my adventure and fulfill whatever need I had to prove myself or get other climbers' recognition. But it felt weird. I was much more comfortable just kicking back, listening to them and smiling to myself. I felt strong, confident and happy. I certainly qualified as a beginner before this venture and was probably lucky things went as smoothly as they did. I had indeed taught myself volumes about the art of climbing big walls. What I hadn't predicted, however, were the most important lessons climbing alone would bring: learning to listen, learning patience and having confidence in my own strengths and abilities. The Captain is quite a good teacher.

My mind returns to the present. I lift my head now and imbibe the awesome beauty around me. I reflect on the lessons Chris learned from this mountain: patience, confidence and courage. They are values every parent wants to instill in his child. Chris's words, "The Captain is a good teacher," echo in my mind.

Tom returns from his latest photography expedition on top of El Cap by mid-morning. It's time to begin our descent if we want to arrive back at Camp 4 before dark. However, hiking down the trail proves to be more difficult than going up. My artificial hip is beginning to hurt from the backpack's downward slams on it. As the hours crawl by, the pain becomes intense. Chris's attitude toward physical hardship comes back to me: "Pain is an illusion. It's the only thing stopping us," he often said. I'm determined to simply slog it out in the best tradition of my son who had learned how to deal with the suffering inherent in forty-mile bike training rides in cold rain, bone cracking, bloody mountain bike crashes and even in the loneliness and fear on a harsh mountain wall.

We finally reach the waterfalls and Tom mutters some words about wanting to change a few things in our packs while I quickly remove my shoes and slip my feet into the refreshing cold water. When we start back on the trail again, my pack has almost no weight in it. I look over at my climbing companion and smile my appreciation. Tom noticed the pain I was enduring and while I was cooling my feet in the water, he shifted all the heavy items to his pack.

"Have you ever read a book called *The Path of the Mountain*?" I ask Tom a short while later as we slowly hike down a stony traverse.

"No, but I've heard of it," he replies.

"It's written by a Polish climber named Voytek Kurtna. He says that mountain climbing is a religious experience, because it enables one to find the truth about himself and the surroundings of nature."

"That's true," Tom agrees. "That's what I was talking about this morning. Chris knew about that. He was there."

"But you don't have to be a climber to have a spiritual experience. There's a Taoist monk by the name of Lao Tzuu who wrote a poem that goes like this:

"The world may be known
Without leaving the house
The Way may be seen
Apart From the Windows
The further you go
The less you will know.

"He feels you don't have to climb a mountain or endanger your life to find God. You can stay right in your own house with the windows drawn and still have a religious experience."

Tom stops and shifts his pack slightly. "That's absolutely true. I'm sure of it. Not everyone can climb a mountain and not everyone is going to have a spiritual experience when they climb. But some do and it's an important part of their lives."

As we turn and step down the trail again, I wonder how many of the great climbers in the world would agree. Probably most of them and yet there have been some very strange motives offered for why people climb mountains, not the least of which was Mt. Everest climbing pioneer George Mallory's "because it's there" explanation.

It's difficult to pinpoint what drove the fifty-eight-year-old school mistress, Annie S. Peck, to climb in 1909 what was then thought to be the highest point of land in the western hemisphere: Peru's Huascarán Mountain. With practically none of the equipment used today for high climbs, she and two male companions suffered under incredible conditions of cold and snow to reach the top and thereby earn for her the title of the "mad schoolmarm of Providence." The fact that a woman had achieved such a distinction at the beginning of the century was sufficient fodder for driving male editorial writers into paroxysms of frustrated rage. As for this extraordinary woman, she could only say that in climbing the impossible she found that she really "lived."

For some climbers, a major motivation has been the fame and fortune that comes from being the first to summit a major mountain. For example, the first ascent of the Matterhorn in the Swiss Alps was won by the Englishman, Edward Whymper, in a race to the top against a former friend turned liar and traitor.

Their rivalry culminated in the middle of the nineteenth century when Whymper beat Italian climber Jean-Antoine Carrel to the top of the Matterhorn by several hours.

In July of 1865, Whymper found Carrel ready to make an ascent on the mountain but unwilling to take the Englishman with him. The Italian, in fact, lied to Whymper about his plans for the summer and his imminent departure for the Matterhorn along with several other climbers.

Suspicious of what was taking place, Whymper hurried to Zermat, Switzerland, and was able to put together a climbing team which left immediately for the Matterhorn. They reached the top several hours before Carrel and were consequently victors in the race to the summit. However, there is an old saying that states, "Mountains are no places for running silly races" and on the way down, the adage proved correct. Four of the victorious English climbers tumbled to their deaths when their belaying rope broke after one of the men slipped.

Before their estrangement, Whymper and Carrel had climbed together in unsuccessful attempts to summit the formidable, and as yet unscaled, Matterhorn located on the border between Switzerland and Italy. Their last try together failed when the Italian quit before they reached the top, because he didn't want Whymper with him as he achieved success. His determination to win the prize solely for himself was a driving force with Carrel, an unsportsmanlike motive which caused others to call the final outcome an example of poetic justice.

Nevertheless, reaction to the successful assault on the Matterhorn brought fame to Whymper. His climb to win the race, to beat his opponent to the top, had succeeded. The price in terms of human lives, though, had been extravagant and even Queen Victoria suggested that mountaineering be prohibited by law. Nevertheless, Edward Whymper won celebrity status and a lifetime income by lecturing and writing about the mountains. However, this would be the last time competitive teams would race to the top of an unclimbed mountain at exactly the same time. "Silly races" would never again be the means for seeking fame on high altitude climbs, although the drive to be the first to reach the summit of an unclimbed mountain would continue to motivate hundreds of climbers worldwide, including my son, to push themselves to the limit in the years to come.

By late afternoon, Tom and I finally reach the end of the trail where the rented minivan is parked safely just as we left it. Happily, we throw our knapsacks into the trunk and soon we're driving back to the Camp 4 parking lot.

In a few days it is time for me to leave for San Francisco. I have several months of training to undergo and I need to get started. I say goodbye to Tim Noonan. Then Tom and I have a final cup of coffee together in the Lodge. His son will be arriving soon and the two of them are going climbing together. I feel a momentary twinge of sadness. It is another reminder of my loss.

"I hope you've found what you came looking for," Tom says as I prepare to leave.

"One thing I found out is what I fool I was to think I could climb a big wall or even a high altitude mountain without proper training."

"It looks easy to all of us before we understand the necessary skills," he replies.

"Well, I'm ready for Climbing 101 now," I tell him. "I'm going to take the next few months to get in shape. Then I plan to go to another place Chris mastered–the Himalayas–and try climbing a high altitude peak. Perhaps I'll learn more about all of this there."

Tom smiles. "Good luck. I know you can do it," he says. Then as we shake hands goodbye, he says: "I'm glad we made that hike together. Chris was a great guy and you should be proud to be his father."

"Thanks Tom. You'll never know how much I appreciate the things you've said about Chris," I reply.

A few minutes later, I'm driving along the Merced River on the way out of Yosemite Park with a sense of awe at how much I've learned in this place. There is still a long way to go before I fully understand what climbing is about and whether I can summit a high-altitude mountain. I'm still not sure I can do it, nor do I know if the answers I'm seeking will be there at the end. What I do know is that the rock walls of Yosemite and the people who climb here have set the stage for a drama that must continue. There are no options left but to "go for it."

9

chapter

Struggling for a Toehold

Now I am to undergo a test of climbing upwards. Is it beyond my capabilities? I will soon know. Zen teaches you to never accept a limit without testing to and beyond that limit.

Neville Shulman, *The Zen in the Art of Climbing Mountains*

A slim young climber with wavy blond hair and a faded rainbow tattooed around his arm pours water into a bowl for his dog. The temperature is hovering around 90 degrees and the large white dog, bred to live in the French Alps, is lapping up the water in a desperate attempt to stay cool.

"Is that a Great Pyrenees?" I ask, after arriving dressed in shorts and a T-shirt outside a small delicatessen near New Paltz, New York. The store is located at the foot of the Shawnagunks mountain area, sixty-five miles north of New York City. Rock climbers from up and down the East Coast come here to try the fine granite walls that emerge from the valley below.

"I'm Rich Shultz and it sure is." The young man looks up with an appreciative smile. "How did you know?"

"I used to own one. It's a great dog. Wonderful around kids," I respond.

"Yeah. Cooper's my buddy," he says, patting the dog. Then he looks at the scrape marks on my knees and elbows. "Have you been climbing?" he asks.

"Trying," I answer.

Rick looks confused. "Trying?"

"I've been top roping here for three days, but I don't think I'm getting much better and I'm exhausted from jumaring up and rappelling down the rock walls along the Carriage Road since early morning."

Then, embarrassed at being a complainer, I switch the conversation back to the dog. "Did you know that every Russian prince had a Great Pyrenees assigned to him when he was a child?" I ask.

"Because it's such a great guard dog?" Rick responds.

"Exactly," I answer.

Rick strokes the dog's head with renewed vigor. "Yeah, Cooper is really awesome."

I soon learn that Rick works at a nearby Patagonia outdoor sportswear store but manages to spend several hours every day climbing the rock walls of the Shawnagunks. I sense that he's an expert.

"You should have a guide to give you instructions," he admonishes me.

After admitting that he's right, I explain, "I'm trying to develop some hand and leg strength by doing low level traverses on my own among the boulders."

"Not a bad idea," he says

"It's been good for me, but now I'd like to move on," I answer.

"Have you ever climbed in New Hampshire?" he asks.

"The 'Gunks' is the only climbing area I've seen in the East."

"You should go to Cathedral Ledge in North Conway. You might like it more up there," he suggests.

The idea sounds intriguing. Unlike the easily accessible climbing community in Yosemite, where I spent each evening around a campfire at Camp 4 talking with other climbers, the "Gunks" has been a lonely place where I've yet to meet someone with whom I can climb and converse. The prospect of traveling to a beautiful village in New England with a variety of rock climbing locations and a large tourist climber population sounds inviting.

"I think I'll go. I need a change of scenery," I tell Rick.

He gives me directions. Shaking hands, I thank him for the advice, then step into my van and start the engine. Suddenly, Rick reappears.

"Are you really going to North Conway?" he calls through the open window.

"Yes. It sounds like a great idea," I respond.

"Any chance I can come along?"

Without hesitation, I turn off the engine and get out of the van. The opportunity of climbing with an expert teacher and having someone to talk with during the trip sounds like just what I need to progress. I tell Rick he's welcome to come along. "I have a tent in the back which you can use and I'll sleep in the van."

Rick hesitates. "Ah, what about the dog? Can Cooper come along?"

"Sure. Definitely bring Cooper. You know how I feel about Great Pyrenees," I answer.

Rick is elated. However, we can't leave right away. I promised to attend a lobster cookout in Greenwich, Connecticut the next afternoon, a Sunday, and Rick can't leave his job until that same evening. The dilemma is resolved when I offer to let him take the van while I take the bus to New York in the morning and then catch a train to Connecticut. We agree that when he's finished work at the store, he will drive the van to Greenwich and pick me up sometime after midnight.

Before starting the engine, I pause. It's time for the explanation, the admission of just why I'm trying to learn the art of mountain climbing. I always hate to bring this up. I still don't like admitting that Chris is gone and I don't want anyone feeling sorry for me. However, Rick needs to know my motivation if we're going to be together for the next few days.

"Ah, Rick," I begin, "there's something I need to tell you. I'm not doing this just for fun. There's a reason."

Rick looks at me suspiciously. "What's that?" he asks.

Then I tell him about Chris's death and why I'm trying to gain some sort of understanding about it through climbing. "It probably sounds like a crazy thing to do, but I wanted you to know," I say.

Rick smiles. "That's really great. You can learn a lot by climbing," he says with such total conviction that I suddenly feel relieved, even convinced that this is not the journey of a man rendered demented and irrational by his loss, but rather a sensible and altogether understandable endeavor.

Admittedly, by the next evening I'm a bit nervous. I've told several women at the cookout about my plan and quickly been admonished for turning over the keys to an unknown young man. "You'll never see your van again," they predict.

However, the plan works and just before one o'clock on Monday morning, my well-used, red van turns a corner and stops at the shopping mall where I'm waiting.

Somehow, I knew Rick would show up. Trust is an important value among climbers, who regularly put their lives in the hands of strangers. If a lead climber says he has placed good protection, a climber coming up next can be killed if the "pro" doesn't hold well enough to break a sudden fall. The leader's promise of good protection must be based on fact. When someone on the ground calls out "on belay" and isn't ready to stop the unexpected slip of a lead climber, a fatal accident can result. Consequently, people who climb rock walls and high mountains learn to keep their word as a matter of survival. So, in reality, I'm relieved but not surprised when Rick appears as promised.

However, I am a bit taken back when I see a pretty young woman with short brown hair and a quick smile sitting next to him as the van pulls to a stop. She casually waves to me and introduces herself. "Hi, I'm Mia."

Mia Croszer, whose parents emigrated from Poland after World War II, is a pre-med student as well as a fine climber. She tells me she met Rick that afternoon at the Patagonia store.

"When I told her about my plans for climbing in New Hampshire, Mia asked if she could come along. I told her that would be awesome," Rick relates.

After negotiating my way over Mia's and Rick's climbing gear and stepping carefully past Cooper, who has by now reserved his own space behind the passenger's seat, I take the rear seat and lean back. I'm ready to enjoy the six-hour, all night drive to North Conway.

"We should be able to start climbing by nine in the morning," Rick announces.

For several hours, we head north through the night, with Mia and I occasionally sharing the driving chores with Rick.

Of course, our conversation soon turns to the subject of climbing. When Rick is asked why he spends so much of his time and energy climbing rock walls, he laughs. "I can't imagine not climbing every day."

"There are a number of well-known climbers who think the whole thing is a sham. One guy, Joe Simpson, called it a mug's game," I mention.

Rick knows about Simpson. Mia, however, wants to know what a mug's game is.

"Simpson almost died while climbing in the Peruvian Andes," I tell her. "He broke his leg during a descent and then fell into a crevasse where he was left for dead by his climbing partner. After an incredible ordeal of pain and determination, he climbed out and then hauled himself down the mountain. After it was all over, he wrote that the world of climbing is an illusion in which you get sucked into thinking it's romantic and courageous. In the end, however, he says it's a dangerous con game which reasonable people should avoid. He calls it a mug's game."

"Did he ever climb again?" Mia asks.

"Of course." I laugh.

"Did he actually call it a mug's game?" Rick wants to know.

I announce that I still remember the words at the close of his book, *This Game of Ghosts,* in which he discusses the loss of so many friends to the mountains. "'One a year. God, it's a mug's game. Where will it end?'"

"But that's mountaineering he's talking about. Not rock climbing," Mia says.

We all agree.

"If people stayed with rock climbing, there wouldn't be so many lost lives. But the trouble is that rock climbing infuses people with the desire to go further and try mountaineering. That's when your life becomes dependent on the weather," I say.

"One of these days, I'd like to try a big mountain," Rick says, as if my previous statement had never been uttered.

"You're not concerned about accidents?" I ask.

"When you're time is up, that's it. It's the flip of a coin," Rick shrugs.

His cavalier statement triggers my memory of a hot afternoon in Vietnam a long time ago when a young photographer and I flipped a coin. I decide to tell Mia and Rick the story.

"During the Tet offensive of 1968, when the forces of North Vietnam made an all-out effort to overwhelm the United States and South Vietnamese armies, an American magazine assigned me to write a piece about the defensive war which U.S. Marines were fighting in I Corps, the northern section of South Vietnam then under heavy attack by Communist troops. I was also informed that Bob Ellison, a tall, skinny and mustached young photographer, whose work had consistently displayed both skill and courage, would take the photos for the story.

"We met at the press center in Danang and discussed our ideas of how the story should be handled. The magazine editor saw the piece as a new kind of war for the Marines who were now fighting in trenches and underground bunkers rather than fulfilling their traditional role of hitting the beaches and charging forward against the enemy. Ellison and I decided we would both fly into Khe Sahn, a Marine outpost to the north which was currently under heavy siege, and I would interview the 'grunts' while he photographed the visual aspects of living under constant bombardment.

"The following day, we inquired about military flights going into Khe Sahn and found that one seat was available for the press on a plane that afternoon. We were both anxious to get there fast since there was no assurance that another seat would be available for days and perhaps weeks. Almost every flight was being fired upon by the North Vietnamese regulars who were dug into the mountains around the Marine firebase.

"There was only one fair solution. We flipped a coin and Ellison won. Disappointed, I shook his hand and he started off toward a waiting jeep. Suddenly, however, he stopped, walked over and handed me several slides which he had already taken of Marines jumping into trenches while under artillery fire. 'These will give you an idea what I'll be shooting up there,' he said. Then he climbed into the jeep with his camera pack and I assured him that I'd be joining him as soon as possible.

"The following morning, I was lucky enough to catch a ride into Khe Sahn and went immediately to the press officer to ask if he knew where Ellison might be. 'No one checked in here by that name,' the Marine captain answered.

"'But he was on a plane that arrived last evening,' I replied.

"'A plane coming in here yesterday took some rounds and crashed. No survivors. I don't have an Ellison on the manifest.'

"In fact, he was on the plane and didn't survive as was later confirmed."

Leaning back in the seat, I tell Rick and Mia, "I can still remember Bob Ellison's happy smile when the nickel came up heads and how eager he was to get on that flight and join the action at Khe Sahn." I pause and look at Rick. "The flip of a coin! I stay. He goes. Tails, I live. Heads, he dies. Is that what you're willing to settle for, Rick?" I ask.

My climbing companion looks off at the roadside. "I guess so," he says.

We arrive in North Conway by mid-morning and, after an ample breakfast, Rick suggests we climb the Sliding Board, a huge slab of granite that stretches upward for 1500 feet at about a forty-two-degree angle. After driving from the village several miles to the end of a dirt road surrounded by trees, we gather our gear in backpacks and walk through the woods for approximately twenty minutes before arriving at the base of the slab. Cooper, of course, comes along. Rick knows from experience that the dog will wait patiently until our return and guard our packs while we're climbing.

Since the rock wall is not vertical, the climb appears deceptively simple, almost a walkup that can be undertaken without the insurance of a belay system. Rick, however, isn't fooled by appearances. Although he moves up quickly on the first pitch, he spends several minutes placing a cam into a small wedge and then testing it before clipping into the protective device. Then he moves up again while Mia remains on belay. I feel more relaxed when I see every safety precaution is being taken.

After twenty minutes of climbing and placing pitons in the rock, Rick has completed the first pitch. He establishes an anchor approximately one hundred feet above us and sets up the belay. Now its Mia's turn. After some initial hesitation on several of the early moves, she climbs the rest of the pitch easily and in a few minutes they call down for me to start climbing.

In a climb such as this, the best procedure is to climb up quickly and aggressively. The forward momentum of one's body will overcome a minor slip whereas the slower one goes, the better chance there is of losing one's balance and falling backwards. Although I realize this, I still haven't developed the confidence to practice aggressive climbing tactics. I move slowly, using both hands and feet like an ape to move up the angular slab of granite. It's slow and awkward, but eventually I reach my companions and Rick descends quickly to clean the placements. Then he starts up the next pitch.

As we go higher, the wall becomes more difficult to climb. There seem to be no apparent cracks or protrusions of rock where a toe or finger can be placed. Yet Rick always finds something to jam his foot into or grab onto where I can see nothing. Soon, he has placed a series of chalks and cams into the wall, secured them with a sling and then fastened this into the climbing rope with a caribiner. "On belay," he calls down, signaling that he can now stop a possible fall of the next climber. Although not as experienced as Rick, Mia, who has been watching Rick carefully, now finds the same holds he used. Amazingly to me as I watch, she climbs well and soon joins him at the next anchor.

After seeing what's involved, I decide I'm not experienced enough to climb this pitch. I call up to Rick, "I'm going to jug it."

"Okay, come on up," he replies.

I take a deep breath. From my harness I remove two hand-sized pieces of metal equipped with spring-loaded teeth that clamp down on the rope when pulled downwards. These "jumars" or "ascenders" easily slide up the rope. However, they grip or hold when downward pressure is put on them. A sling or atrier is attached to the handles and hangs down to foot level. A climber can walk up the side of a rock wall by stepping up in the ladder-like sling while pushing the jumars up the rope. This ingenious device allows the climber to move up any kind of wall quickly, provided the rope is firmly attached at the top. After attaching these "ascenders" to the rope, I push the left jumar up the rope and lift my left leg at the same time.

As a war correspondent in Vietnam, Karl witnessed combat fighting and death firsthand.

Karl, with Chris in his arms, and Alexandra, on her pony, get ready for a gallop across the fields of their Pennsylvania farm.

Like his father, Chris excelled from an early age in sports of all kinds, including tennis.

Both father, left, and son, Chris, right, enjoy playing hockey as children.

Ready to leave for his senior year in France, Chris says goodbye to his father.

Chris, during a visit with his family, is caught having a snack.

Chris and his brother, Justin, enjoy a ski trip to Colorado.

Justin, Karl and Chris enjoy a rare moment when they are all together.

Two days before his fatal accident, Chris relaxes with fellow climbers, Wally Barker and Susan Lilly.

Karl and legendary climber, Tom Frost, high atop El Capitan.

On El Capitan at Yosemite National Park, Karl takes in the beautiful surroundings.

Rick Schulz and his dog, Cooper, accompany Karl on a climbing trip to New Hampshire.

Karl and his alpine climbing instructor, Ivano Ghiradini, in the French Alps.

Karl with a boy believed to be a reincarnated lama.

With prayer flags blowing in the wind behind him, Karl visits a monastery in Nepal.

At the base of the mountain, Jud Millar observes a memorial for German climbers who lost their lives on Pisang Peak.

As they work their way up the Himalayan mountainside with Karl, Ang Sherpa and Jud Millar fight cold, snow and other harsh conditions.

At high camp, Karl prepares for the summit bid on Pisang Peak in Nepal.

The last time the family is together: Justin, Alexandra holding her baby daughter, Karl and Chris.

With new skills, strength and insight, Karl climbs a steep mountain wall.

Then, shifting all weight to the left foot, I push up the right jumar and lift the right leg. Having already practiced this procedure at the "Gunks," I've learned to coordinate the moves. In a few minutes, feeling more secure now, I join Rick and Mia on a small ledge several hundred feet above our starting point far below. Looking down, we can see Cooper patiently waiting near our packs.

"Okay, let's start up again," Rick says.

This time, I'm determined to climb without the jumars. Mia announces that she'll remain below while I climb and then retrieve the "pro" placed by Rick when she comes up. After Rick reaches the top, I check my harness to make sure it's properly secured to the belaying rope and then start up. As I struggle to find a toehold on the rock wall, Mia calls out: "Come on, you can make it." Her encouragement helps and soon I've moved up past two double cam placements. Suddenly, the climb turns easy and, after stretching my legs two or three times as high as I can, I arrive next to Rick. They're both shouting, "Congratulations!" For the first time I'm overcome with a huge sense of satisfaction at having climbed a serious rock wall.

After climbing and removing Rick's placements, Mia joins us on the narrow ledge. Now, it's time for the next pitch.

Surprisingly, it's an easy climb. Over the years, water running over the top of the cliff and dripping down the wall has created a series of steps, carved into the rock every two feet, that provide easy footholds. In another half hour, we have all reached the top where we take a water break and look out over the village of North Conway far below. Finally, we gather up our gear and begin hiking down the backside of the cliff. As we move down the path, Mia mentions that going down the mountain can be even more difficult than going up.

I remind her that many of the clichés and aphorisms about climbing are also metaphors for life.

"Like what?" she asks.

"Falling is not an option," I respond.

Mia laughs and then adds: "In the beginning, this is going to be painful, but in the end, it will be worthwhile."

"Just remember, when you reach the top, you're only halfway there," Rick calls out.

"Gravity doesn't pull you down, it pushes you forward," I retort.

We're all laughing and trying to think up more platitudes when we finally reach the bottom of the mountain where Cooper waits by the packs, eager to welcome us back. Darkness is settling in around the mountain and we decide to go into North Conway for dinner before retreating to the tent and the van for the night.

Mia and Rick share the tent that night. I hear them laughing and making jokes before I finally fall asleep with a deep-felt admiration for these young climbers who can camp out in a tent and have fun without getting confused about the sexual implications of their physical proximity. Perhaps I was born a couple of generations too soon!

In the morning, we find another nearby cliff which turns out to be more of a challenge than I'm ready for. After climbing one difficult pitch and realizing that the wall is getting smoother toward the top, I decide to go back down.

"I'll rappel down and do some bouldering while you all climb," I suggest to Rick.

He agrees and after securing my rope to a bolt, I step backwards on the wall, play out rope carefully through my ATC and quickly rappel down the side of the smooth rock. After approximately eighty feet, I reach a tree growing into the side of the mountain.

"Okay," I call up to Rick.

He unhooks my rope from his anchor and throws it down to me. Then Mia and Rick start their climb while I take a short rest sitting next to the tree.

It occurs to me that I've been moving around on this wall several hundred feet above the bottom with little fear or concern about falling. I can even look down without an attack of vertigo. Slowly but surely, I'm becoming a climber. My thoughts turn to my son. In this clear air, in this place he so loved, I feel his presence and also his absence. Still, though it may be my imagination, it is almost as though somewhere he is aware of his father's trials and successes. Unfortunately, within the next few moments I make a move that almost ends forever my new occupation as a climber.

In order to descend the next fifty feet on my one-hundred-foot rope, I need to secure the rope around the tree and, after arriving at the bottom, retrieve the rope by pulling on one end until it reaches the tree and then falls down on the other side. This will mean placing both ends of the rope in my rappelling device as I go down. With this in mind, I pull the rope around the tree and insert the end through the ATC. Then I step around the tree and prepare to move down the wall. Suddenly, I realize that if I make this move there will be nothing to secure the rope. I will immediately fall a fatal fifty feet. I would land next to Cooper, who would have a corpse to guard until Mia and Rick returned.

Cursing my own stupidity, I unhook the rope, move around the tree and tie in again so that my weight will be held by the tree. Then I rappel quickly down the wall. Cooper welcomes me with a wet lick on the hands.

When Rick and Mia finally return an hour later, I say nothing about my near accident. Instead, we all head for the van and the long ride back to New Paltz where Rick needs to be at work the following morning and I must make plans for the next stage in my training schedule.

As we head back to the Shawnagunks, I have time to think about this journey I've undertaken. Even though I'm beginning to grasp the essentials of rock climbing and have learned to feel comfortable on a rock wall thousands of feet above the valley floor, I know I need a more severe conditioning for alpine climbing. It's time to develop the kind of skills needed on a high altitude, snow-covered Himalayan mountain. I decide that the best place to learn this is in the very birthplace of high altitude climbing. It's time to leave for the French Alps.

When we arrive back in New Paltz, I say goodbye to Mia and Rick. As with everyone I meet while climbing, an unusual bond of friendship has been established. Sharing the dangers and challenges of moving up and down the face of a rock wall creates long-lasting relationships among climbers. Chris knew this and I am learning it, too.

10
chapter

Relentless Sorrow

This week alone, four people fell to their deaths in the Swiss Alps on Wednesday and another climber died in the Italian Alps on Thursday.

New York Times, August 17, 1997

Church bells are clanging slowly through the crisp air of Chamonix as I stroll along a crowded sidewalk on this first morning in the Savoy Valley in east-central France. At the end of the street, men and women of all ages are pushing through the large white doors of the Saint Michel Catholic Church. A hearse is parked in front of the historic building.

Curious, even apprehensive, I approach an aged, craggy-faced woman with wisps of tangled gray hair emerging from her black bonnet.

"What's going on?" I ask.

"Ahh, what a tragedy," she exclaims. "It's a funeral for young Patrick Chatelet. He and his friend, the Ravanal boy, both of them, lost to the mountains!"

Two young girls standing nearby suddenly throw their arms around each other and begin sobbing.

The old woman continues: "They were killed Sunday afternoon. Roped together. When the one boy fell, his friend was pulled down with him."

As my aging informant shakes her head in sorrow, I thank her for the information and edge my way through the throng of mourners and up the stairs of the church. Soon, I'm standing in the packed anteroom listening to the resounding voice of Abbé Dominique Breche, who is once again conducting funeral services for a climber killed on the nearby mountains, a function he performs with alarming regularity in this world-famous cradle of alpine mountaineering, where I've come to learn the techniques of high-altitude climbing.

His words bring back with force the reason I have come here and I'm struck again by the loss of my son.

In fact, it was here in the French Alps where Chris first developed his own love for the mountains. When he was eighteen, after I mentioned that I had attended a French Jesuit school in Montreal when I was eleven and had always appreciated the opportunity to learn to speak French while also becoming acquainted with another culture, he and I discussed the possibility of his going to France for the year. Perhaps, I suggested to Chris, he could have a similar experience in France. He was enthusiastic and so I phoned the University of Grenoble, a large university located in the French Alps, which offered a program of immersion French for pre-college, English-speaking students.

We found that he could be enrolled in this beautiful town surrounded by snow-capped mountains, study French and also receive credits for graduation from high school. By September of 1986, he was on his way, traveling alone to France though he spoke no French and would study in a school he had never seen before.

Despite his tight budget and the need to attend classes, Chris quickly began to develop the irresistible attraction to climbing which would remain with him for the rest of his life. Soon, in fact, he began to aspire to climb some of the famous mountains to the north like Mont Blanc.

Now, as I sit down in the crowded church, I'm once again surrounded by the kind of people with whom Chris had so much in common: climbers and their friends, all here to mourn the loss of one of their fellow mountaineers. Father Dominique's strong and compassionate voice is carried over a loudspeaker as he talks about the young man whose body lies in a wooden casket in the front of the church.

"All of us who have known Patrick since he was a young boy know what a great loss we suffer here today," he says.

Above the pulpit, a chandelier made of tiny crystal balls throws a dim light on the tightly packed mourners while also casting long shadows across the stylized paintings of the Stations of the Cross that hang along each wall. From the ceiling above the nave, a life-sized statue of the Crucifixion is suspended from a wire and beneath the suffering Christ, the all-too appropriate words, *Tout est Consumme* (All is consumed) are painted in block letters on a large ribbon of wood.

"Patrick and Frederick have lost their lives following a path up the mountain and now we must continue on our path of life without them. This is a painful experience which can nevertheless end in joy at the day of our Ascension," the priest promises his attentive listeners.

Memories of a similar ceremony, so recently

enacted in a Quaker Meeting house in Pennsylvania, come back to me as the grief of these French mourners mixes with my own and their tears become mine. There is such an element of deep and irreplaceable loss in the death of a promising young man that even the old, taciturn men of the village are wiping their eyes as the aging priest finally ends his remarks.

After Father Dominique steps slowly from the lectern, an attractive young woman with short brown hair and wearing a black mourning dress takes her place. She begins to speak in clear and carefully pronounced words. Stephanie Ravanal, once the wife and now the widow of Frederick Ravanal, is also, now, the single mother of a four-year-old daughter, Victoria. I would learn later that she is also four months pregnant.

I am told later by the Adjutant Director of the *Gendarmarie du Secours* (Search and Rescue) police that one of the men's crampons had apparently slipped when he stepped on a rock covered by only a half-inch of ice. Had the ice been thicker, the sharp steel point of the special climbing shoe would have held. The police refused to say if they knew who was on the belay and who slipped and said they would not release the report even if they did know because such information might cause dissension among the surviving families.

For several minutes, Stephanie talks engagingly about the friendship of the two twenty-five-year-old men and how they grew up in the valley, climbing the nearby mountains in summer and winter. She tells how they had both landed jobs on the local search and rescue team where they had helped save injured skiers and stranded climbers. Both men, in fact, had hoped to be accepted as alpine guides by the prestigious *Companie Des Guides* which hires mostly young people from the valley. Through all of these times, she says, her husband Frederick had not only been a close friend, but was often a mentor to the unmarried Patrick. Then, glancing down at the closed casket, she continues: "Now, Patrick, you and Frederick have left us but you have gone together to a place where you will have nothing to fear. Frederick will still be with you, Patrick, to listen to your problems, to give you advice and to be your friend forever." Sobs and several cries of anguish waft through the crowded church as Stephanie Ravanal finishes and returns to a seat next to her daughter.

Then Father Dominique gives the benediction and the funeral mass is over. The pallbearers, all wearing the blue, red and yellow ski jackets of the *Companie Des Guides*, carry the coffin from the church and place it in the waiting hearse. Soon, hundreds of mourners join the procession as the hearse slowly makes its way through the narrow streets of Chamonix toward the cemetery located at the end of town beneath the towering walls and slopes of the surrounding mountains.

As the cortege winds toward the Chamonix cemetery, a brilliant burst of sun suddenly breaks through the dark clouds and the glistening peaks of the mountains above us are revealed against a clear sky. A smattering of "ohs" and "ahs" ripple through the long line of mourners at this apparent signal from above that another young climber is being welcomed to his final resting place here in the shadow of one of Europe's highest mountains.

In the center of town, we pass beneath the statues of Dr. Horace Saussaure and Jacques Balmat. The bronze figures gaze upwards at the glistening peak of Mont Blanc, now visible in the emerging late morning sun. It was Dr. Saussaure, a Swiss naturalist, who offered a reward in 1760 to anyone who could find a route to the top of Mont Blanc. The offer was scorned by those who tried and quickly realized that it would be impossible to climb up and down this mountain in one day. Years passed before Balmat, an eccentric local farmer who was trying to figure a way to the top, one day found himself on the mountain when darkness forced him to bivouac for the night wrapped only in his slim blanket. A few days later, he confided to a local physician and aspiring climber, Dr. Michel Paccard, that he had found a way of getting to the summit by remaining for two days on the mountain. Eventually, Balmat and Paccard reached the summit and claimed the prize, twenty-six years after it was offered.

The funeral procession crosses the Cachat-les Geant bridge and winds slowly into the cemetery behind the blue hearse carrying Patrick Chatelet to his grave. Several athletic-looking men in their mid-thirties are sitting in wheelchairs at the gate and will not be able to proceed up the icy path to the grave. These climbers, whose injuries on the mountains have left them crippled for life, have come to pay their final respects to one of their own.

As we shuffle through the cemetery gates, I notice the tombstone of the great English climber, Edward Whymper. The words, "Edward Whymper 1840-1911", are etched into the dark, weathered stone. The simple notation fails to reveal the many dramatic sagas in the famous mountaineer's climbing career. However, the position of his grave at the cemetery entrance is a fitting symbol of this early pioneer's exploits in the Alps, including his first ascent of the Matterhorn.

After the hearse finally reaches the graveside, the pallbearers remove the coffin and the cortege comes to a stop. With only one day's notice, the grave diggers were not able to complete preparations for the young climber's grave, so the lacquered wooden box is placed on a steel stand where it will remain until it can be lowered into the ground. The immediate family stands to the side of the coffin as the other mourners are invited to pass in final tribute to Patrick Chatelet.

They move past the coffin, many whispering final prayers and sliding their hands quickly from forehead to chest and shoulders in the traditional sign of the cross. At the exit gate of the cemetery, everyone is invited to sign the guest registry book. I pick up the small pen attached to the book and, after a moments' reflection, write the words in English: "In sympathy for all of us who have lost a loved one to the mountains."

There is not much time to linger. A second funeral for Patrick's friend and partner in death, Frederick Ravanal, is scheduled for three o'clock that afternoon. The final mass of farewell for the former husband of Stephanie and father of Victoria will be held in the nearby village of Argentiere where hundreds of mourners will have to stand outside the crowded copper-domed church to honor the fallen hometown young man.

The next day, I stop by the editorial offices of the Chamonix newspaper. As a journalist, I know this is the place to glean more information about the mountains and the people who climb them. While researching back issues of the paper, I meet a young reporter who talks knowingly about the popularity of extreme sports in the valley. He also says, "You will probably meet someone who has undergone a loss similar to your own."

I nod but do not comment.

"Talk to Guy Cachat," the reporter says. "He owns a ski lift and restaurant at the edge of town. He, too, has lost a son. Perhaps he will be helpful to you."

Since the first day I learned of Chris's accident, I've wanted to talk with someone who can understand what I'm going through, someone who might offer advice on how to handle the relentless sorrow associated with losing a son. Guy Cachat, I soon find out, is more than qualified to be that person.

After phoning Guy and explaining that I am trying to learn more about mountain climbing and what happened to my son, he replies soberly, "There is no answer to why these things happen, but I'd be glad to meet with you."

Later that day, I meet with him at his rustic, stained-wood restaurant with its large terrace overlooking the ski lift and slopes of Les Plannards. Guy has built this small resort, located on the eastern edge of Chamonix, into a highly successful enterprise over the past eighteen years.

Trim and tall, with a full head of gray-tinged hair, this sixty-year-old Chamonix ski resort owner is still trying to overcome the grief he feels over the recent climbing accident in the nearby mountains in which his handsome, thirty-year-old son, Raymond Cachat, was killed in a snow avalanche. It happened just two weeks before Chris's accident in Canada. Apparently, Raymond, like Chris, was also a high-energy young man who lived life to the fullest.

"Raymond could run this place better than I ever could," Guy tells me with the incomparable pride of a father who has willingly turned over the responsibility of running the family business to a son and found his good judgment borne out. "He knew how to fix the snow-making machine or the ski lift better than any of the employees. And he wasn't afraid to work. He would be here early in the morning until late at night."

"Did you ever warn him about the dangers of climbing or ask him to stop?" I ask.

Guy shrugs his shoulders. "Of course. What father doesn't? But what good does that do? Raymond liked to live on the edge. He drove his car too fast. He loved the mountains. He had such a passion for life! I asked him over and over to be careful, but how can anyone anticipate a sudden avalanche?" he asks.

"By staying away from the mountains," I answer curtly.

"How do you stop the waves of the sea from coming up on the beach?" Guy asks with a sad smile.

It is an answerless question that those like Guy and me who have lost their sons nevertheless still ask.

In our silence a waitress brings us each a small glass of beer at a table overlooking not only the ski slopes of Les Plannards, but also the cemetery at the bottom of the hill where Raymond is buried along with dozens of other climbers lost in the nearby mountains, including their most recent victim, Patrick Chatelet.

"In fact," Guy says, "it was Patrick and his friend, Frederick Ravanal, who first arrived at the scene of the avalanche just after Raymond was killed. The two young men, who would soon lose their own lives, helped carry my son's body down from the mountain.

"What about you?" Guy asks me. "How have you been dealing with your loss?"

This is the first time I've been asked this question and for a moment I hesitate. Then I answer with a certainty born of despair.

"I'm angry. I really hate the whole idea of mountain climbing. I don't understand why people do this, why my son did," I answer.

"And that's why you're here, to find out?"

"Yes. I'd like, no, I need to discover what climbing is all about in order to find out more about my son, Chris, and the kind of person he was," I respond. "I always thought I understood him, until he began this love affair with climbing."

Guy nods with a solemn look of understanding. "When my daughter came to tell me what happened to my son Raymond that Sunday afternoon, I was in the back of the house chopping wood. I had just taken my coat off and still had it in my hand when she told me that Raymond's body had been retrieved from the avalanche. My first reaction was to slam the coat onto the ground. I know what you mean by being angry, but it does us no good," he says.

"Well, what can we do? I've never been in a situation like this before where there is absolutely no way of solving a problem," I confess to Guy, adding, "Death is so final."

Leaning back in his chair with a deep sigh, Guy glances out the window for a moment and then turns his brown eyes back toward me.

"Just after Raymond's accident, my wife and I happened to see a television program on how a loss like this should be handled. It's been a great help to us," he says.

"What was the advice?" I ask.

"They said you have to understand that there are several stages of grief associated with the loss of a child. In the first stage, you find yourself angry, even bitter, about what has happened, just as you are now. There is also a temptation to deny that an accident happened, that your loved one isn't really dead, that a terrible misunderstanding has taken place. That can cause all kinds of problems for you. You lose interest in life. You have no enthusiasm or concern for anything and your sorrow is continuous and overwhelming. Everything you hear or see reminds you of the person who is gone. That's the most difficult period," Guy says. "At this point, many people want to hang onto their departed loved one so they refuse to believe what has happened. They get caught up in anger and guilt, because that deflects them away from facing the death of their child."

"I guess that's where I'm at," I acknowledge. "I'm really angry at the whole idea of climbing and what a waste it is for someone to lose their life on a mountain as Chris did. It also makes me feel guilty that I didn't do something more drastic to stop him. You know, as a parent, my relationship with Chris was based on taking care of him as a small child and if anything happened to him, I was accountable. Well, I can't just snap my fingers and get rid of that feeling of responsibility that has been built up over so many years."

Guy nods his head. "Yes, I have those feelings, too. But you have to work your way out of that, because it prevents you from facing the truth about what has happened and that prevents you from moving on to the next step in the process of grieving."

Guy goes on to talk about the second stage of grief, which he describes as an effort to accept the loss and regain one's interest and zest for life. "Despite our sorrow," he points out, "we still have to go on living. It takes a lot of effort and time to force ourselves back into the old habits of dealing with the everyday details of making a living, running a household and maintaining relationships with other people.

"I think this is where I'm at right now," Guy says. "Coming here to do many of the tasks which Raymond used to manage is taking time and effort, but slowly I'm finding that I can do these things without being swamped with sorrow over the fact that I no longer can see my son every day and enjoy his company."

"Is it harder to do this with Raymond buried in the cemetery at the bottom of the ski slope, which you see every day, where you are constantly reminded of your son's death?" I ask slowly.

"At first, it was. But lately, I've been feeling glad

he's there. Somehow it makes me feel that my son's not so far away and that some day we'll be together again even if it is...only down there," Guy says, looking toward the cemetery.

As we talk, hundreds of intense, brightly dressed skiers are wending their way down the snow-covered slopes, then scurrying like busy ants to the bottom of the hill where they join the long lines waiting at the ski lift. I think about how it must have been a gratifying experience for Guy Cachat to sit in the lounge and watch his son directing the workers, repairing the lift and driving the snow machines that make Les Plannards run so smoothly for the many skiers who come here each winter.

Perhaps only another father can appreciate the deep satisfaction and fulfillment a man feels when his son follows in his footsteps. I suspect that if one were to examine the subconscious frustrations of modern-day fathers, it would be the disappointment inherent in their sons' decisions to move away from home and, both physically and philosophically, choose a career devoid of any connection with the occupation of their dads'. Having experienced the satisfaction of seeing his son follow in the family business, Guy's loss must be exceptionally painful.

Now, as I listen to this other father who shares my sense of loss in so many ways, I realize that I also must attempt to master my anger and bitter sense of loss. As Guy suggests, I need to move on to the next stage. I hope his response to my next question will provide the answer on how to do that.

"What is the final stage in dealing with this grief?" I ask.

Guy pauses and sips his beer for a moment. Then he continues: "You have to learn to remember your son without feeling the pain of his loss. You need to think of all the wonderful times you've had together and how lucky you are to have known someone like the person who is now gone."

"That sounds like a tough thing to do," I say. Then I tell Guy about the reaction I had when the American television personality, Bill Cosby, spoke at the funeral of his son who was murdered in California several weeks after Chris's accident. The grief-stricken father offered a prayer at his son's funeral in which he said: "We now have to give praise to God for letting us know him." "When I read this in a newspaper," I say to Guy, "I asked myself how Bill Cosby could manage to say a thing like that only a week after his son's loss. I mean, how could you feel thankful for anything when your son has just been cruelly taken from you?"

"Yes, that is difficult," Guy says. "But eventually you need to realize that Mr. Cosby is right. We have to understand how much we've been blessed by knowing the kinds of people these fine young men of ours really were. And only when we get to that stage can we really derive any kind of joy from our lives without them. And I think that if my Raymond or your Chris were to speak to us now, that is what they would want us to do."

The afternoon passes quickly as we continue to talk about a subject that is so painful, yet so meaningful, to both of us. I want insights which will make me more philosophical, more accepting as Bill Cosby and Guy Cachat are, but I'm just not ready. I still feel like railing at fate for the unfairness of it all. As usual, despite our conversation, I resort to attack mode by questioning the value of mountain climbing and grilling Guy on the subject of establishing a damage-control system like licensing or requiring guides for everyone.

But Guy Cachat has lived in view of Mont Blanc too

long not to understand what I have so far failed to grasp. "You're thinking of climbing as a sport, a competitive engagement which needs to have rules and regulations we can control. That won't help you to understand how Chris felt about it. Climbing isn't like soccer, where you can change the rules if the goalies are being injured or ice hockey, where checking against the boards can be regulated so no one gets hurt too badly. Mountain climbing represents the ultimate form of liberty. It's a communion. It's a gathering together of everything that makes life worthwhile...like courage and skill and passion. Those are not elements we can regulate."

"That's very interesting," I respond diplomatically, as I try to process what he's saying. Inwardly, I'm thinking that perhaps he's right, that maybe he has put his finger on something which will enable me to understand Chris's attraction to climbing. Yet, I feel Guy is giving me a romantic interpretation, a spiritual justification. I am still searching for an unembellished, factual answer. I need to settle this in my head before I can come to terms with it in my heart. I fear I have a long way yet to go on this journey.

The afternoon sun has moved behind the snow-covered peaks of the Aiguille du Midi when I finally stand to say goodbye to my companion in sorrow. It strikes me how differently we have each approached the passions of our sons and how much courage Guy displays in his continued reverence toward mountain climbing in the face of the enormous loss it has cost him.

This same devotion to mountaineering, despite its high cost in lives, is repeated later in the afternoon when I go to see another man suggested by the reporter at the local newspaper, Dr. Bernard Marsigny, Director of Emergency Services at the small Chamonix Hospital located not far from the center of town. To him, the death of the two young men on the ice-covered slopes of Les Droits the previous Sunday afternoon was not an unusual occurrence.

The tall, angular physician and his staff treat hundreds of climbers each year after the red rescue helicopter of the local *Gendarmerie de Secours* delivers the injured mountaineers to the cement helipad outside the hospital. These doctors sometimes treat dozens of injured hikers, skiers and climbers a day during the summer season, and many who are flown to the hospital have already died or fail to survive emergency help.

Sitting behind his desk not far from a ready-to-go rescue backpack propped against the wall with its red cross stitched on the front, Dr. Marsigny says that each year approximately fifty climbers or hikers brought to the Chamonix hospital eventually end up in the morgue just a few steps from the back entrance to the hospital.

"Fifty to sixty people killed each year just in this area! Isn't that a terribly large death rate?" I ask.

"Of course it is, but this is a dangerous activity. When an accident happens, it can often be fatal. People who climb these mountains know very well that a falling rock, an avalanche or a mistake can kill them, but they come anyway. There are times when I think the proximity of death almost seems like an added attraction to some of the climbers," he says.

"Perhaps there should be some kind of regulation to make sure the climbers are at least qualified to go up these mountains. Would you support the idea of a climbing permit?" I ask.

Dr. Marsigny shakes his head. "It would never work. You have three countries involved: France, Italy and Switzerland. To enact a similar licensing law for each country would be extremely difficult. Also, trying to police such a large area with so many climbers involved is almost impossible. The only thing we can do is provide the very best rescue and medical service for those who have accidents. And I think we do that. After being informed of almost any accident, we can reach injured persons with a doctor in the helicopter, extract the victims from the mountain and have them here in the hospital within twenty minutes."

"But if the police made random checks on permits just as they do with a driver's license, then everyone would at least have some expertise before they started up," I point out.

"It's not just the inexperienced climbers who have accidents, you know. After all, an avalanche doesn't distinguish between good and bad climbers or skiers when it suddenly buries everything in its path," he says.

I nod in agreement. I have researched some tragedies of the past which happened here while at the newspaper office. I remind him of the accident that took place the previous summer when a momentary lapse in normal safety precautions, not inexperience, cost the lives of two climbers. In July, the rescue helicopter was called to bring in the bodies of Clare Kemper, a thirty-one-year-old Australian climber, and an Englishman, Mark Haseler, thirty-nine, when they both fell to their deaths moments after their successful ascent of the 13,291-foot summit of the Aiguille de Blonnassay. The Australian woman asked a third friend in the climbing party, Mike Wigney, to take a picture of her and Haseler in their moment of triumph. Kemper and Haseler began to pose for the picture while Wigney unhooked his carabiner from the safety rope and took the photograph. Just then, however, Kemper noticed that her rucksack was starting to slide down the narrow cliff. Instinctively, she dove for the pack and immediately began to slide down the steep pitch. Haseler lunged after her and within seconds both climbers had vanished down the slope. "I bent down to put the camera away and then all I saw was the rucksack fall. Clare went for the rucksack, head first, down the slope and Mark lunged after Clare. I saw them slip for two or three seconds, then they disappeared," Wigney reported later.

The doomed pair slid down a 1,200-foot vertical slope and then fell another 1,200 feet off the mountain. Other nearby climbers heard the sound of their belaying rope swish through the air as the man and woman dropped to their deaths.

The following week, two French teenagers were killed during a fall, a Chilean climber died of exposure while climbing and three Italians fell 2,600 feet on the Italian side of the Alps. A few days later, a Russian woman was killed outright by a rock fall and her Russian companion had to remain for two days on the mountain in freezing temperatures until weather permitted a helicopter rescue of him and the dead woman.

"There is no room for carelessness or lack of caution on these mountains," Dr. Marsigny says. "A small slip or simple mistake in judgment can easily cause a fatal accident. In some cases, of course, it's just a matter of being at the wrong place at the wrong time."

"But what about the people who come here to climb?" I ask. "If they know about the danger, why do they continue to challenge the odds?"

The doctor, who has been a climber since his youth, looks out the window where the mountains are shrouded in clouds on this particular morning.

"Not everyone who comes here to climb has an accident," he says defensively. "During the summer months, there are thousands of people climbing in the Alps every day. If a hundred are killed, that is not a large percentage. I can tell you that there are more people killed in one week driving their cars in France than there are climbers who lose their lives in these mountains throughout the entire year."

It's the same kind of comparison with the number of people killed in other activities which I heard years ago from my son as he tried to justify his climbing activities. I respond now just as I replied to Chris by reminding the doctor that in our society, we have to drive cars and walk across the street.

"Those are necessary activities, but climbing is not," I say.

"For most people, you're right, but for some of these climbers I suspect that climbing is as necessary as breathing," he answers immediately.

Dr. Marsigny has obviously had good cause for thinking these questions through. I decide to get personal. "And what about you, Doctor? I understand you're still a climber. Is it as necessary as breathing for you to go to the mountains on your day off?" I ask.

He smiles and folds his hands on a cluttered desk. "There was a time when that was true, but not now. I think most climbers, like me, go through a stage where being on a mountain is their first priority. They need to prove to themselves that they can get to the top of a high peak. Then, as they get older, develop careers, get married and have children, their priorities change. They no longer have to prove to themselves they can do it, because they already have. That's how I feel now, although I still climb occasionally for pleasure."

"Do you mean it's still fun for you after all the accident victims you've treated?" I ask somewhat incredulously.

"Unfortunately, I've cared for climbers who were injured or killed on just about any route I can take in these mountains and that memory is always there. Sort of takes the fun out of it," he admits, "but nevertheless I still want to climb. Once you've felt the thrill of it, it's hard to relinquish."

In the distance, I can hear the whirling blades of a helicopter approaching from the Chamonix Valley. Another accident victim has been pulled off the mountains and is on the way to the hospital. Dr. Marsigny glances nervously out the window and I realize it's time for me to go.

"A final question, Doctor?" I ask.

"Sure."

"Do you like this job, with all the trauma and tension that accompanies every emergency coming in here by helicopter?"

Dr. Marsigny glances slowly out the window again where the sound of rotator blades slapping against the still air is getting louder.

"I've been here for ten years...and I'm still here," he says with a smile and a final, hurried handshake.

As I walk outside the hospital, the helicopter bumps down on the painted red cross of the landing pad. A doctor dressed in a blue ski suit jumps from the passenger seat while two nurses from the hospital push a gurney to the helicopter as the whirling blades come to a stop. A stretcher loaded with one more victim of the day's mountain activities is pulled from the helicopter, placed on the gurney and quickly wheeled into the emergency room.

Meanwhile, on the other side of town, the grave diggers must be finished with their work. By now, Patrick Chatelet is in his grave. A few miles up the l'Arve river, in the small village of Argentiere, Frederick Ravanal will also be in his final resting place. From now on, the price of their climbing passion must be borne by fathers, mothers, brothers, sisters, relatives, close friends and, in Frederick's case, a wife and daughter. Stephanie Ravanal will have to face the duties of caring for little Victoria alone. In the meantime, she must wait for the day next summer when another child will arrive whose father is gone forever, because for him and his friend, Patrick Chatelet, climbing was apparently as necessary as breathing. I feel angry for her; I feel angry for myself. And yet, I must go on.

11 chapter

Glistening Peaks, Twisting Trails

You may be whatever you resolve to be.

General "Stonewall" Jackson

The crowded, cog-rail train for Montenvers jolts slowly out of the small station in downtown Chamonix and begins its steep twenty-minute climb to the Sea of Ice. With ropes, crampons and ice axes tied securely against our packs, Ivano Ghirardini, who has agreed to be my instructor, and I lean toward each other on the wooden seats in order to be heard above the clanking and rattling of the thick, cog chain pulling us upward to Europe's longest glacier.

I found my instructor the evening before while strolling through downtown Chamonix. In a small store window was the picture of a solidly built, middle-aged man who advertised his guide business with a montage of photographs and newspaper articles pasted on a large piece of cardboard. This highly personal and individualized form of self-promotion was appealing so I tried to open the door. It was locked.

At a small bar next to Ivano's shop, however, a waitress informed me that he usually arrives there around six-thirty in the evening after a day of guiding clients. Before I could order an espresso, Ivano suddenly appeared and joined me at an outside table.

"So you want to learn alpine climbing," he asked with a friendly smile.

"Yes, but first I must tell you why," I responded.

A mystic and philosopher who has written an excellent book about climbing, Ivano immediately took an interest in my situation.

"You are doing the right thing in searching for the meaning of your son's life," he assured me. "The mountain will give you the answers you are looking for."

He instructed me to purchase or rent some climbing gear that evening and meet him early the next morning at his shop. "A client informed me that he must cancel an appointment for tomorrow so I am free to go with you," Ivano told me.

This morning, as we lean back in our seats on the way to the glacier, Ivano, his handsome face deeply tanned, lights a well used wooden pipe and calls to me over the noise of the train: "Today, we'll practice using the ice axe and crampons. Tomorrow you can come up by yourself and practice. If you're ready, we'll go to Mont Blanc at the end of the week."

"Great," I reply, little realizing that the training schedule Ivano is proposing would be challenging even to Chris who was a young, seasoned climber in perfect physical condition.

After a twenty-minute ride through the steep and heavily forested slopes we arrive at the Montenvers station above the Chamonix Valley. Chalets, hotels and shops are spread three thousand feet below us in the valley like small match boxes scattered about by an unruly child. After the train stops, several other climbers like us, with backpacks and ropes, separate from the tourists who have come for the view and begin hiking along a trail leading to the glacier.

In a few minutes, we arrive at a vertical cliff where a steel ladder has been bolted to the rock. Ivano sends me down first. Carefully, I descend one hundred feet to the first ledge and look up to where my guide is walking down the ladder facing outward without using his hands. One misstep and he would fall sixty or seventy feet.

"Climbing is all about balance," Ivano calls to me as he casually steps down the rungs as if he were descending the stairs of an elegant hotel.

I turn my eyes away, unable to watch. In a few minutes, however, he's standing beside me and suggesting that we now climb the rock wall we just descended.

"I thought we were working on alpine techniques," I respond.

"In alpine climbing, you must do everything," he answers. "Sometimes you have to climb a wall that is part ice and part rock."

"But I'm wearing these huge, clumsy mountain boots," I answer with fond memories of the flexible, rubber climbing shoes I have come to depend on for vertical ascents on the rock walls of places like Yosemite, Cathedral Ledge or the Shawnagunks.

Ivano hands me the end of his coiled climbing rope and smiles. "So you must learn to use them."

After carefully watching me tie a figure-eight knot into my harness to be certain that I'm properly secured, he approaches the wall with the rest of the rope slung over his shoulder and begins to climb. Without hesitation, he places the tip of his heavy boot on a small rock protrusion and steps up.

"You see, the tip of your boot will hold on even a small stone extension," Ivano says.

Then he moves up the face of the smooth cliff for approximately fifteen feet without protection before clipping into a small bolt drilled into the rock. I put him on belay with my ATC and he climbs upwards again. In a few minutes, he arrives at the top and slips a nylon sling into a steel ring imbedded in the rock. He clips a carabiner to the sling and his climbing rope so he's ready to secure my climb.

"Okay, now I've got you on belay. Come on up," he calls down to me.

Totally convinced of the impossibility of following his lead, I place the tip of my thickly soled boot into a small crack and step up. Surprisingly to me, the boot holds. The soles are so rigid that even placing the tip of the boot on a rock will carry my full weight. I move up again and soon arrive at the first anchor where there now seems to be no foothold to proceed. I grab a small ledge and try to pull my weight upwards.

"No. No. Use your feet, not your hands," Ivano calls from above. It's familiar advice. Climbing techniques are obviously no different in France than in the United States. Eventually, I find a better foothold and push up with my legs. Again, the boot's sole holds and I step up.

"Good. You're doing fine," my guide calls down.

Encouraged, I climb to the top ledge where Ivano has been watching my moves. He tells me to rappel down and try the route again. "Sometimes the holds are hard to find, but you have to keep looking," he advises. Then, looking out over the glacier field, he says: "The mountain is like a book. You have to read it and study it chapter by chapter as you climb."

I try to put into practice what I have learned.

After an hour of rock climbing, Ivano is satisfied with my progress and suggests that it's time to move onto the glacier.

We walk down a rocky path. Soon I can feel the cool air coming off the Sea of Ice as we tramp past several deep crevasses. Ivano stops to throw a piece of ice into one of these gaps in the glacier. It takes several seconds before the ice splashes into the water far below.

"Falling into a crevasse is not a good way to die." He shakes his head and looks at me to see if I have taken in his admonition. I nod.

Soon we strap crampons onto our boots and then proceed up and down several slopes of the snow-covered glacier.

"Keep your feet flat on the ice so that all ten points of your crampons dig in. When you move down, turn your toes out like Charlie Chaplin and keep your weight distributed evenly on your feet," he calls out as he easily demonstrates each of his instructions.

"I understand the theory, but trying to walk like the famous comic actor is difficult and tiring."

It's a relief when we turn to the various uses of an ice axe.

"This can save your life if you fall," Ivano says. Explaining that the pointed tip enables a climber to walk along the edge of a vertical ice slope and that it can hold a climber's weight if it's slammed into the ice, he demonstrates a series of moves which I then try to copy. "If you ever fall and begin to slide down a slope, roll over on your stomach and slam your axe into the ice," he says.

We go to a small slope. "Practice this maneuver several times to get the feel of it." Little do I realize how important this self-arrest technique will become in the very near future.

Ivano is patient, but demanding. Finally, we stop for a lunch of water and sandwiches which he brought in his pack.

"Do you like doing this?" Ivano asks with a smile.

"It's not easy," I reply.

Ivano turns philosophical. "Alpine climbing isn't just a foolish pastime. This is serious business. It's a journey to find the most hidden part of one's self. It's a search for the soul," he says. "But to do this, you must first suffer. It's a natural law of man. Nothing worthwhile is given to us without pain."

I nod, realizing how similarly Chris and Ivano view the concept of pain.

However, a short while later after we finish our lunch and go back to the mountaineering lessons, I call out so Ivano can hear me: "Hello, soul, I'm suffering. So where the hell are you?"

Ivano laughs. "You are a funny guy," he says.

By mid-afternoon, the stretching of so many muscles I've never used before is taking its toll. Ivano notices my tiring condition. He decides that we've had enough for the day.

"For the next few days, you can come back and practice on your own although I suggest you hike up instead of taking the train," he says.

I groan. He reminds me of my Harvard hockey coach, "Cooney" Weiland, who used to say: "When you're too tired to skate anymore, skate two fast laps around the rink."

Nevertheless, the following day, I take Ivano's advice. Instead of the twenty-minute train ride, I hike three hours up to the glacier with a heavy pack. Two more hours on the ice walking in crampons like Charlie Chaplin and practicing various moves with the ice axe again leaves me tired and sore. I stop for a long drink of water.

Then, while leaning against a rock, a surge of depression and doubt washes over me like a tidal wave. Suddenly, I'm convinced that climbing is simply too tough. It's hard, exhausting work. I'm too old for this, too far out of shape. I have started to feel maybe it's an impossible goal to walk in Chris's shoes! Perhaps I should quit, just give up. Perhaps I should abandon the whole project. I imagine how pleasant it would be to return to Chamonix, shop in some of the elegant stores in the village and have a grand lunch of onion soup *gratinee*, quiche, a salad and a fine bottle of local wine. But then my thoughts return to my lost son and my mission—to find out why all this was so important to him—and I realize I've come too far to stop. The training schedule has got to continue. I've got to get as physically fit as possible. I repeat to myself Ivano's words about the necessity of pain. Somehow, they make a difference.

Screwing the lid back on the water bottle, I hoist the pack onto my shoulders and start hiking up the frozen snow once more. For another painful hour I push myself up and down the slopes and around the crevasses of the Sea of Ice.

When my watch finally shows four o'clock, I hike back to the Montenvers station for the last train of the day to Chamonix. As the train rumbles down the steep slope, I tell myself again that no letup can be tolerated. In three more days, Ivano and I are slated to go to Mont Blanc.

The next morning, aching muscles and all, I manage to hike five thousand feet up a twisting trail to the Junction, overlooking a huge glacier which Balmat and Paccard crossed on their first ascent of Mont Blanc. On a large stone near the path, a brass plaque informs me that the two climbers bivouacked here on the first night of their climb. Later, when I reach the Junction, I look out over the huge crevasses that had to be crossed by these early eighteenth century climbers with their primitive equipment and find it difficult to believe they were able to accomplish their goal.

That night I soak in a hot tub and sleep well and heavily. For the first time in a long while, I sleep deeply and soundly.

The following day, I return to the Sea of Ice for a second day of trekking on the glacier while wearing heavy boots and crampons. Afterwards, on the train coming down from Montenvers, I realize I feel tired, but not totally exhausted. *It's getting better*, I tell myself. My replacement hip is no longer a hindrance. My other hip, the one which should be replaced, is functioning perfectly and without pain. The constant struggle is paying off. Chris was right. Pain is a state of mind. By overcoming it, I'm breaking the barriers which could prevent me from reaching my next objective, the summit of Pisang Peak in Nepal. The handicaps I started with are beginning to disappear. The joy of being physically fit is beginning to replace the misery that accompanied those first days of the conditioning program.

By the end of the week, in fact, Ivano is ready to take me up to the Aiguille (Needle) du Midi for a day of high-altitude climbing and, possibly, a summit bid on Mont Blanc.

I rise early the morning we are to go and, nervous with anticipation, decide to stroll through the streets of Chamonix. The shops are not yet open although a few climbers with bulging packs are moving through the village on their way to an early start on the nearby mountains. The smell of fresh bread and strong coffee wafts through the cool air from the bakeries already open for business. High above us, the glistening peaks have already emerged from the clouds. I stop for a moment to look at the pointed top of the Aiguille du Midi. It's frightening and yet the excitement of knowing that in a few hours I'll finally be climbing up a snow-covered glacier at a high altitude is exhilarating. To my surprise, I find that I share Chris's contradictory emotions described in his Christmas letter before the final ice climbing expedition in Banff: "I'm psyched and scared."

By eight A.M., with climbing equipment secured in my backpack, I arrive at Ivano's shop where we spend several minutes organizing and checking the gear. We take a *café* and then walk two blocks from his shop to the *telepherique* station where we purchase tickets and board a gondola for the 3,300-foot ride to the mid-station leading to the Aiguille du Midi. Then we get on a second cable car which rises another 6,300 feet. Within twenty minutes we've arrived at an altitude of 12,678 feet. Although this rapid ascent can eliminate two days of climbing, it cancels any opportunity for slow acclimatization to the altitude.

Except for those alpine climbers who have unlimited time to practice climbing at heights above 12,000 feet, the problem of becoming acclimatized to the altitude is undoubtedly the biggest challenge. There is simply no training program that prepares one for breathing in thin air. The best conditioned athletes have no advantage over any other climber if they do not have time to become accustomed to breathing and hiking at a high altitude.

After arriving at the upper station of the Aiguille du Midi, we exit the cable car and pass through a permanent tunnel carved from glacier ice, emerging onto a snow-covered platform overlooking a spectacular view of the Alps, including sections of Italy and Switzerland as well as France. My interest in the scenery is quickly eclipsed by Ivano's crisp instructions. "Strap on crampons and clip my rope into your harness. We'll stay roped together for the next few hours," he says.

In the distance, I can see the long, snow-covered slope leading first up to the Mont Blanc Tacul at 14,200 feet, then down to the Col Maudit (the Cursed Mountain Pass), then up again to Mont Maudit and finally up to Mont Blanc. I simply cannot imagine walking that distance and yet the tiny specks on the ridge indicate that people are that very day traversing southward and up to the 15,779-foot summit of the famous mountain.

After securing our gear and making sure crampons are properly fit to our mountaineering boots, we start down the ridge, placing the right foot on the northern slope leading sharply down 1,000 feet to the Col du Midi and the left foot on the southern slope which drops sharply to a glacier far below. As we descend toward the aptly named Glacier du Geant, a thousand feet below our starting point, I concentrate on my boots and where to place my feet. It is simply too terrifying to look down on either side where a fall would be fatal.

By the time we arrive at the bottom of this "arret" and begin moving slowly upwards along the Col du Midi, I'm beginning to gasp for breath, the inevitable result of breathing at a high altitude before undergoing an acclimatization period. Even an athlete who can run several miles at sea level or climb all day at a low altitude is not in condition for the 12,000-foot altitude we have gained via the cable car. The pressure to breathe after only the slightest exertion quickly forces me to stop every five minutes. Ivano says nothing, although we are now both aware that summiting Mont Blanc by that night is becoming a questionable goal.

Still roped together, we nevertheless keep moving upwards, step by step along the glacier. The sun has come out and far to the south, the rounded summit of Mont Blanc is glistening in the light. Almost an hour passes when suddenly we come to a small crevasse, perhaps five feet wide. Ivano moves away from this danger point and steps ahead.

"Stay in my path. Place your boots in my footsteps," he orders.

I obey and we move forward. However, I see that I can save several yards of walking by placing my foot down on the snow approximately ten inches from his mark. Without thinking, I take the shortcut. It's a huge mistake.

Instantly, the snow collapses beneath my feet. I struggle to jump forward but it's too late. My entire weight begins plummeting down a section of the crevasse where a small snow bridge had concealed the icy fissure. For two or three seconds, I'm totally out of control, falling toward a cold chamber of ice and water perhaps fifty feet below. There is no time to react nor is there time to sense the terror of dropping into the freezing tomb of this massive glacier.

Suddenly, the harness snaps securely around my waist as the rope attached to Ivano's gear pulls tight. My fall is broken. Now, I'm dangling approximately ten feet down the ice wall of the dark crevasse. Quickly, I kick the toe points of my crampons into the ice wall, grab the rope in my gloves and begin climbing upwards. Ivano has braced his legs in the snow and can hold my weight. I raise my left foot, push the points into the ice and step up. Then I repeat this motion with my right points. In less than a minute, I climb up the ice wall and, in violation of proper climbing technique, throw my upper body onto the ledge of the crevasse. Wet snow works its way quickly inside the front of my down jacket sending a stream of cold water down my chest. It's a welcome trade-off against a fatal fall into the mausoleum of ice far below.

As I crawl out of the crevasse and onto the solid snow again, I sense that Ivano is annoyed with my carelessness. However, he remains patient. *"Ah mon amie, je ne crois pas que tu est un alpinist,"* (My friend, I don't think you're a mountain climber) he mutters.

"That's why I have you as a guide," I stammer.

Ivano does not smile. *"Allons, on y va,"* he says. Without another word, we start out again marching slowly across the ice and snow.

However, the gravity of what happened to me at the crevasse is not lost on Ivano. He calls for a rest stop to announce the inevitable. "I don't think we should try for Mont Blanc today. I think it's better for us to climb here for a few hours and then go to the refuge where I'll make some coffee for us," he says. "Then we'll take the train back down."

I agree, although the prospect of giving up the goal of summiting Mont Blanc is a disappointment.

To make sure I get more experience, Ivano decides that we should rock climb across a jagged series of stone cliffs leading to the *Refuge des Cosmiques,* a small chalet where climbers and skiers can sleep and find food without descending to the valley. For the next hour, we move across the face of these stones. Far below, I can see Chamonix. In the best tradition of an ostrich, I don't look down. What you don't see can cause no harm!

When we finally enter the refuge, I order a bowl of onion soup while Ivano brews some coffee on his small stove which he intended to use on the climb up to Mont Blanc. As we sit on the wooden porch outside the refuge, I turn to Ivano. "What was the most important climbing experience of your life?" I ask.

He lights up his pipe and without hesitating, he replies: "The Shroud. Years ago, I had a big problem up there," he says.

"What happened?" I ask.

Ivano draws on his pipe and leans back against the wooden bench. "When I was nineteen years old, I decided to solo in the middle of winter. It was not a wise thing to do, but at that age...well, everything seems possible."

I lean forward to listen.

"Several of my friends started with me for this high-altitude ascent, but they decided to turn back after the first few hours of climbing. Then I elected to attempt what no one had ever accomplished on this mountain: solo climb the Shroud in the middle of the winter without using siege tactics and fixed ropes."

The first day went well as he ascended almost 3,000 feet through deep snows. By evening, however, he was beginning to understand the danger of his undertaking.

"That night, I began to think that I was a fool to be doing this. The temperature dropped to below zero and to avoid the bitter cold, I pitched my small tent in the snow and tried to stay warm. In my imagination, I started hearing voices of other climbers who had lost their lives in these mountains. I began thinking that this was a dream, that I was someone else, that the real me was not really climbing the Shroud."

Despite these warning signs, the young climber was determined to move forward. In the morning, he resisted a strong urge to return to the warmth and comfort of the valley and began working his way upwards in a monotonous but steady pace toward the top. He continued for two more days.

"After the third day, I was beginning to lose all track of time. Sometimes, I stopped for an entire hour to look at the landscape or examine the small lichens on the rocks or the bubbles in the ice," Ivano relates.

Nevertheless, he kept moving up the difficult pitches and ice-covered slopes of the Shroud. Then, as he began to believe he could reach the summit, a small but serious accident occurred. He mistakenly allowed the fuel to escape from his propane stove. That meant he could no longer melt snow for drinking water. Even worse, his food was gone, except for several sugar cubes. Sensing that serious trouble was developing, he realized he should get off the mountain, but still he kept moving up. On the fifth day, in the freezing temperature, Ivano was getting desperately weak and he decided to give up.

In the middle of the afternoon, a helicopter appeared. The young climber waved desperately and made the V sign with his arms, indicating he was in distress. However, the pilot never saw him and continued on. Rather than give up, Ivano decided to make one more bid for the top. After climbing until dark, he pitched his tent and fell into a deep sleep. In the morning, he made one last attempt and by midday he reached the summit.

Totally exhausted and dehydrated from lack of water, Ivano dropped to his knees and kissed the snow. He had made it. He had reached the top of the Shroud in a way no other human being had climbed the massive mountain. For several minutes, he was euphoric. Then he began his descent.

Almost immediately, he made a mistake by descending to a position below a snow ridge where he became trapped. Ivano could not go up or down.

"I realized that, very soon, I would be dead. After so much time on the mountain in a debilitated condition, I could no longer feel the pain of hunger or thirst. I made a hole in the snow and tried to keep from freezing to death. It was tempting to just fall asleep and let the warmth of permanent sleep take its course." Ivano pauses. I know the train we will take back down to Chamonix will soon arrive at the station overlooking the glacier, but I urge him to continue telling the story.

"I wasn't ready to die," he says with a smile. "So I began to pray to the infinite gods to save me. Every time I prayed, it helped me to stay alive. After a short time, however, I could feel death coming back, working its way up my arms and legs and I knew the time was fast approaching when I could no longer fight for life."

Then, just before dawn of his sixth day on the mountain, as he lay dying in his small one-man tent, he heard a loud, clear voice speaking to him from the void in words that would resonate in his head for years to come: "Get ready! They're coming to rescue you at ten-thirty this morning."

Sure enough, a helicopter appeared in the sky at ten thirty and rescued him.

The medical community was astounded that Ivano lived through his experience on the Linceul. "You should have been dead two days before they found you," one of the doctors told him later.

Yet, not only did Ivano survive, his passion for the mountains became even stronger, particularly after being chosen to join an elite French team of climbers who went almost to the top of Annapurna II in the Himalayas before a storm forced them to turn back. Now, more than ever, he sees his daily life of guiding clients on the ice and snow-covered slopes of the Alps as voyages of discovery. *"L'alpinism n'est pas un conquet de l'inutile, c'est la rechereche de la partie la plus chachee de soi-meme, son ame,"* he says. Alpine climbing is not a foolish pastime, it's a search for the most hidden part of one's self, one's soul.

This statement prompts me to ask a question of Ivano I've been trying to pose since we first met and he told me about the confusion and troubles he had to deal with during his youth. "You stated earlier that you believe climbers are different from other people. Why did you say that?" I ask.

Ivano leans back in his chair and puffs slowly on his pipe. Then he answers with an almost rehearsed fluency.

"Part of that answer is easy. By definition, anyone who is willing to climb a treacherous mountain has got to possess courage and determination. When you meet a true mountaineer, you meet someone with a real passion for life, someone who is desperate to prove themselves and find out who they are," he says.

"I've heard that from others," I reply, trying to keep my voice steady. "But what is the other part?"

Now Ivano leans forward, his elbows on the table, and begins to speak with a sudden intensity that suggests his strong feelings on this topic.

"Most of the climbers I know have a father problem. Either they come from a broken home where they didn't get to know their father or else, for one reason or another, they're trying subconsciously to prove their strength and courage to the man who brought them into the world."

His words hit me like a two-by-four. "That's a pretty big generalization, Ivano," I protest.

"Yes, but it's right. Talk to any serious climber and he'll reveal a childhood filled with family trauma. Its almost always true. The result is that climbers are looking for self definition. It's a spiritual thing. They're really searching for their souls like no other category of people you'll ever meet."

Could Ivano be describing Chris, who underwent so much conflict because of Janey's and my contentious separation and divorce? And as I think back about all the stories related at Camp 4 in Yosemite each evening by so many young climbers, I realize Ivano could be speaking of many of them as well.

"Interesting," I say in my most noncommittal voice. I don't want at this moment to tell him how acutely his words describe my son and perhaps even myself.

My guide smiles. "These are things to think about. Now we must go back," he says.

We take almost an hour to walk up the arret to the the Aiguille du Midi *telepherique* where we can ride down to the village in fifteen minutes. By late afternoon, I say goodbye to Ivano and return to the hotel. In two more days, I'm scheduled to catch a plane from Geneva to New York and from there, fly to the Himalayas where I plan to climb Pisang Peak while I'm still in good physical shape.

The ten days of climbing in the Alps are hardly sufficient for becoming an expert mountaineer. Yet, Ivano's lessons will surely go a long way in helping to accomplish the expedition I plan in the Himalayas. Learning to feel comfortable in crampons, using mountaineering boots for rock climbing, wielding an ice axe effectively, setting up snow anchors and roping together with other members of a team will all be necessary skills needed for my upcoming climb. Furthermore, an understanding of the tough mental attitude required to move steadily upwards hour after hour at high altitudes is an essential ingredient for getting to the top of a 20,000-foot peak. Of course, there should be more training, but the opportunity for preparation is running out. The climbing season in the Himalayas is about to begin. It's time to leave for Pisang Peak, a mass of rock and snow which twice defeated Chris and is undoubtedly now waiting, relentless and implacable, to deal with a father who is determined to conquer its summit in this increasingly personal family feud.

12

chapter

Star-Crossed Encounters

What fates impose, that man must needs abide,
It boots not to resist wind and tide.

William Shakespeare, *Henry VI*

The plane drones through the night as the passengers sprawl, doll-like, in the seats of the darkened cabin of a Boeing 747. It's been more than twenty years since I last made this trip across the Pacific Ocean. My mind spins back to January of 1968 when the Tet Offensive was just breaking out in Vietnam and I was returning for a second tour of reporting on the war. Knowing that major fighting was already underway throughout the country, I was anxious to arrive in Saigon as soon as possible. There would be plenty of big stories that could boost the career and reputation of a young reporter. I also knew that a lot of people would be killed before this major offensive ended. Like Chris heading off for his climbing expedition in Canada, I remember being "psyched and scared."

Tonight, however, there is probably more "scared" than "psyched" in my feelings. In two more weeks, Pisang

Peak will be in my view, high above a valley floor, challenging me to attempt the same snow-covered slopes that Chris tried and failed to climb and where climbers regularly lose their lives.

As the plane slips easily through the darkness toward Southeast Asia, I realize that no longer can I muster the youthful confidence and feeling of invincibility that once allayed the fear of danger. During the past thirty years, too many disasters, reversals of fortune, unexpected failures and even death itself culminating in that worst blow, the death of my son, have tempered my ability to remain optimistic in the face of peril. No one, I've learned, escapes the dark side of life. No matter how secure the dream, how careful the dreamer, the nightmare inevitably intrudes. Now, as I lean back in my seat, it's not an image of posing for a picture on the summit of a high altitude mountain which keeps me awake. Instead, visions of tumbling down steep slopes, being ploughed under by an avalanche of snow or just freezing to death in a windstorm prevent me from sleeping.

It is late afternoon when the plane lands in Bangkok. Quickly, I check my bags through customs and catch a taxi to a downtown hotel. In the morning, I'll fly to Kathmandu, gateway to the Himalayas. In the meantime, Bangkok is the "City of Pleasure," the "Butterfly of the Orient." And the plane to Nepal doesn't leave until morning!

It's a warm, early evening by the time I'm walking along the crowded downtown streets. Young couples from Germany and Sweden, older tourists with French and English accents, all kinds of people from throughout the world are crowding the narrow sidewalks that are jammed with small kiosks selling a variety of name-brand bargains. Ralph Lauren, Tommy Hilfiger, Chanel, Gucci! Overruns or knock-offs, the quality is good and the prices are ridiculously low.

Hardly in a shopping mood, I push on toward the nightclub area of Patpong when suddenly I'm overwhelmed with the impression that everyone seems to be a couple this evening, everyone except for me. I wish I had some company, a wife, a girlfriend, someone with whom I could share this experience. Later, I'll stop at a good restaurant for a wonderful Thai dinner, but there will be no talk, no laughter. I'll be eating alone. It occurs to me that making this trip without someone with whom to communicate is compounding the difficulty of trying to extract meaning from the events I'm seeking to understand. After I arrive in Nepal, there's going to be a five-day trek on the Annapurna Trail, which I'll have to navigate alone. Day after day of solitary hiking will be a trial, an exercise in mental toughness that I'd like to avoid. I should be with someone like Chris's mother, a person to talk with, a person who knows and understands the unshakable and constantly returning grief that occurs after the loss of a child. But I'm not–I'm alone.

I pass nightclubs, or more precisely, strip-joints, which line the streets of Patpong. I know they are filled with slim and aggressive Thai girls who dance to the blaring rock music of a revved-up sound system. Each evening, all traffic is banned from this four-block area and more shopping stalls are set up in the middle of the famous concourse.

I make my way slowly down this street and soon stop at a stand to look at a pair of hiking trousers. Suddenly, however, I notice an attractive woman with dark hair, wearing a long skirt and a well-filled tank-top shirt, examining a silver bracelet in an adjoining booth. She appears to be in her forties although her slim figure and strong arms suggest a woman who works out and takes care of herself.

She catches me watching her. Instead of looking away, she smiles. Then she moves to the next stand. The game is on. I move behind her for a few steps, careful not to appear overly aggressive. She stops to look at some jeans.

I move towards her and say, "Pretty good bargains."

Without looking up, she sighs and responds in English, "Oh, I'm so tired of shopping."

"Well, there are lots of other options in this city," I parry.

She turns and looks at me with sparkling blue eyes. "For you maybe. But for a woman alone in Bangkok, it's a different story."

I detect an accent and assume it's British. "Are you from England?" I ask.

"No. South Africa. I'm with a tour group, but no one wanted to go anywhere this evening," she replies.

For a moment, I'm not sure how to proceed. Do you ask a woman you've just met to join you for a drink in a club filled with naked women trying to arrange a fifty-dollar assignation for the rest of the night? That's the only choice on this street and I don't know where else to take her.

"Are you an American?" she asks.

"Guilty on that one," I reply.

"Oh no. Not guilty. Lucky. I've always wanted to visit the States," she says.

The salesgirl is getting anxious. "You wanna buy? Nice jeans. Maybe he buy for you," she says, nodding in my direction.

The woman from South Africa shakes her head and laughs. "So what are the options?" she asks.

"Well, we could try one of those," I respond, pointing to a nearby bar.

"That's great. I was dying to go in one, but I didn't want to go alone. Will you come with me?" she asks.

Stunned and hopeful because of how quickly my luck has changed, I quickly agree. In a few minutes, we're seated at a small corner table where gin and tonics soon arrive via a scantily clad waitress. Above us, on a small stage, several skinny and topless Thai girls are grinding their silicone-filled breasts and frail pelvis bones back and forth to rock music.

My new and unexpected date announces that her name is Victoria Irving and that her group has been traveling throughout Southeast Asia for the past two weeks. In the morning, the tour leaves for the resort area of Pattaya where they'll spend two days prior to a final departure for Johannesburg. Victoria is disappointed with the trip.

"I should have come with a friend. The people in the group are all pretty old. They only want to eat and go to bed early every evening. It's not much fun." She grimaces.

The waitress comes back and asks if we want another round of drinks. "Maybe in a few minutes," I respond.

Then the young girl moves in closer to us and asks seductively: "You and lady want massage?"

"No thanks." I laugh, remarking to Victoria that, in Bangkok, there are no limits.

Victoria, however, is ambivalent. "Are you sure? I've heard so much about Thai massages."

I explain to her that, in Bangkok and particularly here in this nightclub, the expression "massage" is a code word for sex and the action would probably be in a seedy room upstairs. However, I also point out that there are some very good massage parlors nearby and if she wants, we can go to one.

"Really? I'd love to do that," she answers.

That sounds fine to me although a series of questions immediately arise in my mind: Will we have separate rooms? Will the masseuses give us the traditional bath before the massage? Victoria doesn't seem much concerned about these details. Apparently, "go for it" is also part of her lexicon. I'm beginning to be more and more impressed with this South African woman. Perhaps she would take a similar attitude toward mountain climbing.

It's still early evening, however, so we decide to have some dinner before seeking a massage. We finish our drinks and call a cab to take us to the famous Oriental Hotel where a buffet of exquisite Thai food is served each evening along the Chao Phraya river, a fast-moving body of water that snakes its way through the entire city before emptying into the Gulf of Thailand forty miles to the south. Strings of colored lights are woven through several trees planted in the middle of the restaurant while a three-piece band plays background music next to the river.

After we've been seated, I order a bottle of wine and then we pick out our first course from the buffet table. As we begin eating, Victoria asks, "Why have you come to Bangkok?"

I hedge. My story is so complicated, so filled with ambiguities.

"I'm on my way to the Himalayas for some trekking and mountain climbing," I say, giving only half the truth.

She turns enthusiastic. "Oh, that would be so great. I wish I had planned on something like that," she responds.

"How did you happen to take this Asian tour?" I ask.

Victoria looks out over the dark water. A sparkle of light reflects on a silver bracelet she wears on a bare arm. She pauses for several seconds and then turns toward me, a sudden look of sadness on her face.

"I'm a high school English teacher who has been divorced for several years, and my nineteen-year-old daughter was staying with some other girls in Johannesburg. Something pretty terrible happened several months ago. She was living a pretty fast life and not taking care of herself. Then, one evening, she went to a party where people were using drugs. Something went wrong. Maybe it was her health, maybe an overdose. Who knows? Anyway, my daughter passed out and they called an ambulance. By the time they got her to the hospital, she was dead.

"The shock was terrible. The whole thing was too much for me. I decided to quit my job and just go away, you know, take off. Leave South Africa for a while. See the world and try to accept reality. I broke up with the man I'd been seeing for several years. It wasn't going well anyway. Then I signed up for this tour," Victoria says. She sighs: "I'm going back in a few days."

The sound of the band playing selections from *Cats* floats through the warm evening air. The clarinetist swings into the sentimental theme song, "Memory."

Words to fit the torrent of thoughts within me triggered by Victoria's story are illusive, but finally I blurt out, "I have something to tell you." I confess, "It has to do with the real reason I'm here." After we have chosen our second course, a mixture of seafood seasoned with red pepper and curry, I tell her about Chris and why I'm on the way to Nepal. As we eat, I continue.

She listens carefully, occasionally asking for clarification with hard questions that force me to think beyond the replies I've been using up till now. "You've already been climbing and training for four months. Have you found any real answers about you and your son?" she asks.

"No, not really. But I haven't reached the top of a big mountain yet," I respond.

"What happens if you climb this...ah, Pisang Peak and you still don't understand why your son is gone?" she asks softly.

"Of course, I've thought of that. But I'm hoping..."

"Hoping that your Faustian bargain won't produce a Mephistopheles," she interrupts with a smile.

I ask her what she means and Victoria responds with a question.

"Do you know the story of Faust?"

"I think so. Didn't Faust make a bargain with the Devil in which he would sell his soul to him at the end of his life if he could have the ability to acquire magical powers no one else could achieve?"

"Precisely," she says.

"But I'm not asking for absolute power and I'm not offering my salvation to a Mephistopheles as payment, " I respond.

"Are you sure?" she asks. "I mean, aren't you asking for a kind of knowledge that no human being can have and are you not risking your life for it?"

Until now, I never thought of my commitment to climb a mountain in order to gain understanding of Chris's life and death as a Faustian bargain. And yet, I have to admit to Victoria that I am expecting a *quid pro quo.* "When I reach the top of the mountain," I tell Victoria, "I want an answer. What's the alternative? Do nothing?" I ask her.

Victoria sighs. "These are difficult issues. I'm not sure you can find the answer to someone's life and death like this. I know I can't."

"So what should I do?" I ask.

"I think you should climb your mountain," she responds quietly.

"Are you sure?" I ask.

Victoria pauses for a few moments and looks across the river. Then she turns and asks if I understand what causal thinking is.

"Cause and effect. If something happens, there has to be a cause," I answer.

"That's right and it can lead you into some very wrong answers, because there isn't always a cause," Victoria responds.

She sips at a glass of wine and then turns to me with an unexpected question. "Do you know much about love?" she asks.

"Probably not," I respond with a laugh.

"Most people don't, although they're always looking for it," she says. "The reason they don't understand is because they think love has to be reciprocal. You know, you love me and I love you, but if you don't love me, then I don't love you anymore. That isn't love. Real love isn't dependent on anyone or any place or any thing," Victoria says.

"What is it then?" I ask.

She smiles at the impossibility of answering my question, but nevertheless offers a definition: "Love is a strong feeling of caring which one can have toward another person and it doesn't stop because of a particular event."

"Even death?" I cut in.

"Even death. If you really loved your son, then you still do even if he's not here anymore. That kind of love can be sustaining and meaningful as long as you live," she states.

"Is that how you feel about your daughter?" I ask.

"Yes. It isn't easy. And lots of times I ask myself where I went wrong, why did she turn to drugs? But those aren't helpful questions. They produce wrong answers. So I just try to concentrate on my good memories of her and how much I love her even if she is gone."

"Your words remind me of what Guy Cachat, a man who lost his son, told me in Chamonix and what Bill Cosby said at his son's funeral. 'We have to be grateful for the memory of our child and how fortunate we are to have known them.' That's tough to do," I respond.

She reaches across the table and takes my hand. "Of course it is, but you'll get there. You just have to keep on climbing."

I realize that we've hit on some very deep bases very quickly. Slowly, I recite to her the words from one of my favorite poems, written by a former teacher, May Sarton, and published in *May Sarton: Collected Poems, 1930-1993*:

Twin trees whose pollen has been swiftly crossed
And all this sumptuous flowering of the heart
Will grow rich fruit, not anything be lost.

"That's beautiful," she says, still holding my hand.

Emotions are stirring too fast. A mutual need to slow down takes over. She removes her fingers from mine. We move the conversation to lighter topics: "Where are the best bargains in Bangkok? What is Johannesburg like now that apartheid is finished? What is life really like in New York?"

In each case, the answers we give to each other seem just right, a perfect fit of cultural and artistic attitudes. I'm beginning to hope that this evening will not end with the coming of dawn.

Finally, dinner is finished. We've consumed several glasses of wine. I realize that I could talk with Victoria for twenty-four straight hours without stopping.

"Ready for your massage?" she asks.

"That's right." I answer, realizing that I had forgotten about our plans. "Let's get a cab."

On the way out of the hotel, I pick up a copy of a local tourist publication filled with advertisements for massage parlors. Afterward, I hail a cab and show it to the driver. He looks briefly at the magazine and shakes his head. "Not good places. I take you better massage," he says.

"What's wrong with this spot" I ask, pointing to a full color ad displaying dozens of beautiful girls.

"Not good for lady. Girls there only make love with guys. I take you velly good place. Clean. Many ladies go there have massage."

He sounds convincing so we tell him to take us to his choice, well aware that his prime motivation will be the commission he earns by delivering customers to the massage parlor where he has a deal.

After a long ride through the nighttime traffic, the driver deposits us in front of a two-story building with blinking Christmas lights strung around the door. Inside a glass window, we see a counter and a row of chairs where several Thai girls are talking. As we enter the door, these masseuses look up with more than casual interest, undoubtedly wondering what kind of arrangement we're looking for.

The manager, a middle-aged Chinese woman with dark hair wrapped around her head, asks: "You and lady want massage together or maybe you want one room for each." Victoria looks at me to make the decision. I take the high road.

"A room for each of us," I answer.

The manager smiles. "Maybe I give you one big room with curtain. Then you can talk and have massage same time," she says.

"That sounds perfect," Victoria responds quickly.

Two masseuses are summoned and immediately lead us up a flight of stairs to a room where foam mattresses covered by white sheets are placed on the floor. One of the girls drags a mattress to the far wall and pulls a curtain, strung to the ceiling on a thin wire, across the middle of the room. Victoria and I are now separated by the curtain.

Another of the girls, heavyset and strong by Thai female standards, hands me a white terry cloth robe. "My name Mai. You put this on and come with me," she says. In a few minutes I've hung my clothes on a hanger and she's leading me to a large room with a Jacuzzi bathtub and shower where, for the next ten minutes, I am hosed down with a spray shower attached to a long hose, scrubbed with soap, a sponge and Mai's uninhibited hands. The warm water and her strong fingers explore and knead everywhere. I wonder if Victoria, who has gone to the Jacuzzi in the adjoining bath, is getting the same treatment.

Then, Mai leads me back to the room where the massage gets underway as she begins to pull and stretch the toes and soles of my feet. In a few minutes, I can hear Victoria returning with her masseuse.

"How was it?" I call to her.

"Wonderful. A little awkward at first, but then totally good," Victoria responds.

Slowly, Mai works her way up my legs, occasionally squeezing so hard against calf and thigh muscles that I grunt with pain. Victoria hears me and laughs. "Does that sound you're making represent suffering or ecstasy?" she asks.

"Both. They're always related," I answer.

For almost an hour, we undergo a massage that is so relaxing I could easily fall asleep. However, when Mai has finally worked over my shoulders and finished with a bone-cracking series of karate chops on my neck, the massage ends. I dress and in a few minutes, the curtain is pulled back and the masseuses lead Victoria and me down the stairs.

"Well, how did you like it?" I ask, as we step into the street.

"So good I'd stay in Bangkok forever," she laughs.

It's past midnight now. The sky is filled with stars and the streets are still filled with people. Even the kiosks are open for the constant flow of pedestrian traffic crowding the sidewalks. We walk in silence for several minutes. I suspect, or at least hope, Victoria is sharing my thoughts. I suggest we stop at a small bar overlooking the street. She nods. We enter through the open door and take a seat by the window.

"Victoria, this is a very unusual situation," I say.

She responds by reciting Juliet's balcony statement to Romeo:

Good night, good night!
Parting is such sweet sorrow
That I shall say good night
Till it be morrow.

I take her hand. "Actually, the problem is tomorrow. It is going to be here very soon."

"And you're leaving for Nepal while I go back to South Africa," she answers.

"Isn't there anything we can do about that?" I ask.

"What do you suggest?" she queries.

"Victoria, I'm going to ask you something that will sound really crazy. I'm asking you to leave your tour and come trekking in Nepal. It could be the right thing to do."

She pauses for a moment. I sense that she too has thought of coming with me. "You can't imagine how much I'd like to do that," she answers.

"Then do it. I'll postpone my flight to Kathmandu until we get you a ticket. After that, we can get you outfitted with trekking gear and you can even climb to base camp with us if you want."

"I've always wanted to go to the Himalayas," Victoria exclaims. Then she pauses and looks into my eyes. Finally she says: "Okay. I'll go. In the morning, I'll tell the tour leader that I'm staying on." She pauses again then continues. "I'll meet you after they leave."

It occurs to me that Victoria and I are being not only hasty but overly trusting. How does she know I'm not a psychotic ax murderer who will attack her when we're alone? By the same token, how can I be sure she's not some crazy bitch-woman who will turn on me? Neither of us can be sure, of course. However, it seems to me that in one evening I have found that elusive person who can share this difficult journey. A journey which has been so difficult to endure.

Victoria takes a pen from her purse and on the back of a matchbook writes the phone and room number of her hotel. Then she says in a crisp and determined voice, "I'll talk to the tour leader at seven-fifteen in the morning. The bus leaves at seven forty-five for Pattaya. So you can call me at seven-thirty and we'll make our plans. Maybe we should go straight to the airport and I'll try for a standby ticket on that ten-thirty flight to Kathmandu you were talking about."

The remaining moments with Victoria are a blur of more plans finalized by a quick hug and kiss on the cheek. "Until the morrow," she whispers. Then she's gone and only the phone number written on the back of a matchbook connects us. For a few minutes, I walk along the street trying to decide whether the whole evening has really happened or whether it has been some kind of dream which will soon terminate. I finger the matchbook in my pocket, assuring myself that it did exist and that a real phone number is scrawled on its cardboard cover.

Soon, I hail a cab and am whisked back to my hotel where a uniformed guard salutes and nods respectfully as I cross the foyer and head for the elevator. It's two A.M. In five-and-a-half more hours, I'll call Victoria and we'll arrange to meet before leaving for the airport.

The hotel room is more luxurious than I prefer. The brass fittings on the sink faucets, the heavy curtains, the huge bed and the refrigerator bar filled with champagne are of little value to me as I crawl between the crisp white sheets and try to sleep. Of course, I think how fine all these extravagances would be if Victoria were here. Perhaps, tomorrow night in Kathmandu!

I set the mahogany-covered radio alarm clock on the bedside table to seven A.M. That will provide ample time to wake up and call Victoria.

The hours pass slowly with only fitful sleep. Five o'clock shows on my self-illuminating wristwatch. In two-and-a-half hours, I'll hear her voice again. Then, sleep takes over until five forty-five A.M. I don't want to be totally exhausted for the rest of the day. I go back to sleep.

Suddenly I wake and sit up in the bed. Sunlight is filtering through the brocade window curtains. "Oh my God," I gasp through the silence of the room. Quickly, I hit the illumine button on my watch. It's seven forty-five. The alarm never went off.

I grab at my trousers, pull the matchbook from a pocket and dial the number. A Thai woman answers and I ask for the room number scribbled on the cardboard. "Just a moment please" echoes through the phone's receiver. It rings. Then it rings again...and again. Victoria doesn't answer.

I hang up and dial once more, this time to ask the hotel operator if Victoria Irving is still registered. "No. Check out. They go in bus," the woman responds.

I stare out the window. A diminutive man with stooped shoulders and thin, rounded legs is watering the grass with an old hose. I watch his slow movement while my brain desperately searches for a plan. She's gone. The bus is on the way to Pattaya, a three-hour ride from Bangkok and I don't know the name of the group or the hotel where they'll be staying. *Why didn't Victoria wait for me? She knew I would call. Or did she? Was there a last minute change of mind on her part or did she assume that since I didn't call at precisely seven-thirty I had decided not to follow through on our plan?*

For several minutes, I consider catching a bus to Pattaya in a desperate attempt to find her. However, I realize the impossibility of success. There are hundreds of hotels in Pattaya and the chances of running into Victoria would be infinitesimal. Furthermore, I have a plane reservation for Kathmandu at ten-thirty. I know now that the beautiful English teacher from South Africa who seemed so perfect and wonderful will not be coming to Nepal with me after all. Perhaps this is the way it is meant to be. Never again will I see Victoria Irving. My journey, if it's going to continue, must be undertaken alone.

Later that morning, as the plane begins its three-hour flight to Kathmandu, I lean back in the seat of the airplane and try to assess the meaning of my previous night's encounter with Victoria in Bangkok. Her words come back like a sledgehammer slamming on top of my head: "Love is a strong feeling of caring which one can have toward another person and it doesn't stop because of a particular event." The craziness of it all makes me want to cry and laugh at the same time. What an ironic ending to our evening in Bangkok! Yet, inwardly I know that a message has been sent. Perhaps later, I'll be able to hear and understand what she was saying. For now, I call the stewardess and order a glass of wine as the plane gains altitude and flies northward toward the Himalayas.

13
chapter

Death-Defying Thrills

Oh, that I were as in months past,
As in the days when God preserved me:
When the Almighty was yet with me,
When my children were about me.

Job 29:2

Pisang Peak is not a well-known mountain in comparison with its famous Himalayan neighbors. A few miles to the south of it across the Manang Valley, for example, the colossus 26,493-foot Annapurna II looks more like a spaceship riding above the clouds than something actually attached to the earth. A hundred miles to the east, lies Mt. Everest, the highest mountain in the world at just over 29,028 feet. Each climbing season this tower of ice and snow randomly selects who shall die and who shall live among the world's most renowned climbers who try to reach its summit.

Yet, for me, it is Pisang Peak, a 19,983-foot mountain that is the goal. Spiraling upwards above the ancient village of Pisang, the mountain is best known for its location near the Thorung La pass, a rocky slash in the Himalayan mountain range where trekkers cross each season from the Annapurna Range into the Kali Gandaki Valley. Crossing this high altitude pass is usually considered the hardest day's trek on the final leg of a three-week hike in the Annapurna Range.

I think back to Chris's attempts to climb Pisang Peak. Both times, he was forced to turn back without reaching the summit. On his first attempt in early 1989, he stopped at approximately 16,000 feet, because deep snow delayed his progress and depleted his supply of stove fuel and food. A month later, however, he returned more determined than ever to reach the top. In a letter, he wrote:

> I went back to Pisang Peak, this time with an English guy named Colin. No deep snow problems now. We had some good death-defying thrills. At 18,000 feet, six o'clock at night, storm setting in fast, we are hanging off ice axes on sixty-degree blue water ice, my crampons popping off my left boot, altitude causing deliriousness. Tired. Hungry. Unroped. Six thousand feet straight down is the village of Pisang. Yee haw! Well, good judgment finally overruled sheer determination and we quit only sixty feet from a chance to watch the sun set in Tibet. We had to down climb what we up climbed and then we faced a seven-hour descent in the dark since our headlamps were in the tent at advance base camp.

As with most of Chris' early climbs, I'm glad I knew nothing about it until he returned safely. However, his attempt on Pisang surprised me. After all, I thought he was taking his college junior year abroad in Nepal in order to study Tibetan Buddhist art and architecture. He wrote in another letter to his family:

> If parents or grandparents reading this are worried, you should get used to it as I plan to do a lot more and a lot harder Himalayan climbing. After you try it here, everything else is boring.

Like most fathers, information imparted to me by my son was released on a "need to know" basis. Consequently, I didn't find out until a year later that Chris had really chosen to study Buddhist monasteries in order to climb high altitude mountains. But that is precisely what he did. In fact, he later wrote a letter which expressed his determination to become a climber.

It all began in 1989 when he was feeling frustrated as he completed his sophomore year at Penn State University. Although he was doing well in his geography major, he longed for a more interesting study program and lifestyle. He found the answer after learning about the Junior-Year-in-Nepal program offered by the University of Wisconsin in Madison. In the book-length report Chris eventually submitted at the end of his year abroad titled *Tibetan Religious Architecture of Northwestern Nepal,* he explained in the foreword just why this choice was made:

> I became intrigued by Tibetan monastery architecture in somewhat of a roundabout way. My parents had been to Nepal twice in the late 1960s. The first time, I had not been born, but I was taken along on the second trip. So I was fortunate to be exposed to Nepal rather early on. Having artifacts and books around the house added to my knowledge of Asia as I grew up.
>
> Probably the strongest "pull factor" in going to Nepal were the mountains. I'd lived in the French Alps before and grew quite fond of mountain sports such as

skiing and mountaineering. How great it would be to travel to the highest mountains in the world! I thought. So when my friend told me of a college-year-in-Nepal program, I didn't hesitate to apply.

He was accepted into the program and after spending the summer of 1989 at the University of Wisconsin studying the Tibetan language, Chris traveled to Nepal in September. For the next four months, he studied Tibetan art and culture and further increased his language skills, particularly when he went to live with a Tibetan family in nearby Bodhanath. He also elected to do research on Tibetan monasteries located near the Himalayan mountain range. He described his less than scholarly reasoning behind this choice:

> We were asked to tentatively decide the topic of our fieldwork project before leaving. I thought about doing a cross-regional study of monastery architecture, primarily because it would involve traveling in the mountains. It sounded so exotic at the time, trekking from monastery to monastery, photographing and documenting structures that had never been documented before. Well, with the encouragement of the program directors, the plan was put into action and I was on my way.

Now, eight years later, I seek to know why he came here and what he found. I'm ready to follow his path. My guide will be his report. I'll go to the monasteries where he studied and talked to the lamas he visited. And...I'll try to climb Pisang Peak just as he did in the hope that some kind of understanding will emerge as to why Chris became so impassioned about mountaineering.

It's a warm afternoon in early October when I

finally arrive in Nepal. A frenzied crowd of taxi drivers are waving and shouting outside the Kathmandu airport at the latest planeload of passengers from Bangkok.

"You come with me. I get you good hotel. Very cheap."

These are the frantic calls of the desperate young men who can make a week's wages by delivering a foreigner to a hotel where a finder's commission is paid. Fortunately, I know my destination and easily secure a taxi ride to the Kathmandu Guest House, a small oasis of hospitality and comfort in the city's crowded tourist area of Thamel. The ride from the airport to downtown Thamel provides a quick introduction to motorized transportation in Nepal. The taxi dodges through a screeching phalanx of bicycles, pedicabs, people, trucks and occasionally comes to an abrupt halt for a lethargic cow slowly crossing the street. Unable to watch the unfolding drama of near-accidents, I look to the side rather than through the driver's window.

It's been almost thirty years since I last visited Kathmandu with Chris, his sister and his mother. The deserted walkways and spacious boulevards of the early seventies have given way to traffic-jammed streets filled with black smoke belching from ancient buses, taxis and motorcabs powered by two-stroke engines. The old Hotel Royal where the famous Russian hotel owner, Boris Lasinsky, presided with dignity and grace is gone. In its place, the ornate and impersonal Yak & Yeti Hotel now serves as an impressive monument to Western material comforts with its pool, tennis courts, shops and restaurants.

After settling into my room, checking my E-mail at the busy hotel computer center and unpacking my climbing gear, I call a taxi and negotiate a price of one hundred rupees ($1.50) for the fifteen minute ride to Bodhanath, a section of the city where Tibetan Buddhists have developed a strong presence since the Chinese invasion of Tibet in 1959 when so many refugees fled to Nepal.

As the taxi begins to negotiate the narrow streets, I repeat the destination to the driver: "Double Dorje." This small restaurant, with living quarters upstairs, is located a block from the famous Buddhist stupa, a shrine where four sets of blue painted eyes stare imperiously from each side of the white cupola. Most tourists to Nepal manage to visit the stupa where they can observe the Tibetan faithful circumambulating this huge round structure while spinning dozens of tin prayer wheels mounted on the side of the building. In fact, while walking past this stupa later in the day, I see the film star, Steven Segal, dressed in a monk's robe walking around this holy shrine with prayer beads and followed by a small retinue of admirers. Later, when I relate this Hollywood sighting to a friend, she informs me that when Segal, the star of many violent movies, comes to Nepal, one does not hear the traditional Buddhist sound of one hand clapping, but rather the noise of two heads cracking.

During some of the time Chris studied in Kathmandu, he lived with the Tibetan family who owns the Double Dorje, a restaurant that attracts many of the Western students of Buddhism who come for retreats and seminars in the nearby *gompas*. In the acknowledgment to his report, Chris thanked his hosts as follows: "Dorje, Tsering, Trashig and Kaydrop Sangpo, the Tibetan family in Bodhanath with whom I lived for several months. If you are in Bodhanath, go to their restaurant, the Double Dorje, for great food."

It's more than great food that I'm looking for at the Double Dorje. After pushing through a narrow doorway into a small room that is capable of seating no more than fifteen customers, I find Dorje, a small Tibetan man with a mustache and sparkling white teeth, standing behind a narrow counter in the far corner.

"Many years ago, a student lived here. His name was Chris," I say slowly.

Dorje places a finger to his lips and thinks for a moment. Then he smiles. "Ah, Chris. Yes...yes...Chris. He stay here. Live upstairs."

"I'm his father," I explain as I show him Chris's report and point to the names of Dorje's family in the acknowledgment section.

Dorje places a finger on each word and with obvious astonishment at seeing the names of his family in a book, exclaims: "Ah, yes, yes. Dorje. Tsering. Tashi."

Then Dorje's dark eyebrows come together in confusion. It's time for the dreaded question, the one that is always so difficult to answer. "Chris. Where is he now?" Dorje asks.

After I explain that my son has died, Dorje stares at the rough plank floor, shakes his head and expresses his sorrow in the few English words he can muster for the occasion. "Ahh...no good. I remember Chris. Live here. Very funny. Laugh many times. No good what happens to Chris. No good." Then he excuses himself and goes to find his wife, Tsering, also called Emala, Tibetan for respected mother.

In a few moments, the cloth curtain is parted in the rear of the restaurant, and a middle-aged Tibetan woman, dressed in a traditional long brown skirt and colorful, horizontally striped apron appears. Emala takes my hand and shakes her head slowly. "Chris. My family," she repeats twice, her soft brown eyes revealing a deep and genuine sorrow at what she has just heard. She turns to Dorje and speaks rapidly in Tibetan, which he translates: "She says she is very sorry about Chris. She says he was like a son. Help her in kitchen. Always make jokes and laugh. Some nights wait on tables."

Emala also informs me that since Chris was part of her family, therefore I am too. Whenever I come to visit, she and Dorje will not allow me to pay for meals at the restaurant. Through her husband, she also informs me that she will go to the temple and light a butter candle for Chris. In accordance with Tibetan Buddhist tradition, this *choeme* will provide light for deceased loved ones as they travel on their journey to the next life. I thank her for her kindness.

Since the restaurant is also the gathering place for the western Buddhist community of Bodhanath, I soon meet or am offered directions to almost everyone I'm looking for. Dorje introduces me to Tenlay, Chris's handsome, middle-aged former language teacher who lives with his parents nearby and who still teaches Tibetan at the University of Wisconsin extension school in Kathmandu. Tenlay sadly tells me, "Chris and his friend, Dan Whaley, were always looking for adventure during the field studies which the school group took outside the city." He invites me to visit the university's house behind the royal palace. We go there and I soon meet the program's new director, Pam Ross, a devout Buddhist of many years.

I also meet Lothro, an American Buddhist nun from Oregon who has come to organize a teaching tour in which she will talk to religious groups around the world. With her shaved head and red robes, it's difficult at first to recognize she's a woman and not just another Tibetan monk of which there are so many in Bodhanath. She tells me the story of her three-year retreat on Vancouver Island.

"Several years earlier I went there without speaking to anyone except an occasional lama, a monk who came to give me teachings. Groceries were left on the doorstep of my cabin each week by someone I never saw or talked to. When the retreat was over, it took me another three years to readjust to a world filled with people who speak with each other."

When I inform her I'm headed for northern Nepal to climb Pisang Peak and visit the gompas, the Buddhist monasteries described in Chris's report, she studies my face intently. Then she says, "Something will happen, an unexpected event that will be important to the purpose of your journey." Lothro's prediction represents the intuition of a woman whose awareness level has been developed through years of meditation. Her words resonate in my mind as I make my way back to the Double Dorje restaurant.

"I take you to meet Chokii Nyingma Rinpoche (highly regarded teacher). He will help you," Dorje says later while we both sip tea in the restaurant. The renowned lama is the reigning abbot at the nearby Ka Nying Shedrub Living Monastery.

The following day we climb the stairs of the monastery to a small waiting room filled with Westerners waiting to visit the sought-after lama in his private quarters. After a short wait, we're admitted to a large room adorned with parquet flooring, colorfully painted walls and crystal chandeliers, all highly unusual symbols of wealth in a country where dirt floors and mud walls are the norm. At one end of the room, the small, somewhat square-headed Rinpoche is seated at a low table in front of several visitors who have come to make offerings and receive his blessing. When it's my turn, Dorje explains to the lama in Tibetan that I am here searching for the meaning of my son's death. He hands the senior monk a copy of Chris's report on Tibetan monasteries. After glancing at it and asking me a few questions about where I come from, Chokii Nyingma promises, "I will pray for Chris." I am surprised at how good his English is. Then he focuses his brown eyes on me and says, "Your son is not lost. Death is only another stage in the endless cycle of our lives. When you learn that, you will understand the meaning of what happened."

Just as he finishes this sentence, handing me a dilemma for which I'm not prepared, the sound of a phone ringing interrupts the Rinpoche. Reaching into his saffron robe with a bare arm, he extracts a small cell phone and flips open the lid. After listening to the phone for a moment, he announces: "Excuse me, it's a call from America."

My time is finished and as I retreat to the rear of the room, the Rinpoche talks on the cell phone for several minutes in English. A few giggles from an impressed and adoring audience resonate through the room. Chokii Nyingma may be preaching an ancient religion, but he apparently has no compunction against the use of modern means of communication to further his cause.

Shaken and disturbed by the words so confidently expressed by the Rinpoche, I leave the monastery with Dorje and soon we're dodging in and out of the human and vehicular traffic of the narrow and dirty alleys of Bodhanath on the way back to the restaurant. The idea that Chris is not gone, that he might actually be reincarnated is a comforting thought. Belief in the rebirth of people is widespread among Tibetan Buddhists. Their spiritual leader, the Dalai Lama, is supposedly the reincarnation of a previous lama who lived in Tibet. Certainly, the emotional devastation of Chris's loss would be mitigated if I thought he has been reincarnated as the Rinpoche suggested. For that matter, it would also be wonderful to believe that he has gone to Heaven and I might be able to join him there someday as some of my friends have suggested.

Skepticism about religious assumptions and theologies is so strongly embedded into my rational Western mind, however, that it's hard to accept these optimistic views. If I'm not sure that I believe in reincarnation, then how can I take comfort in the thought that Chris's death is only a passing stage of perpetual life? Even as I ask myself these questions, the words of the Rinpoche keep swirling around in my mind: *Death is only another stage in the endless cycle of our lives. When you learn that, you will understand the meaning of what happened.*

Did he mean that Chris has been reincarnated and is once again living somewhere on this earth, perhaps right here in Nepal? Is there any chance that I could see my son?

The most important book for Tibetan Buddhist scholars is the *Tibetan Book of the Dead*, a compendium of ancient teachings by high lamas written over the centuries. I am familiar with this Tibetan "Bible," which offers a detailed description of what happens after death and provides instructions on just how the process of reincarnation takes place.

During the first forty days after death, according to these teachings, the spirit of the deceased travels above the earth during a transition stage called the Bardo. At the end of this period, the reincarnation process begins. People who have led exemplary lives may go on to permanent nirvana, similar to the western idea of Heaven, but most are destined to return to life on earth. After the forty days, the spirit of the deceased flies over the land until an ideal mother and father are found who are in the process of making love. The spirit enters the mother's womb at the moment of conception and becomes the embryo. The Tibetan book describes how the choice of one's future parents must be made:

> You should use your clairvoyant powers to choose a suitable womb in the best of places in the human realm. Your future mother should at least live in a place where advanced spiritual teachings are widespread. Before you enter her womb, you should resolve to devote your future life to the practice of whatever is wholesome and will benefit others. This resolution is very important to ensure entry into a suitable womb.

Could this be the process that Chris went through? If the answer is not available in Kathmandu, at least there is the consolation that I'll have more time to reflect on the lama's statement over the next few weeks when I travel to the remote area of northwestern Nepal, where the life of the spirit has flourished for so many centuries among the Tibetan Buddhists.

"How you like Rinpoche?" Dorje asks when we arrive back at the restaurant.

"I'm not sure. It doesn't help much when someone says Chris isn't lost when I feel he is," I respond.

"Rinpoche is a very wise man. Maybe it takes time to understand what he says," Dorje answers.

"You're probably right. Perhaps the answer is at the top of Pisang Peak," I respond.

"Yes," Dorje says solemnly. "Mountains are wise, too."

With that consolation in mind, I leave Dorje at the restaurant and return to the Kathmandu Guest House to complete final arrangements for the climbing expedition. Unlike Chris, I have no intention of simply trekking to northwest Nepal and climbing Pisang Peak either by myself or with one other person. Climbers regularly lose their lives on this mountain. My attempt needs to be taken seriously, with all the proper organization and personnel needed for a major Himalayan climb. Consequently, I've asked Judson Millar, a six-foot, two-inch, handsome and powerfully built young man of twenty-eight, who is also best friends with my son Justin, to be the guide for this expedition. A former football and rugby player, Jud is also a trained Outward Bound instructor and experienced mountaineer whose most recent job has been as a guide at California's Mount Shasta.

I first met Jud at the wedding of my son Justin and his wife, Kathryn, in Asheville, North Carolina. We hit it off right away and spent a lot of time talking about climbing. Jud told me his dream was to someday climb in the Himalayas. I looked at his strong shoulders and clear blue eyes and immediately realized this was the kind of person I would need as a companion in order to climb a high altitude peak. Not only would his technical knowledge and experience be valuable, but his physical strength and youthful exuberance might be the difference between a foolhardy effort on my part and a successful expedition.

"Jud, how would you like to come to Nepal in October and be my guide?" I asked him.

Jud looked carefully at me to determine if I was joking.

"I'll take care of all costs," I added.

He realized I was serious. "I'd love to," he said eagerly.

We stayed in touch for the next few months and by late September I sent him an airplane ticket and arranged to meet him in Kathmandu.

Jud has already arrived at the guest house and is standing with friends when I get there. I, along with Ang, a climbing Sherpa guide whom we have hired, have arranged to spend the afternoon picking out the equipment we'll need for our high-altitude climb. Ang Sherpa has recommended a small climbing supply store run by a Sherpa woman from his village in the Solu Khumbu region of eastern Nepal. We spend several hours there, trying on climbing shoes, fitting crampons, selecting down jackets, warm gloves and ice axes.

By late afternoon, everything we'll need on the mountain has been packed in three duffel bags. We're ready. Jud, however, has an opportunity to guide a group of climbers on another expedition later in the month and needs to remain in Kathmandu for two more days to finalize plans for that group. We decide that I'll start out in the morning with the porters. He and Ang Sherpa will leave two days later and by a quick "forced march" catch up with us in Pisang.

That evening, Jud and I have dinner at a fine restaurant in Thamel where a variety of Tibetan food is served. We're both in a good mood. And yet a slight touch of fear and anxiety are beginning to settle in the back of my thoughts. In five more days, the climb will begin. Will I find the answers to Chris's passion for which I so desperately search? Has my training prepared me for the arduous climb which he attempted but was unable to complete? I order a bottle of wine for Jud and myself and force these thoughts from my mind. I try not to think about anything beyond the pleasures of the evening.

14 chapter

A Heavy Pack

The monastery is like a huge bird. No words can describe its splendor. May it last forever.

Tibetan Song

It is time to depart. Over the desperate squawks of chickens, the shouts of late-arriving passengers and the bleating of a terrified goat, the bus's engine crackles into action. The ancient, faded green vehicle jerks forward and begins to sway down the rut-filled road in a westerly direction toward Besi Sahar. At last, my journey to the high mountains along the Tibetan border is underway.

After several quick stops, or more accurately, "slow-downs," additional passengers swing on board and push themselves into the crowded aisle. Soon the vehicle emerges from the smoke and dirt of Kathmandu and enters a valley of small villages surrounded by terraced patches of ripe wheat, corn and barley.

For the first few hours, the trip is no different than any ride on a Nepalese road. Seemingly inevitable collisions with trucks, taxis, meandering cows and pedestrians are miraculously avoided with last-second turns by the unflappable driver. By noon, however, the bus turns turn north along the west bank of the Marsyangdi River. Now, the level of both beauty and insanity increases. The majestic valley below the road with its green fields and rampaging river turns more scenic. The road also narrows and becomes increasingly dangerous.

We reach a switchback high above the river where a small creek rushes from the mountainside across a twenty-foot section of the road and then spills over the edge and down the steep slope. Looking out the window on my right, I see only the terraced fields and a small village several thousand feet beneath us. If the bus crowds against the mountainside on the left, there can be no more than six inches beyond the right side tires and the edge of the road. Even this narrow margin is under water. The driver stops the bus to ponder how to proceed.

Realizing that he's planning to move forward in a few seconds, I immediately decide to jump up and exit the open door of the bus while the driver crosses the washout. If he makes it safely, I'll wade through the water and return to my seat on the other side of the stream. If not...well, only my pack will disappear into the valley below along with all the passengers, the chickens and the goat.

Before I can make this move, however, the bus lurches. It's too late for any desperate leap to safety. I suck in my breath and close my eyes. The other passengers turn silent as the motor growls and backfires in protest. We begin to move forward, pushing slowly through the running water. I try to devise a plan of action for the moment we begin crashing down the cliff. Should I hang on to the seat or try to jump out the window as we roll over and over, tumbling into the valley? Before the impossibility of either option becomes obvious, the bus miraculously passes through the washout and once again begins to jolt and sway upwards along the dirt road.

Slowly I exhale and sit back against the seat. (The next day, the bus traveling this route slips off the road killing eleven passengers. The day after this accident, Jud, driving this route to catch up with me, comes through here and photographs the upended bus lying on the slope below the road.)

We cross several more washouts on the way to Besi Sahar, narrowly surviving additional crises when oncoming buses and trucks need to squeeze past us on their way to Kathmandu. Each time, I'm convinced it can't be done and one of us will be pushed off the road. Yet, in a few minutes, the oncoming vehicle edges by and we're on our way again.

By the end of the day, I'm exhausted from the mental strain and anxiety incurred not only by my anticipation of the climb to which I'm committed but the constant threats of an accident. I've also become a firm believer, however, that our agile driver could probably fly the bus if necessary. Still, it's a relief to finally arrive at Besi Sahar and exit the battered vehicle. Heavy darkness and an unrelenting rain have enshrouded the village, causing the electricity to fail.

Quickly, I go to a nearby hotel and secure a small, dank cubicle equipped with a single candle for light. After gulping down a bowl of hot garlic soup from the hotel's primitive kitchen, I retire to my room and roll up in my sleeping bag to the comforting sound of raindrops smacking against the tin roof.

I awake in the morning to see a warm and welcome sun emerging over the valley. After a quick breakfast of two boiled eggs and a cup of lemon tea, I walk down the main street of Besi Sahar in search of the porters. A

Buddhist monastery glimmers in the bright light on a cliff a thousand feet above the village. If there's time before we leave, I want to look at it more closely, but there's no time now.

After inquiring at several hotels, I find the porters and my guide, Prem, a handsome twenty-year-old Buddhist who speaks good English but whose native language is Gurung. Prem tells me that the first day's trek will take only four hours.

"In that case, I'm going to hike up to the monastery," I tell him.

Prem offers to come along and soon we're climbing rapidly up the path to a group of stone buildings with multi-colored Tibetan prayer flags hanging from poles next to the *gompa*. A school is located close to the monastery and just as we arrive, approximately twenty high school age students begin filing into their classrooms.

A small mustached Nepalese wearing a white shirt approaches me. "Where are you from?" he asks.

"America," I respond.

"Oh, you American?" he asks in astonishment. "I am English teacher. My name is Sonam."

We shake hands and then I make him a spur of the moment offer. "Would you like me to talk to your class?" I ask.

Sonam hesitates to see if I'm serious, then smiles. "Yes. My students would like that."

After entering a small stone classroom where several rows of well-used school desks are lined up on a dirt floor, I step before the twenty girls and boys, all of whom are dressed in white shirts and blue skirts or pants.

"Good morning," I call out.

The class repeats my greeting in unison: "Good morning."

After picking up a piece of chalk and quickly sketching a crude rendition of several travel modes on the blackboard, I ask: "How do you think I came from America. By airplane, by horse or by walking?"

One of the students calls out, "Airplane!" and the class all laughs and nods.

"I've come to your country to climb a mountain. Do you know what the highest mountain in the world is?" I ask.

Three students pick this up quickly and shout, "Everest."

"Exactly. And can you name the first person to climb Mt. Everest?" I ask, fully expecting the answer to be Sir Edmund Hillary.

Instead, the entire class responds in unison: "Tenzing Norgay."

The answer is offered with such pride and assurance that I wonder if they have ever heard of the famous New Zealander, whose unparalleled act of sportsmanship in making sure his guide joined him at the summit enabled the Sherpa to share the Everest triumph.

After a half hour of more questions and answers, I say goodbye to the class and then Prem and I start down the steep path to Besi Sahar where we find the porters, gather our equipment and prepare to leave for the first day's march to the north. As I separate my high-altitude climbing gear for the porters to carry and place basic necessities into my own pack, I wonder how Chris ever managed to carry his huge pack when he made this trip eight years earlier.

Here is how he described the beginning of his trip to Pisang Peak in 1989:

> I left Kathmandu in February 1989, right after the Tibetan Lo-sar (New Year) celebration in Kathmandu.

> My pack weighed about seventy pounds. I carried notebooks and pens, hard and soft-covered books and a Pentax KH000 camera with several lenses and twenty rolls of film. I also carried a lot of climbing gear, durable plastic boots, ice axe and crampons, a Gore-Tex suit, a pile suit and lots of dehydrated food. My trekking permit was good for two months.

In my case, I've given the heavy stuff to the porters, but still the pack weighs almost forty pounds. In addition to a sleeping bag, a high-altitude down jacket, wool hat and gloves and Chris's report, I'm bringing two paperback books, the Dalai Lama's *The Four Noble Truths* and Maurice Herzog's story of his first ascent on Annapurna. Additionally, I have a small recorder, a Nikon 400sl, a portable CD player with discs from several favorite operas and most controversially, an eight-pound Presario laptop. Serious climbers would scoff at the foolishness of this last item, but the potential for taking notes and writing during those long hours of waiting for dawn, resting by a path or sitting in a cell-like hotel room, if not a dark, smoke-filled shepherd's hut for the evening, was a trade-off I couldn't resist. As for the CD player, the promise of listening to a selection of operas ranging from La Boheme to Aida while trekking or lying sleepless in a cold tent at high altitude was also irresistible. The climbing gear, including mountaineering boots, crampons, ice axe, gloves, wind-breaker, harness, etc., has been packed in a larger bag to be carried by the porters. On this trip, the father is willing to enjoy luxuries the son would not have considered.

The sun is glistening against a blue sky when we finally start up the trail. I'm wearing light hiking shoes, khaki shorts and a polo shirt to stay cool plus a baseball cap to keep from getting sunburned. Without any ceremony, we begin putting one foot in front of the other, which we do for the rest of the day.

Walking long distances has a way of slowing down the mental process, allowing thoughts to emerge that have previously been suppressed. As we begin hiking through the Nepali villages, crossing and re-crossing the Marsyangdi River on wire-rope bridges and stopping occasionally for water from mountainside springs, a series of questions begin to fill my mind. Am I really going to discover something important about Chris if we succeed in climbing Pisang Peak? Will proof of the Rinpoche's statement about Chris not being lost suddenly pop up the moment we reach the top? If we don't reach the summit, will this entire journey be a waste of time and effort for me?

That first day, after Prem's promised four hours of walking, which actually turns into five, we arrive at the small village of Boughla Boughla where he arranges for us to stay in a trekking hotel. The porters deposit our equipment bags in my small room and we all go to the dimly lit dining hall for *dal bat,* the traditional Nepalese lentil soup served with steaming rice. Each of these trekking hotels gives free quarters to the guides and porters and they normally disappear in the evenings to sing, drink rice wine and chat up the hotel waitresses by the kitchen fireplace.

My own night is more contemplative than exciting. Since there's no electricity in the hotel, I spend the evening reading *The Four Noble Truths* by the light of my climbing headlamp. The Dalai Lama's explanation of Buddhism seems like a reasonable antidote to many of life's problems. If we want to rid ourselves of unhappiness and find serenity in our lives, we first have to get rid of our desire for things we don't need. I immediately think of the CD player and laptop computer I take everywhere. I decide they are necessities for me.

Eventually, I turn off the headlamp and extract the CD player from my pack. I play Madame Butterfly's final aria on the disc player in order to fall asleep. Poor Butterfly! She decides to commit suicide when she learns that her son will soon be taken away by Pinkerton, his American father. Her problems were far greater than mine. Or were they? We both had to give up a son.

In the morning, we leave by eight and mount a steep trail that winds through several villages to a police checkpoint where we're charged ten dollars to continue. Then the path leads upwards again through a spectacular valley of terraced corn and wheat fields, which are beginning to ripen. Eventually, we arrive at Bahunadu, a Brahmin village located at an altitude of 3600 feet where we stay the night.

The next day we do some steep climbing which goes on for several hours. It's tiring, but I'm glad to be pushed physically. Every opportunity to get fit for the final climb needs to be taken. Finally, the path levels out and by mid-afternoon Prem finds a place for us to stay in a village next to the Marsyangdi River where the constant noise of the rushing water forces us to shout at each other in order to be heard.

As the days pass, we trek along the endless trails through lush hills and valleys, and the riddle-like questions I had when we began redirect themselves to me in a dozen different ways. No matter how they're phrased, however, I fail to come up with answers. Sometimes the questions disappear for a few hours, but they always return and understanding continues to be elusive. Despite my growing doubts and questions, however, each hour is bringing me closer to my destination. Then I hope the questioning will end and the climbing will begin.

With only two more days of hiking left before we arrive in Pisang, I'm beginning to develop serious doubts about the upcoming climb. Although I am committed to this endeavor, I ask myself, Can I really do this? Am I in good enough shape? Will I be able to breathe sufficiently in the high altitude to continue climbing at 18,000 feet? Do I have sufficient technical skills to handle the crampons, ice axe and ropes? I even wonder if my time on earth is up like Chris's was and death is only a few hours away. Visions of my son's final climb and my potential disaster on the mountain are beginning to dominate all other thoughts.

By mid-afternoon of the fifth day, we arrive at our destination, a small village with a few trekker hotels and one-room shops on each side of a dirt road. Above this commercial strip, the old village of Pisang is nestled comfortably on a sloping hill. In the fields around the ancient stone houses, Tibetan men and women are beating wheat shocks into reed baskets to separate the golden kernels from the chaff. Like so many other Tibetan farming villages where few if any modern conveniences have yet penetrated, the struggle to survive is dependent on a modicum of wood and dried yak dung for heat, the meager harvest taken from small plots of terraced gravel and occasional meat from a slaughtered yak, mountain goat or scrawny chicken. Little change has taken place here during the past few centuries. Even the wheel has yet to replace the backs of men and beasts for transportation.

Unfortunately, on this day, Pisang Peak itself is enveloped in a mass of clouds. The monsoons are late in departing the valley this year and the clear October weather we had hoped for has yet to arrive. Consequently, there's no way of knowing what the mountain looks like.

Will we have to undertake a long, gradual climb to the top or must we negotiate short vertical pitches over ice and loose rock? How much snow is on the summit? Is the final ridge serrated and severely angled or is it more of a flat ramp? None of these questions can be answered because, even with binoculars, we can't see our objective through the clouds.

To fight my disappointment with the bad weather, I decide to hike up a nearby slope to visit a memorial built in honor of eleven climbers–nine German climbers, a Swiss woman and a Sherpa–who died on Pisang Peak in 1994. The entire group, roped together, fell two thousand feet to their deaths. The tragedy happened when the lead climbers moved onto a snow ridge that collapsed beneath their weight. Friends and relatives arranged for the construction of a stone memorial at the foot of the mountain which I find after a fifteen-minute hike from the village. A plaque on the face of the gray stone obelisk states: *In memoriam der Verungluckten am Pisang Peak 13 November 1994.* The names of the victims are listed and at the bottom is the inscription in German: *Sie leben, auch wenn sie nicht mehr unter unds sind!* (They still live although they are no longer with us.) Glancing from the memorial up to the cloud-covered mountain, I'm reminded once again of the old climbing adage: "When you reach the top, you're only halfway there."

Returning to the village in a somber mood, I watch the sun slide behind the western end of Annapurna. Soon Jud and Ang Sherpa arrive. Moving fast for three days without porters, they walked as far as we did in five days. After the relative solitude of my own trek, it's good to see Jud's confident smile again and have someone to talk with. Immediately, we retreat to our small room to discuss whether to wait in the village until the clouds disappear or begin immediately and hope the weather will change as we move up the mountain.

"Sitting here at 9,000 feet isn't going to acclimatize either one of us," I point out.

Jud agrees. "That's true. We could at least go up, establish a base camp and then see what happens," he says.

We decide that in the morning we'll have the porters carry the tents, the climbing equipment, water and food to the first camp site at 13,000 feet. Then we'll decide whether the weather conditions will permit us to go further up to high camp. Despite this possible impediment, momentum is building rapidly within us for an immediate assault on the mountain. Having spent our youths playing contact sports like hockey and football, Jud and I have developed the ability to get psyched for the Big Game. The adrenaline is pumping and we're ready for the opening whistle. We tell the porters to plan on an early departure the next day.

However, the following morning after we pack the equipment, both Prem and Ang Sherpa, who are devout Buddhists, insist on a *puja* before we start. They suggest we go to Pema Lama, a chubby, rather gruff monk who has a small prayer room in the Maya Hotel where we're staying. We agree and enter a dark room filled with wall paintings depicting the life of the Buddha, as well as a brass Buddha surrounded by *choeme,* votive candles. Prem, Ang Sherpa and Jud all sit cross-legged on a rug in front of the small altar where the lama is seated. Unable to assume this almost lotus position because of my unbending replacement hip, I simply stretch my legs out and lean against the wall as the Lama begins to read the traditional prayers of Tibetan Buddhist ceremonies from a stack of old papers the size of postcards. Although the actual words are mumbled rapidly in the atonal chant of Tibetan monks, their meaning conveys a series of prayers to the Lords of Dharma, asking these enlightened spirits of another world to be with us in the coming days. Pema Lama assures the deities that we will try to rid ourselves of egocentric behavior and thought: "We seek your blessings to blame, begrudge and destroy the monstrous demon of selfishness."

As the lama reads on, he occasionally throws small pinches of rice toward us, the symbol of prosperity to Tibetans who for centuries had to import rice from India. Once in a while, the lama hits a small drum, a symbolic gesture aimed at getting the attention of the gods. Finally, he asks: "Make us meet no untimely death, sickness, demons or interfering spirits. See that we have no bad dreams, ill omens or calamities."

Then the *puja* is over. The lama stands, mutters a final blessing on us and places a thin silk scarf, *kata,* around our necks to bring us good karma during the upcoming climb.

The porters have already started up the sloping path leading from the village when the four of us also get underway. Clouds are still covering the mountain as we cross the river on the wire-rope bridge and hike past the old village of Pisang. Soon we are climbing through a forest filled with tall fir trees. Then we move onto a large slope covered with closely cropped grass where several yaks are grazing quietly in the misty air. Every move brings us upwards. Even the traverses require stepping up one foot at a time. After an hour of steady climbing, in which we pass the porters, Ang signals that it's time for a rest.

We draw together. Jud reaches for a pack of diamox and gives me two pills. "Here. This will help your respiration and may also prevent some altitude sickness," he says.

I take the two tablets with gratitude. Any advantage I can gain over the odds at this point is welcome.

By mid-afternoon, we arrive on a small plateau where a U-shaped wall of large rocks has been constructed as a shelter against wind and snow. "This is base camp," Ang Sherpa announces. Several minutes later, the porters arrive with the camping and climbing equipment. After we all take a short rest, the tents are pitched under Jud's directions and hot water is boiled on the small gas-fired cook stove he brought with his climbing equipment. Carrots, cabbage and garlic cloves, purchased the previous evening in Pisang village, are sliced and thrown into a pot along with a bag of powdered soup. Since the ground is wet from recent rainfall, we eat this dinner standing as darkness sets in around our bleak, but semi-comfortable camp.

Soon Jud and I retire to our tent and attempt to read with our head lamps before finally getting to sleep.

"Think you're ready?" Jud asks as he closes his book.

"As ready as I'll ever be," I respond.

After the day's tiring activities, a welcome and dreamless sleep soon comes.

The next morning, we take an early breakfast of tea and porridge. Then we break camp and, by eight-thirty, we're on our way to high camp. For the next few hours we move steadily upwards. More and more we gasp for breath in the thin air. As we climb, we can see Annapurna to the south of us, occasionally visible through the clouds, looking magnificent with its snowy peaks glistening in the sun. The northern ridge is usually visible first. It's like a slide show or slow motion movie, as the clouds present different views of the awe-inspiring mountain first climbed by Maurice Herzog and his French expedition in 1950. Never do we get a clear view through the clouds at Pisang Peak, although occasionally we see glimpses of the approach route, an intimidating sight.

It's cold and wet when in the late afternoon we make our final camp at 15,000 feet. There's time for an exploratory climb, so Jud hikes another thousand feet above camp, where we'll be climbing in the morning. When he returns, we repeat the dinner menu of the night before.

"Tomorrow we go to summit," Ang Sherpa declares.

"What's the weather going to be like?" Jud asks.

"Maybe okay," Ang answers with a confidence we all recognize to be unjustified optimism.

The clouds above us are dark and the wind is picking up. There is no way of knowing what will happen six hours from now. We go to our tents and try to get some sleep since we're planning on a five o'clock departure.

"I wish we knew what's going on up there," Jud says wistfully as he turns on his headlamp and opens his book.

"What's the worst possible scenario?" I ask.

"The worst would be rain, then sleet, then snow," he replies.

I turn on my own headlamp, wishing that I hadn't asked the question.

15

chapter

To the Summit

Those who care not for comfort can do a thousand deeds.

Tibetan Proverb

There is little rest for me tonight. After a fitful nap throughout the early evening, I'm soon lying wide awake, staring up at the inside of the tent. The effort to breathe in the high altitude, plus the realization that all my long training sessions are finished and in the morning, my long-awaited climb will begin, prevents any possibility of sleep. In the morning, my long-awaited climb will begin.

For now, the vision of me slipping and sliding on crampons over sharp, snow-covered ridges with thousand foot slopes on either side crowd into my innermost thoughts. Fear of the pain which accompanies total exhaustion stirs another set of anxieties. I don't tell Jud, but the truth is that I am truly frightened. Despite my resolve, despite how far I've come in my journey to make understand Chris's life and death, I'd like to get out of this. I have begun to hope that Ang will postpone our departure because of the weather.

Paradoxically, I know I need to make this climb. I want more than ever to conquer Pisang Peak and stand on its summit. I tell myself I've sacrificed too much to turn back without even trying. I've got to be ready to do whatever it takes to succeed.

In an effort to suppress my fears and doubts, I try to concentrate on how well prepared I am for the mountain. I think how hard I have trained over the past year to become a climber. The first lessons at Yosemite National Park with Tim Noonan. Tying knots, securing carabiners and controlling rappels with the ATC all provided important lessons on basic techniques. The solo top roping at the Shawnagunks in northern New York State forced me to trust my gear even when climbing alone. Rock climbing with Mia, Rick and his faithful dog, Cooper, at Cathedral Ledge in New Hampshire taught me to climb with confidence at hundreds of feet above the ground.

I remind myself of Rick's words, "There's no difference between falling forty feet and a thousand feet. Either way, you'll be dead." I hear Mia's "You-can-do-it" calls from the top of the Sliding Board, proving to me how seemingly impossible moves can be done if one tries hard enough. I go over again the proper use of crampons and ice picks, taught so well by Ivano near Mont Blanc in the French Alps.

These were critical aspects of preparing me for the upcoming climb through snow and ice. I recall also running around tracks combined with sprints up and down the steps of football stadiums wherever I happened to be staying during the training period. Those sessions forced me through the various levels of pain by racing two steps at a time...up and up, until nothing hurt anymore. The sore muscles and stiff joints, stretching my legs up onto a chair each morning, lifting weights and spending hours on artificial climbing walls were all painful ordeals, experiences that were part of the training routine that got me here. It's done, and the result is a body that's prepared to reach the top. Despite the high altitude, I'm breathing reasonably well. There are no headaches, no throwing up. The murderous training sessions have paid off. I'm in shape. I'm ready.

The problem I can't stop thinking about, despite Ang's optimistic prediction that we will reach the summit, is that we have yet to see Pisang Peak. It's been hidden in the clouds since we arrived. The late monsoon storms have deprived us of clear weather. Consequently, we have no idea what weapons the mountain will use against us. Will the clouds and sleet prevent us from finding the correct approach to the top? Are the ice-covered ridges waiting to turn our crampons into snowboards that can send us sliding down the 2,000-foot slopes? Maybe it will take only the age-old barriers of high wind and driving snow to keep us from the summit. We have no answers, nor can we find any without undertaking hours of upward climbing in constantly changing weather conditions.

Suddenly, I hear the zipping sound of a nearby tent being opened. A few moments later, Ang Sherpa calls out, "Jud! Weather okay. Today we climb."

"Are there any stars out?" Jud calls from his sleeping bag. No response. Ang doesn't understand. Jud tries again. "Weather. Are you sure it's good?"

"Yes–good. Good for climbing," comes the response.

Jud sits up and opens the tent flap. The sky is clear except for some clouds rolling across the blue expanse above us, though Pisang Peak and the Annapurnas remain invisible.

"Okay. We'll go," Jud says. Then he asks: "What time is it?"

Ang hesitates and tells us he doesn't know because

his headlamp isn't working. Since Jud has no watch and mine isn't working at this altitude, I hand Ang my headlamp so he can look at his watch. After focusing the light for several moments on his wrist, he chuckles and then calls out: "One-thirty."

"One-thirty!" Jud exclaims in disbelief.

Ang is obviously embarrassed by his mistake. He calls to us without hesitation: "Yes. Too early."

We decide that Ang will keep my headlamp and go back to his tent until four-thirty. Then he'll come for us and we'll start the climb. We all return to our sleeping bags.

Unfortunately, the good weather we witnessed at one-thirty changes. Rain begins to smack against the tent. The wind increases and is soon howling across the campsite. Then, a drilling sound against the tent replaces the softer patter of rain. Freezing sleet is now slashing our high camp and undoubtedly, the entire face of Pisang Peak. This continues for about an hour. Then silence. Only the sound of wind tugging at the tent flaps breaks the early morning quiet. That can mean only one thing. The sleet has turned to snow. Jud's description the previous evening of the very worst scenario we can face is now a reality.

Anyone who has driven a car or walked on a surface covered with sleet and snow knows what happens under these conditions. It occurs to me that on a day like this at home, I wouldn't think of walking my dog or even going to the mailbox.

This morning, however, I must venture out. There's no choice. In a short time, Ang will inform us that it's four-thirty and time to begin the long grind up the side of the mountain. I turn over on my right side and wait. I flip to my left and wait some more. Finally, with the wind still howling outside, the sound of a tent flap being unzipped is audible. Our Sherpa is coming for us. The appointed hour has come.

Ang's strong voice calls from the darkness. "Jud!"

Jud sits up and calls back. "Time to go?"

To my astonishment, Ang responds: "No, Jud. Bad weather. No climb today."

"No climb? Why not?" Jud asks.

"Much snow," Ang calls to us.

Jud opens the tent flap and we both peer out. The ground is covered with at least three inches of snow and visibility is limited to approximately twenty feet. "You're right. We can't climb in this," Jud says.

"We wait for another day. Maybe weather changes," Ang responds.

He goes back to his tent and we close our own flaps. Like a death-row inmate reprieved by a last minute call from the governor, I sigh with relief. Yet I wonder how I can get through the rest of the night. The prospect of remaining in the tent for another twenty-four hours is even more depressing.

The minutes inch by. I'd like to sit up and read, but Ang now has my headlamp. There is nothing for me to do but lie still and wait for sunrise. The wind continues to howl and groan outside and the soft brushing against the tent indicates continual snow. Then, just before dawn begins to filter light into the tent and I'm sure I cannot remain another instant within its narrow confines, Ang Sherpa calls once more.

"Jud. Jud. Weather okay. Today we go."

Jud sits up for the third time that morning and opens the flaps. The snow has stopped and once again the sky is clear. However, even if we hurry to get ready, we cannot possibly leave before seven-thirty. That is a very late start. If everything goes well and we reach the summit in six hours, it will be two in the afternoon before we begin our descent. Under the best of conditions, it would be dark before we returned to high camp.

Ang tells us that it may be now or never. "Maybe tomorrow, weather get worse. More snow. Then no climbing possible," he says.

We have food and water for only one more day. If bad weather prevails, we would have to give up without even an attempt at the summit. There's another persuasive, if unspoken, argument in favor of immediate departure: No one wants to spend another day and night waiting here encapsulated in a tent.

Jud turns to me.

"Why not? This may be our last chance," I respond immediately.

Then he looks out at Ang and gives his assent. "Okay, let's go for it."

Relieved that the long hours of preparing and waiting have ended, we all jump to the work of getting ready for the summit climb. High-altitude fleece jackets, sunglasses, water bottles and crampons are placed in our packs along with cold weather gloves, a 200-foot rope, ice screws, pickets, biscuits and several candy bars. We'll be ascending another 3,000 feet where the cold will increase significantly. To save time, we put on our climbing harnesses with attached carabiners now to facilitate roping ourselves together later in the morning.

Ang boils some water and throws in a packet of porridge. After we eat this quick breakfast, we strap on our back packs and by seven forty-five we're prepared to leave high camp.

For a moment, we all pause as Ang Sherpa looks up. The entire mountain is still covered with clouds. Turning to Jud and me, he issues final instructions: "Climbing slowly.

Up, up, up." Then he steps toward the snow-covered slope as Jud and I follow. My attempt to triumph over Pisang Peak has finally begun.

Climbing a high-altitude mountain in bad weather is a radically different experience from other kinds of climbing. The difficulties are not only more numerous, but they continually get harder to overcome as one approaches the summit. Snow impedes each step. Wind makes it difficult to stay balanced. Crampons get stuffed with ice and fail to hold. Lack of visibility creates mistakes in finding the proper route. And all the time, one's strength and stamina is diminishing from the constant struggle to move higher.

Along with the physical difficulties of climbing comes the actual pain of moving oneself forward under these conditions. The torturous effort to breathe in the thin air, the fatigue caused by limited oxygen filtering through the bloodstream to arms and legs, the stinging wind and increasing cold all combine to raise the suffering aspect of mountain-climbing to a higher level.

Chris used to say that pain is a state of mind and it's the only thing holding us back. Perhaps, I think, remembering his words now, he's right. As we begin to move, step by step, up the side of Pisang Peak this morning, I try to remember his advice about overcoming pain. Perhaps it will be the secret ingredient that can get me to the top.

As the first hour of "slowly climbing, up, up, up" gets underway, the level of snow increases. We stop to attach the crampons to our climbing boots. Then, as we begin climbing again for a second hour, I realize that despite all the training of the past year, my reserve of strength and energy may not be the only key to success on this final attempt to reach the top of Pisang Peak. Other factors, like snow and wind or the difficulty of climbing up a ramp covered with sleet on the bottom and snow on the top, may eventually stop us. In short, neither our skills, our endurance, nor our equipment can dictate the final outcome. The mountain is now in control.

After climbing approximately 1500 feet along a relatively safe side of the northwest ridge, we come to a steeper ramp with sharp slopes falling off on each side. A fall from this route could be serious. Ang and Jud decide it's time to establish an anchor and rope ourselves together.

Ang goes up first with one end of the rope and an angled piece of aluminum in which several holes have been bored. After climbing 150 feet, the length of our rope, he drives this 'picket' into the snow and ice with his ice axe until it's secure. He slips the end of the rope into this anchor, secures it with a carabiner and then wraps several feet of rope around his waist. He can now hold either Jud or me if we fall.

"Okay. Climbing up," he shouts to us.

I slip the rope through the carabiner attached to my harness and start up.

At first, I move quickly. Then the angle changes, and suddenly the route is so steep I have to drive my crampons and ice pick deep into the snow and ice in order keep from slipping back. The effort to push my entire weight up on each step at this altitude quickly turns my breathing into a series of gasps. Nevertheless, I keep moving, stopping only twice to rest. In perhaps fifteen minutes, I reach Ang Sherpa and sit down to restore oxygen and strength while Jud moves up to join us.

When Jud arrives, Ang immediately gathers the rope and picket and moves up again. Meanwhile, the wind is picking up and the cold is becoming more intense. We go up another pitch, and then another. In each case, I take the middle position so that I've got Ang at the top and Jud at the bottom to arrest a fall. It's comforting to know that even if I do slip, they will be there.

By late morning, however, the worst of my fears is beginning to take shape. I'm getting tired. Each step up the sharp slope is becoming more difficult. Deep gasping for oxygen is replacing the normal breathing cycle. I try to establish a slow rhythm. Right boot up, left boot up. I do this twenty times and then stop to rest on the ice axe. My legs now feel as if they've turned to soft jelly. My chest seems to be on fire. The twenty steps become too much. I cut back to ten steps, then rest. Finally, I'm down to three steps before collapsing on the ice axe. The diminished lack of oxygen moving through my bloodstream is taking its toll and I'm frightened I won't be able to continue.

It's well past noon when we finally reach the huge *couloir,* a deep gorge, that lies in front of Pisang Peak's summit. We need to descend about 200 feet and then move up along a narrow ridge another 1500 feet to the top. On both sides of this ridge, snow-covered slopes drop off thousands of feet. Perhaps in good weather, under the right conditions, this would not be so difficult to navigate. Today, however, a thirty-mile-per-hour wind filled with stinging snowflakes is whistling up the *couloir*. Furthermore, clouds are still swirling around the summit which we can finally see, though not clearly.

This is the final approach to the top, the same place where Chris had to turn back when he saw a storm fast approaching from the Tibetan plateau. This is also the ridge where the group of eleven German climbers, who were roped together, fell to their deaths. The words etched on their memorial plaque far below is still in my mind: *They still live although they are no longer with us.*

Despite all this, we can now see the summit shining

through the snow and clouds. It's tantalizingly close. A final push could get us there in less than an hour. This is the goal we've been working so hard to achieve.

But I now have a serious problem. Even if I can force myself to keep climbing for another hour, the actual strength it would take to maintain proper balance crossing the narrow ridge against the force of the wind is gone. I will drastically slow down the time required to summit. I will also be a threat both to myself and to the others. This is the moment Tom Frost talked about on top of Yosemite's El Cap. *If we have a feeling that we shouldn't make a certain move or that we should not even climb that day, we need to heed that advice. If, on the other hand, our inner voice tells us to move forward, to go up the next pitch, then we must listen to that as well.*

Now is the moment when I must listen for the inner voice. It comes through as clearly as the yak bells ringing through the early morning air down at base camp. No matter how much I want to triumph at the top, I know it's impossible in this weather. The strength to take one more step upwards, and then another, and another, against this wind is simply not there. *Climbing slowly...up, up, up* is no longer an option. And if I did somehow struggle to the summit, what reserves of energy would be left to propel me down again? After all, the Germans who died here several years earlier were on the way down. They fell to their deaths after reaching the summit. *When you've reached the top, you're only halfway there*!

Reluctantly, I turn to Jud who is standing nearby. "I need to talk to you," I call through the wind.

Jud approaches. "What do you think?" he shouts into my ear.

"Okay...here it is. I've reached the end. The wind is really moving on that ramp. It's going to be tough. I haven't got enough strength left to make it under these conditions."

"Are you saying you can't summit?" Jud asks.

"That's right. But there's a mountain up there. It's yours now. I want you to go up and get it," I reply.

Jud pauses. This is a difficult decision for him. An unspoken rule exists among mountain guides that a client should never be left alone. Yet our relationship is far more complex than that of a client and his guide. I had clearly stated to him at the beginning of this expedition that I would be treating him with the same trust and care I would accord to one of my own children. So, in a sense, the father is now passing on the torch of leadership to the son here on top of this storm-swept mountain. If Chris were standing in front of me, I would be repeating his words, the words which inspired me to come this far: "Go for it."

Jud understands, but again he wants clarity. "Are you telling me you want me to summit and you want to wait down here until we return?"

"That's right. I'll wait for you on the other side of the ridge where there isn't so much wind," I respond.

Reluctantly, Jud agrees. Quickly, he tells Ang about our plan and, in a few moments, the two climbers start down the *couloir* and disappear into the driving snow.

For a few minutes, I remain on the rim looking up at Pisang Peak which has once again scored an unconditional victory. The mountain will no more allow the father to stand on its summit today than it had the son eight years earlier. Neither revenge nor redemption is being permitted. The massive pinnacle of dark stone smeared with patches of snow looming in front of me is offering only the bitter fruit of defeat and failure on this miserable, stormy afternoon.

There is nothing left now but to wait and then climb down to high camp while the others go on to the top.

Slowly, I begin picking my way down the snow-covered slope that was gained at such physical cost only an hour earlier. The harsh depression that comes with losing is hammered into my consciousness with each step. In desperation, I devise a plan for staying in Pisang for another week. I'll become better acclimatized to the altitude and surely the weather will change. Then I can try again. The idea is exciting. Momentarily, it removes the sting of defeat. However, after a few minutes of down climbing through the snow, reality returns. I know very well that the porters, Ang Sherpa and Jud, are all scheduled to return for other expeditions. Jud has been hired by a Canadian adventure tour company to lead a group of climbers to Island Peak, an 18,000-foot mountain in the Everest region.

No, I can't possibly mount a second expedition without walking five days back to Kathmandu. By then, the altitude conditioning I've already attained will be lost. Jud will be gone and climbing without him would be unthinkable. Any plans for a second chance are based on myth. There will be no victory on Pisang Peak now or in the future.

As I down climb, I recall a letter I received written after the memorial service we held for Chris. A friend of his wrote the following:

> Chris loved being in the mountains, loved climbing more than anyone I've ever met. Once, on Mt. Rainier, we were bivied at 10,000 feet and woke up to a snowstorm. Down was the logical choice, but as we were preparing to leave, a small break appeared in the clouds. It was Chris's enthusiasm that got us going upwards again. We climbed all day, until one last barrier blocked our route. I took a fall, sliding down before being held on belay. Chris's grin and laughter at the episode rescued it from being a bad experience to a

beautiful one. He asked me if I was spooked, which indeed I was, and without another word we retreated down the ridge. That was very typical of Chris, pushing the limits, finding out what they are, but not being ashamed to retreat from them.

Now, I need to follow Chris's example.

As I descend further, the snow turns wet and begins to pack under my crampons. I move carefully since there are no anchors, ropes or climbing partners to check a fall. A prudent climber would stop now and wait for the others to return. I'm feeling too discouraged to sit and wait and I decide to keep going down despite my promise to Jud.

For perhaps ten minutes, I descend without incident. Then, a large rock, covered with snow, appears in my path. I shift my weight to the right and step forward. As my right foot hits the snow, my boot slips from under me and I fall, totally out of control. Instantaneously, I begin to slide down the slope on my back. Two hundred feet below, the slope ends with a vertical drop of another thousand feet. Within seconds, I'm picking up speed.

Immediately, my physical reflexes respond to the advice Ivano repeated several times on the Mer de Glace. *If you fall and begin to slide, you must turn over facing the snow and hit down hard with your ice axe.* Quickly, I roll over and slam my ice axe into the snow and ice. The steel point sinks several inches into the ice. I squeeze the handle with both hands as the ice axe catches my weight. I hang on and the fall is momentarily broken. Then I slowly try to shift some weight onto my crampons. The moment I move, however, the axe slips through the soft ice and the slide begins again. Once more I hammer the axe into the ice. This time it holds. Apparently, today is not the day I am meant to die.

Shaken, and determined not to descend any further without protection, I stand up, clean the ice from my crampons and traverse carefully along the slope to a large rock where I now decide to stay until Ang and Jud return from the summit.

The wait is not long. Suddenly, I hear Jud calling from far up the slope. They're on their way down. I can't believe they reached the top in such a short time. In a few minutes, they arrive.

"It can't be done today. The wind is too strong and the snow is getting heavier. We couldn't see the route," Jud explains.

"I'm sorry...I was hoping...," I stutter.

"There's nothing to be sorry about. This isn't our day," Jud interrupts. "We've all done our best."

We break out a power bar, take a long drink from the water bottle and then start down again.

Jud knows what I'm thinking. He attempts to be comforting. "Sometimes you learn more from failure than you do from getting to the top," he says when we pause for a momentary rest behind some large boulders.

"You're probably right. It's just that we tried so hard and I so much wanted to reach the summit for Chris's sake as well as my own," I reply.

"You did well. You gave it your best shot," he says.

Once more we move downward. Perhaps Jud is right. Maybe it's better that we didn't get to the top. I stop and turn around. The clouds have suddenly drifted clear of the mountain above. There, towering high above us, is Pisang Peak, shimmering triumphantly in the sunlight.

As the light begins to fade against the cloud-filled sky and we continue slogging down the steep slopes, I try to assess the damages caused by the day's losses. All along, I assumed that victory on the mountain would deliver the comfort, the understanding, even the peace of mind I desperately need to find. All my expectations were based on getting to the top. I was planning on success, on winning, on beating the mountain. There were no contingency plans for defeat. Like my reaction to Chris's fatal accident on the ice column at Kicking Horse Pass, I wasn't prepared for this. I didn't think it could happen.

Faced with the fact that I didn't reach the top, that I didn't find the answer to what drove my son on, I don't know what to do, to say, to think. Is this the end of a wasted year? Has this huge expenditure of time, money and effort all been for nothing? Was there really a message waiting for me at the summit of Pisang Peak? I'll never know. I didn't climb that far.

When we finally arrive at high camp, darkness and a wet mist have closed in around our tents. I try to act pleasant and upbeat. In reality, my mood reflects the weather. Jud and Ang cook some soup, using the last of our water. We'll spend tonight in the tent and then leave early in the morning for another day of downhill trekking until we get to Pisang village.

The climbing expedition is finished. If there's a lesson from or about Chris to be found at the top of Pisang Peak, I tell myself, it will remain forever a mystery. Yet, that night as I push down into my sleeping bag, I lie there very much awake. I realize there is another truth that Chris knew and every climber must eventually deal with. Failure. Defeat. Difficult as failing to summit may be for me, perhaps the lesson being taught is learned in the doing, not the end result. After all, has this trip not been a journey to learn how to deal with loss? How could a high-altitude victory be the great teacher in my search to understand? It occurs to me, as the wind begins to rustle along the roof of our tent, that perhaps today's defeat may offer more wisdom in the long run than a victory on the top of Pisang Peak. It would be, I can't help thinking, just like Chris, with his infectious, dark sense of humor, to find the irony in this situation.

Early the next morning, the porters and Ang Sherpa prepare to leave for Kathmandu via the same route along the Marsyangdi River which brought us to Pisang. Regretfully, we shake hands goodbye. They've worked hard, undergone difficult climbs with heavy loads and never complained. Jud and I are sorry to see them go. Then Prem, Jud and I leave for a three hour hike to Manang, a village to the north, where we stay overnight before tackling another day of climbing up a steep, winding trail which eventually crosses the Thorung La pass, a snow-covered gash in the Himalayan mountain chain which Tibetan porters and yak caravans have used for centuries. Crossing the 15,500 foot pass with its four hour descent to the Kali Gandaki is considered the toughest one day trek in Nepal.

By late afternoon, after seven hours of hard up and down climbing to cross Thorung La, we arrive in Muktinath, the first village in a string of Tibetan communities throughout the valley. Since Jud needs to return quickly in order to guide another group of climbers on another high peak not far from the Everest Base Camp, he leaves in the morning while I make plans to visit several *gompas* which Chris described in his report.

16
chapter

"Ah So"

Nothing can be loved or hated unless it is first known.

Leonardo DaVinci

With one worn tooth occasionally protruding from a wrinkled mouth, the old lama sways back and forth at the entrance to the monastery. He wears a long, saffron robe and a worn red coat vaguely resembling a ski parka. When I point toward the inside of the monastery, signaling that I would like to enter, the caretaker nods and steps to one side of the aged, wooden door.

Finally, I've arrived at the Sakya monastery which Chris visited and described in detail during his study tour of this valley in 1989. This is the structure which he termed a "power place" in his 125 page report written for his Junior-Year-Abroad project. On the cover page of his report is a picture of the very monastery I'm about to enter.

Unfortunately, the building is doomed to eventual extinction because of its precarious foundation on an eroding cliff. This weakness will soon send the entire structure crashing into the valley below. For now, however, I'm sensing a feeling of reunion at being in this place which Chris wrote about with such passion.

Removing my shoes, I step inside. From the prayer hall, I hear the barely audible mumbling of the monks chanting their morning prayers. Immediately, I sense a closeness to Chris that is relaxing and harmonious. I can hear him telling me to come on in, assuring me that this *gompa* is really "cool."

Through my mind runs the question: *Chris! How did you ever find this place?*

As I enter the main prayer hall, called *Chaitya* in Tibetan, a brilliant glow of golden light from the morning sun shines through a skylight in the roof. It illuminates the young monks sitting with crossed legs in front of two benches on each side of the room. On an elevated pulpit to the right and front of the prayer hall, the monastery's Abbot also sits in the lotus position. He chants in unison with the young boys in the morning prayer session, the *puja,* which is now in progress.

For several minutes, I stand transfixed by the mesmerizing sound of the chanting monks. Memories flood back to those days more than half a century earlier, when I was an eleven-year-old student kneeling in the chapel of a French Canadian Jesuit school in Montreal, listening to the Gregorian chants of the choir. Then it was a statue of the Virgin Mary, bathed in light from dozens of candles burning at her feet, which held my attention. Now, a bronze statue of the Buddha in front of the prayer hall, also illuminated by candles on the altar below, imparts the same transfixing feeling of reverence and awe.

Several young monks look up at the stranger who has entered their sanctuary to watch. They shift their legs, one stretches a shoulder and then they all return to their chants. I know about the kind of discomfort they must be feeling. I can still recall the sharp pain in my knees caused by interminable kneeling on a hard bench during early morning matins. How well I can empathize with these young boys trying to concentrate on their prayers when the desire for breakfast or playing outside in the courtyard becomes overwhelming. It occurs to me that Chris has brought me back to the beginning, to the completion of a cycle, which is about to impart an important lesson of the spirit.

Slowly, I move to the side of the prayer hall and sit on a cushioned bench with my usual stretched out legs which refuse to cross into a lotus position. Suddenly, the first blast of a long horn shatters the somber calm of the room. Several bells ring. A small drum is struck. Cymbals clang and the horns shriek again. The evil spirits are being driven away by the noise-making instruments played by the young monks. The devils and demons who would harm all sentient beings are being frightened into retreat. Then, calm returns again to the room. The monks pick up their atonal chants as the *puja* moves into the final stage of the morning ritual.

I sit back and look around the room. On the walls, I can barely discern the outline of a series of paintings depicting the life of the Buddha. I check Chris's report in the dim light and I read his observations of a decade earlier.

> Dzar has a beautiful interior space that represents some of the better artwork to be found in the region. Some of the internal elements such as murals are new and intact: others are ancient and crumbling.

On one wall, I see that several paintings are marred by streaks of white caused by water, probably from a leak in the mud roof covering the *gompa.* In some instances, the paintings have disappeared. All of this damage is undoubtedly worse than it was eight years earlier when Chris was here. Still, some of the work is in good shape, although even these paintings are difficult to see in the darkness of the interior walls. For a moment, I wonder why the artists were so foolish as to paint in an area where there was not enough light for the viewer to enjoy and appreciate the work in question. Then, I check Chris's report again and gain insight:

> It is important to note that most murals are painted on walls that see little light. Temples are usually illuminated by a skylight in the middle of the room. While this provides adequate light for the monks to read, the perimeters of the room are in near total darkness, no matter the time of day. One may conclude then, that the murals do not exist for a decorative purpose and seemingly not even for use in any type of ceremonial ritual or exercise in meditation. The reason is simple–it is often impossible to see more than vague outlines. This would suggest that the purpose of the murals is for their spiritual presence alone. As a representation of a deity in any religion, these murals have power. The conception of an inanimate object having a sort of power is not unusual. What is unusual is that there can be power by the sheer existence of that inanimate object–whether or not the image can be seen by a human being.

A painting that is not made to be seen but that has power! This is quite different from my own Western training, which insists that a painting or work of art exists only for me, the viewer. Chris's suggestion that "the purpose of the murals is for their spiritual existence," strikes me as potentially far more rewarding than a mural whose objective is limited to my own immediate enjoyment. It also occurs to me that someone who could understand the concept at the age of twenty-two might easily be able to touch a rock wall and feel its mood several years later while climbing in Yosemite National Park.

When the chanting finally stops and monks file out of the prayer hall, I am left alone in the silence and tranquility of the *Chaitya*. I stand up and slowly begin to wander around the inside of the *gompa*. I notice that several of the wall paintings are relatively primitive and not equal to the fine work done in some of the older renditions. Chris, too, was aware of this:

> The murals were apparently repainted twenty years ago and a fair job was done, It must be said that these murals, or the other art encountered, would not be considered "fine Tibetan art." Any especially talented painter or sculptor could usually learn his skill only in a larger city, and could support himself only in a larger city as well. Therefore, the art one sees in these temples is beautiful, but not comparable to the best examples of Tibetan art. Nevertheless, an image of *Sakyamuni* is an image of *Sakyamuni,* and has spiritual value no matter the quality of execution.

Here, Chris is reminding me to put aside the Western mind-set that the value of art is determined by how it looks or what it does for the viewer. The spiritual value of these wall murals *in situ* are the most important part of their worth.

There's a particular room in this monastery that I'm looking for. It's the *Srung Kang* in the south-east corner room which Chris described as the most fascinating room he encountered in Nepal. He explained:

> It is the temple's *Srung Kang,* a room dedicated to *Mahakala* and wrathful deity worship. There are murals on the wall, but the style is much more "folk" looking. Here, nothing is geometric; everything is painted freehand. This is significant because almost never have I seen Tibetan art that does not follow prescribed rules. The "rules" of Tibet's art have prompted some to argue that Tibetan art is not really art. That would be oversimplifying it; there is much room for an artist's own input in his creation.

This classic argument over the definition of art held special meaning to Chris, since he had spent several months during his fall study program in Kathmandu painting a *thanka,* a painting on cloth which can be rolled up and carried. The rules of painting in this form have been formalized over the centuries. Yet, he was aware that choices had to be made in the use of colors, the method of depicting characters such as the Buddha and even the overall structure of the painting. I sense that his defense of the creative potential in Tibetan painting, whether on a *thanka* or wall, was a position he would have defended with passion.

Yet, as I continue wandering through its rooms, reflecting on the meaning of the priceless *gompa* with its centuries old icons and works of art, it suddenly occurs to me how unfortunate that it will soon be destroyed by the erosion of its outer foundation. I read Chris's words:

> The old temple will soon crumble until it is unrecognizable as a man made structure and will be one more lost monument to the crumbling Tibetan world.

But the building has not yet been lost! Admittedly, it's only a few feet from the edge of the cliff on which it was built a half century earlier. In a few more years, this frail foundation will be worn even further by the severe wind, snow and rain whistling down from the Tibetan mountains a few miles to the north. Then the *gompa* will simply crash over the cliff and disappear into the valley below.

Discouraged, I stop near a shaft of light and open Chris's report to check on what he had written in the introduction. Incredibly, his words stand out as clearly and irrevocably as the horns, the drums, the bells and the cymbals played by the monks during their *puja* earlier in the morning.

> We cannot afford to let Tibetan Buddhist monasteries and temples deteriorate and disappear. It is wonderful to see the community of Dzar (Jharkot) undertaking renovations to their temple, their heritage, and I hope I will be lucky enough someday to get involved and aid in the preservation of these remarkable feats of mankind.

Suddenly, I realize that perhaps this is a directive from Chris, a mandate that should be considered. After more reflection, I understand that these words constitute an opportunity to carry out the hopes and plans of my son who is no longer present, but whose spirit so clearly exists here in the foothills of the Himalayan mountains.

As I look up at the peaceful statue of Buddha, a promise suddenly runs through my mind. *I'll do it, Chris! I'll make sure the monastery is restored just as you wished. I'll start a foundation and raise enough funds to do the job. It may take some time, but eventually I'll come back here and make certain your dream is carried out.*

Then, to cement the promise, I walk to the front of the prayer Hall and light a candle. As the flame bursts from a thin, wooden match which I strike against the altar, the small wick begins to glow at the feet of the bronze Buddha statue. Chris and I both know that this promise will be kept. I'll "go for it." The monastery will be saved.

Later, in the fall of the year 2000, I would be present to witness the first stones being carried in baskets from a quarry a half mile away to the foot of the monastery's cliff on the backs of dozens of young porters. The cliff will eventually be supported by thousands of these stones, packed in wire, to insure the stability of the monastery's foundation. Then, the Sakya Monastery itself will be restored according to carefully engineered architectural plans. A small school will be constructed on adjoining grounds. This work is being financed through grants and donations being made to the Christopher Purnell Foundation which is carrying out the restoration with the approval and cooperation of the Abbot and village elders of the surrounding area.

On the front wall of the *Chaitya,* a large bronze statue of the Buddha has been placed behind a glass wall. The imposing and silent figure sits with legs crossed and hands pointing down, suggesting the importance of earthly beings. I'm reminded of the Buddhist concept as interpreted by the Dalai Lama in *The Four Noble Truths,* which I've been reading for the past few days. As His Holiness has written, "If we want to rid ourselves of unhappiness and find serenity in our lives, we first have to get rid of our desires for the things we don't need."

This teaching now seems more relevant than I had previously supposed. As I look at the calm presence and serene posture of this bronze statue, it occurs to me that perhaps my own unhappiness and misery over not summiting Pisang Peak is being caused by a need that was not essential. As Chris wrote in the first chapter of his report:

> Existence and the eternal cycle of birth, death and birth results in inevitable suffering. Suffering is caused by craving, and the right way to absolve suffering is to follow what is known as the Eight fold path, right views, right intention, right speech, right action, right livelihood, right effort, right mindfulness and right concentration.

Perhaps it was not, after all, so necessary to climb a mountain in order to find the truth. Even Tom Frost agreed with that when we discussed this very subject back on El Capitan.

I remember telling him, "You don't have to climb a mountain or endanger your life to find God. You can stay right in your own house with the windows drawn and still have a religious experience."

Tom had responded with unqualified conviction. "That's absolutely true. I'm sure of it."

It occurs to me that perhaps my need to climb a mountain to know my son was misplaced. Then, the hard question arises: Could it even be said that my craving to have Chris back again is also a need which is not essential, a negation of all the underlying principles inherent in *The Four Noble Truths*. The idea seems shocking, almost blasphemous. Yet, as I continue examining the artifacts of the monastery, this thought continues to brew new ideas about the meaning of the journey which I've been taking. Perhaps, I have been wrong in refusing to accept Chris's absence.

I remember the "Ah so" story which I related to Chris when he was in his mid-teens. It's a Zen parable about a young Japanese monk who suddenly found himself in trouble after being unjustly accused in a paternity dispute. It happened one day when the village elders arrived at the monk's cottage with a pregnant woman who claimed the monk was the father of her forthcoming child. The elders told the monk he would have to support the mother and child. Rather than protest and argue that he was innocent of the accusation, the monk merely nodded and said "Ah so." A year later, the elders returned with a young man and told the monk that the woman had lied. Furthermore, the young man now acknowledged that he was the father. The monk was told that he would no longer have to care for the mother and child. The monk simply nodded and said, "Ah so."

This example of the Buddhist concept of calmly accepting the ups and downs, truths and mistruths, of life was often helpful to Chris and me. The story reminded us that the good and bad events of our lives need to be taken in stride and are even of little concern to those who truly seek enlightenment. The lesson of this parable, that acceptance is the key to a harmonious life, was one we both felt important.

The story became a kind of symbolic, verbal shorthand between us. If something happened that I didn't like, but which I was determined to accept, I would say to Chris, "Ah so." He would smile and yet also understand I was foregoing my personal desire in a particular situation and that I would accept whatever was necessary. On the other hand, Chris might tell me about a failure or set back that he regretted and then he would sigh, "Ah so." I would understand that he was going to accept his loss with patience and understanding.

As I stand in this place where Chris found so much enlightenment, I see that now I'm faced with the necessity of accepting my son's loss. I ask myself, *Am I sufficiently enlightened to say "Ah so"?* I can not seem to say yes. Not yet, anyway.

After a tour of the inside rooms, I walk outside into the bright sunlight to the courtyard and decide on a prayer tour of the temple. This rite of circling the *gompa* is practiced faithfully throughout the day by the Tibetan Buddhists. Particularly in the morning and the evening, the devout can be seen walking slowly around the sacred building. Chris described this practice in a section about the various uses of the temple.

> Another way a monastery is used in its concrete sense is as a path of circum-Ambulation. The people of the village, mostly older, will walk around the monastic complex, always with their right shoulder closest to the building, in a form of praying. Mantras and short sayings with religious implications are repeated as the person walks along and around the loop formed by the monastery.

After circling the monastery, I stroll through the village past the stone huts where women are huddled over open fires in the dark and smoke-filled kitchens as they prepare the evening meal. Many of the men are removing the heavy yokes from their yaks after a day of plowing in the nearby fields. The centuries-old cycle of plowing, planting and harvesting, cooking, washing and raising children remains unchanged even by the constant flow of trekkers from around the world who walk through the village each day during the dry season.

Finally, I come back to the hotel where a group of trekkers are huddled around a candle-lit table eating dinner prepared by several women who are cooking over a small, wood-burning fireplace in the kitchen. They're making a variety of local dishes such as potato omelets, noodle soup and vegetables as well as the standard *dal bat.* All of this can be had with tea and milk, tea and lemon, tea with cinnamon or tea with honey. In some cases, even a coke or an orange soda is available. Considering the fact that all ingredients, except local vegetables, have to be carried to these mountainous villages either on the backs of porters or by small mules, it seems miraculous that so many culinary offerings can be made.

I settle for *dal bat* and then retire to my room. From a small window in the narrow cubicle, I can see stars shining above the distant mountains as I roll out my sleeping bag on the narrow bed. Soon, the old questions come back again. *What am I doing here? Why did the fatal accident have to happen? What can I do about it? What is the meaning of Chris's loss on the mountains and why did he even have to be there?*

The answer is that I still don't know. My failure to climb to the summit of Pisang Peak awakened in me some knowledge, but not the final solution. In the morning, it will be time to leave. There will one last trek to the airport village of Jomsom. The following morning, I'll take a flight past the Machhapuchhare mountains back to Pokhara and then to Kathmandu where my journey will end.

Like a football player with only one play left before the game is over, I'm overcome with desperation. As I turn over in the sleeping bag and begin to drift into unconsciousness, I haven't the slightest hint that the ball has been thrown. In fact, it's spinning through the air now, ready for a receiver to race into the end zone. But I do not suspect for a moment that before another day ends, an opportunity to open my arms and catch the ball will finally present itself.

17 chapter

The Final Message

You have done wisely to invite the night before the darkness came.

Edna St. Vincent Millay

The next morning it's time to leave Dzar and hike down the river valley to Jomsom where a small plane leaves each day for Kathmandu to begin the final leg of this long journey.

As I pack my gear on this cool, misty morning, however, little do I realize that the trek to Jomsom will soon become a blueprint for disaster. The potential for trouble starts when I decide to visit the ancient village of Lubra, an hour's walk to the east of the main trail. Chris spent several days there during his study tour, became friends with the resident lama and even stayed in his small, dark, smoke-filled house. He included a description of the Lubra *gompa* along with several photographs of its interior in his report. I want badly to see the place and meet the lama. Chris wrote:

Lubra is a small community tucked away in its own river valley, about two hours' walk from Kag. The people of Lubra are not Buddhists, they are Bon-pos. The religion of Bon, often described as "shamanistic" and "animistic," existed in Tibet before Buddhism was introduced. Over the past several hundred years, the two religions have influenced each other to a point where they are essentially identical. Variances do exist, but they are largely cosmetic; having different names for the same deity, for example.

A huge cliff across the river bed to the north in front of the village is full of niches, many of which have served as caves for lamas in retreat. Up the river, to the east, is a long wall of mountains all above twenty thousand feet high. To the rear of the village to the south is a steep hill with many terraced, rocky patches of mediocre soil that provides Lubra with a meager daily sustenance.

At the top of the hill are the somewhat hidden ruins of an old fortress. Although it's difficult to see from below, a view from the fortress encompasses miles all around, in any direction from where one would approach the village. Going west from Lubra leads down the river valley for about forty-five minutes, where the river meets the larger Thak Khola (Kali Gandaki). So, unlike Dzar and the whole Muktinath Valley, Lubra is essentially free of the tourist flow.

For these and many more reasons, Lubra has a captivating magic all its own. Though geographically no more isolated than the other villages in the region, staying in Lubra "feels" like being in another world.

It is Lubra with its' "captivating magic" that I want to see on my way back to Jomsom. By eight in the morning, I zip up the backpack and say goodbye to Hira Gurung, the charming twenty-two-year-old Tibetan waitress and manager of the hotel.

I'm planning on a fast, tough march to Lubra where I'll spend an hour at the *gompa* and then make a quick hike to the airport village of Jomsom later in the afternoon. I know that the wind will begin to blow through the river valley at noon. Despite this, I figure that putting up with the cold blast from the south for the final hours of the trip will be only a minor inconvenience. The following morning, I'll catch the plane back to Kathmandu and my journey will be completed.

After hiking several hours south along the river, I reach a small, one-room restaurant at noon where I stop for a hurried lunch of curried vegetables on rice and lots of lemon tea. It's taken longer than I expected to trek this far, so I eat quickly and then shoulder my pack for a hike to the rock-filled river bed where the Panda Khola flowing from the northeast feeds into the main Kali Gandaki. A strong wind has begun whistling down the valley now. It's one-thirty and I'm running an hour behind schedule. One hour to the east, or forty-five minutes according to Chris's report, the village of Lubra is located along the river bank.

Because I'm late, I consider aborting the trip. It might be impossible to visit Lubra and still get back to Jomsom before the sun sets. I pause and look toward the valley, trying to decide whether to hike up to the village or head down to the comfort and security of the airport village, an hour's walk to the south. If it takes more than an hour to reach Lubra, I could be in the dangerous position of having to trek back to Jomsom after nightfall. The most reasonable solution at this point is to forget about Lubra and instead, undertake an easy one-hour walk down to the airport village.

For several minutes I stand at the river junction trying to decide which way to go. Chris's words prior to his solo ascent of El Capitan come back: *Go for it.* I say to myself: "I'll solo it." And so, I decide to head upriver to Lubra by myself. I'm still feeling strong. If I can reach the village by two, have a quick tour of the gompa and leave by three-thirty, I will have two hours before dark to hurry back down the river and hike into Jomsom. And if this doesn't work, I can stay in Lubra overnight in a villager's hut and then depart early in the morning. Or so I tell myself.

My decision is made. I heave my shoulders forward into the pack and start up the mostly dry riverbed with a very distinct feeling that Chris would be proud of me. The hike north immediately turns out to be a lot tougher than I imagined. A fast stream runs through the middle of the riverbed while huge cliffs rise on each side. The wind is blowing really hard now and there's little sheltered space walking among the large riverbed stones. I'm forced to jump regularly from one stone to another while balancing my heavy pack. I trudge on, but the village doesn't appear. I cannot remember ever feeling so alone, so isolated. Chris's words used to describe climbing alone on El Cap come back:

> Soloing is really amazing. Since human interaction is nonexistent, your perceptions become much more focused on your surroundings. In fact, I believe I have a more clear visual memory of climbing Zodiac than I have of subsequent walls done with partners. Your emotions are tempered when you're alone; there isn't as much of a thrill when you finish a hard pitch. You also don't get as frustrated when, say, your rope gets tangled. You just deal with it. It's much easier to maintain your concentration when the distraction of a partner is eliminated.

Chris may be right, but hiking solo in the Himalayas is also a decidedly lonely experience and right now more than ever I wish I had someone with me. The one comforting feeling comes from the knowledge that he also made the same trip through this desolate valley just a few years earlier.

On I go. A second hour passes and fatigue is beginning to take over. The straps are cutting into my shoulders. My legs are resisting forward movement. Then, as I wearily take one more step through the riverbed, a mysterious voice becomes audible. Someone is talking! I stop and look up and down the valley. There is not a living thing anywhere, and I can see clearly for at least a mile in both directions. The voice continues! I can't understand what it's saying but I know it's a human voice...a man's voice.

Perhaps it's the computer! Could the CD player have switched on? Could it be Puccini! Or is it Chio Chio San expressing her mistaken joy at the return of Pinkerton who has come to claim her son? I shake my head. It can't be that; the voice is speaking, not singing. I must have forgotten to turn the laptop off early in the morning when I wrote a few notes before leaving Jharkot. Quickly, I take the pack off my shoulders and reach for the laptop. It's definitely turned off. In fact, I realize, the battery would never have lasted this long if the computer was on.

The voice is still talking. Again I look around, but there's no one in sight. Then I look at my pack and realize where the sound is coming from. It must be the recorder! I pull the small device from the bottom of the pack and sure enough, it's playing the voice of Tom Frost which I taped while we were sitting on top of El Capitan several months earlier. He's discussing the third principle of climbing mountains. His words come through clearly now:

All of your ambition urges you on. But if you're motivated by ambition, you'll hear ambition. If you're climbing for the right reasons and you're ready to listen, you'll hear your inner voice. The one can cost you your life, the other can save you.

Stunned, I shut off the recorder and return it to the bottom of the pack. Now questions arise faster than I can articulate them in my head. How did this happen? Who or what turned on the recorder? Why was it playing that particular selection? The words of the American nun, Lothro, come back to me: *Something will happen. You're going to experience an unexpected event that will be important to the purpose of your journey.* Is this what she was talking about, a recorder that turns itself on in the middle of a trek and plays a message about hearing an inner voice?

In a few moments, I shoulder the pack once more and begin moving up the river toward Lubra. Like the glacier waters rushing along the riverbed a few feet from the rock-filled path, my mind is now a torrent of conflicting thoughts. What is the significance of the message that played on the recorder? Or is there no meaning? Has some strange force from the other side interceded in order to send me a message about hearing an inner voice? Or was this purely mechanical–the recorder bumped when I jumped from one rock to another? Is it pure chance that the tape recorder was playing Tom's words about climbing for the wrong reasons when I pulled it from the pack? Like all the questions which have arisen during this trip, no answers come.

However, I suddenly see some holes in the cliff to my left and surmise that these are the caves which Chris described in his report. Is this not another strange occurrence to add to my dilemma–that I would be so near a place where my son walked when the recorder came on? I see with his eyes: "A huge cliff across the river bed (north) in front of the village is full of niches, many of which have served as caves for lamas in retreat."

If these small monk cells dug from the cliff are the "retreat" locations, I realize, then the village of Lubra must be around the next bend. Indeed, a colorful *chorten* covered with prayer flags suddenly appears in the distance and behind this shrine, the busy village of Lubra fits snugly into the surrounding hillside. The "forty-five-minute walk" has taken two hours and it's now three o'clock.

The monastery is located at the top of a hill overlooking the village. Treading past small and dirty urchins, goats, undernourished cows and an occasional Nepalese porter staggering along the narrow twisting path with a huge load of hay on his back, I finally reach a rock ledge beneath the *gompa* where a young Tibetan appears and asks me in fairly good English what I'm looking for.

"Lama Tsulsterin," I reply, referring to the monk who had been so helpful to my son ten years earlier and given Chris a place to sleep in his house.

"Lama Tsulsterin go to India. Leave this morning," I'm told.

"Oh no," I reply with disappointment at missing Chris's teacher. Then I ask if there's a house where I might stay for the night.

My host tells me that Lama Tsulsterin's wife will undoubtedly allow me to sleep near the fireplace. It is the same location where Chris had spent his nights when he lived in this household. I really don't want to do that, however, because I remember too well Chris describing the solitariness he felt there in a letter about his evenings in the lama's residence:

> Living with a family like this is an incredibly lonely experience. I speak Lhasa Tibetan. That means, when I

talk, they understand me, and when they talk to me, I understand them. But when they speak local dialects among themselves, I don't! So, sitting in a smoky, dark room around a mud-sculpted stove, drinking rice alcohol, rice beer or butter tea, I am lost as to the nature of the lively conversation among the family. So I watch and listen and taste and smell, trying to understand. Is it clearing my mind? Is it confusing it? What do I understand?

I decide to tour the *gompa* and then remain in Lubra until morning. I ask a very old monk for a tour of the *gompa* Chris termed "a power place."

It is, as Chris reported, in good condition. However, the sun has already dropped beyond the distant mountain range. I can see almost nothing of the finely painted murals on the side and rear walls of the monastery. It's disappointing not to view these paintings, but then I remember again what Chris wrote about this dilemma:

> It is important to note that most murals are painted on walls that see little light...One may conclude then...the purpose of the murals is for their spiritual presence alone. As a representation of a deity in any religion, these murals have power. The conception of an inanimate object having a sort of power is not unusual. What is unusual is that there can be power by the sheer existence of that inanimate object, whether or not the image can be seen by a human being.

Again, Chris's observations awe me. To have such depth and insight at such a young age is so unusual.

As I continue through the inside of the *gompa*, I notice that, as in the Sakya Monastery, some of the wall paintings appear to have been the work of very skilled artists, while others are more simplistic. Again, I reflect on Chris's insights on such disparities in the artwork:

> The art one sees in these temples is beautiful, but it's not comparable to the best examples of Tibetan art. Nevertheless, an image of *Sakyamuni* is an image of *Sakyamuni* and has spiritual value no matter the quality of execution.

I am reminded once again by my son that the value of art is not necessarily determined by it's appearance and what it does for me. Chris understood that the spiritual value of the works of art on the temple walls is an intrinsic part of their worth.

It is almost five in the afternoon when the tour is complete. As I emerge from the dark building, the young man who has been watching over me approaches with a friend and communicates bad news.

"Snowstorm come," he announces solemnly. "Tonight much snow."

Looking up the valley, I can see dark clouds appearing in the distance. It's apparent that remaining in Lubra for the night might force me to stay here for several days, perhaps a week if there's a sizable amount of snow.

I decide to leave immediately before the storm arrives. There is still another hour of daylight. Conceivably, I could hike down to the Kali Gandaki riverbed before dark. However, it would take an hour more to turn south and walk the riverside path to Jomsom. Not only would this be impossible in the dark, but I'm too tired to try. After carrying the pack up and down the mountain and riverbed all day, I simply cannot go on another two hours. Not only am I worn out, but my replacement hip is sending a loud and clear message through the age-old signal of pain. The nerve endings around the titanium ball, where my hip joint used to be located, have clearly had enough trekking for the day.

At this moment, my self-appointed interpreter, sensing my desire to leave Lubra before the snow arrives, makes an inviting offer:

"Maybe you go now. My friend will carry pack," the young Tibetan suggests.

His friend, Gira, a small but strong looking youth who probably has not yet reached his twentieth birthday, shows his perfect white teeth, a common characteristic among the Tibetans, and nods his head. If he carries the backpack and we hurry downriver, we might be able to catch the main trail to Jomsom in one hour. By then, however, it would be dark, with still another hour of walking needed before arriving at our destination.

"Too late," I reply.

However, the more I think about spending a week holed up in a cold, smoke-filled room unable to communicate with the Tsulsterin family or anyone else, the more I want to go.

Reaching into his pocket, Gira announces: "I have torch." Indeed, he takes out a flashlight, however slim and worn.

The Yosemite climber, Royal Robbins, once wrote of El Cap: "We were finding reasons not to do it because we were misperceiving it. If you really want to climb it, you start looking for the ways you can do it; if you don't really want to climb it, you start looking for the ways you can't do it."

In this case, I am the one who is trying to escape. I am desperate to leave Lubra immediately and get back to the airport village before the storm hits, even though I know it will be almost impossible to do so before dark. I realize that it's foolish to leave, but I refuse to listen to my inner voice. As the Yosemite climber would suggest, I'm looking for a way to leave, so I am ready to believe a flash-light and a porter will make it feasible.

"Okay, let's go," I say to Gira.

Quickly, we negotiate a fee, which is twice what a porter would make on an ordinary day. However, anything now seems better to me than remaining in Lubra.

Gira smiles briefly, picks up the pack and together we hurry through the village and down to the riverbed. Fortunately, he's good at finding paths through the heavy stones and we move without delay toward our destination, sometimes half-running over level patches of ground when they appear. The absence of the heavy pack on my shoulders is a relief and allows me to travel easily over the rocks.

We move rapidly, although the sky is becoming darker and the path more difficult to see. At one point, we come to one of the streams running through the riverbed and Gira, in the best tradition of Tibetan porters, signals me to hop on his back so he can carry me through the water and spare me the discomfort of walking the rest of the way in wet shoes. Earlier in the day, I would not have considered accepting his offer, but now, tired and desperate to get away, my morality has become more flexible. I hop aboard his incredibly strong back as he splashes through the stream and drops me on the far side with sore but nevertheless dry feet.

We reach the confluence of the Panda Khola and the Kali Gandaki rivers by six. It has taken us one hour, which, I believe, must be a record for that trip despite Chris's claim that it can be done in forty-five minutes.

Now, however, the sun has fallen over the western mountain ridge and darkness is setting in quickly. Without stopping for a rest, we move down the main riverbed as the blasts of cold wind seem to pick up speed and intensity. I put on my down jacket, gloves and wool hat.

After ten minutes of moving toward our destination, the moonless night has made almost everything invisible. I can barely see Gira ahead of me so we stop and he pulls the flashlight from his pocket. He pushes the switch to "on." A dim light flickers for a moment and then goes out. The batteries are dead. It is the final signal that I may have acted in haste. I haven't prepared properly for the trip by making even a minimal check on the flashlight batteries, nor have I listened to my better judgment which clearly stated that leaving Lubra so late in the day with a storm coming was foolish.

That foolishness is now compounded. Not only is there another hour of hiking left under the best of conditions, but now the river itself begins to flow next to the base of a large cliff. This means we must climb several hundred feet above the rushing water along a narrow path that has been cut into the side of the cliff. Before we start up, however, Gira loses the trail, and for the next fifteen minutes we stumble around looking for it. Finally, he calls out, "Hello!" By now all visibility is gone. I can no longer see my feet which seem to be kicking painfully against every stone on the path.

We begin groping our way along the side of the soft mud and rock wall. Five hundred feet below, the Kali Gandaki river is rushing across the stone-filled river bed, ready to finish off any living thing that is still alive after dropping from the edge of the narrow path we're desperately trying to negotiate.

Gira is a few steps ahead of me. I can no longer see him, but, thank God, I can smell him. It's the same smoky smell of burning yak's dung, dried sweat and caked mud that Chris reeked of when I met him at Kennedy Airport years ago after he returned from Nepal. That evening, I politely said nothing of my son's powerful smell, but I had to open the car windows while driving him home. Now I'm feeling grateful for that same smell. It tells me that Gira hasn't yet stepped off the edge with my pack, smashed against the rocks and disappeared into the glacier-fed river far below.

One step forward. Easy. Slide the left foot across the stony path and then ease the right foot sideways again. I'm moving from left to right like a ballet dancer doing a *glissade lentement.* When I try feeling my way with the right hand, I start a minor landslide that almost knocks me off the path. By using my left hand, soon scratched and bleeding, the rocks tumble behind me.

Arduously, we move another few feet along the trail. The sound of the rushing water far below seems to get louder, more menacing. I slide to the right another few inches. My weight holds. I move my left foot over and stand quietly for a moment. This is a serious problem. There is no rope from my harness to a "bomber" anchor. Ivano is not here, braced to arrest my fall, nor can I rely on the strength and technical knowledge of Jud who is also absent to solve the problem of getting out of this predicament without a fatal plunge into the river below.

I'm lost and stuck on a soft cliff wall in the Himalayas on a moonless night with a snowstorm approaching. There's no way of retreating. I have no idea how to proceed without simply stepping forward and hoping my foot hits the ground instead of the empty space a few inches away.

Now I know the desperation Chris must have felt when he was climbing El Capitan and thought he had forgotten to bring the "angles" necessary for going up the next ledge. The same sweat-producing feeling of fear he described has raised my adrenaline level, pushed fatigue aside, creating energy for one more step forward, and then another.

Slowly I proceed, right foot sliding sideways, left foot dragging across the pebbles until my full body weight is equally shifted on both legs and my left hand is moving gently along the wall of the cliff. I repeat the process. Again and again. Suddenly it occurs to me that we could stay on the ledge and bivouac for the night. After all, I have a sleeping bag in the backpack. Trying to sleep on a narrow rock trail for one night is better than getting killed. Then I remember Gira has no camping gear. He would freeze by morning. We have no choice but to go on.

Despite the necessity of concentrating solely on the situation at hand, my mind flashes for an instant on the thought that finally I'm learning about a new aspect of climbing mountains. This is the focused experience which Tim Noonan spoke about in Yosemite several months earlier when he said: "Because if you ever learn how to focus, if you can get yourself into the zone I'm talking about, then a whole lot of other things start happening. Experiences take place that can really change your life."

Tonight, I'm totally concentrated, completely aware of each movement of my feet, my hands, my fingers. I'm in the zone. Now I have time to consider the possibility of falling. The other mishaps of the past year happened so fast I had no time for reflection. Slipping into a crevasse in the French Alps took place so quickly I didn't have even a second to reflect on the possibility of dying in a tomb of ice. Sliding out of control on Pisang Peak was over before

I could consider the consequences of a 2,000-foot fall. Here in this windswept cocoon of darkness, however, there is plenty of time to reflect on the possibility of a fatal drop into the Kali Gandaki river.

How ironic! This morning, I thought my journey was finished, that danger and discomfort were over with. Now I'm trapped on a narrow foot path which has none of the lofty goals associated with a high-altitude climb. This moment is not remotely related to conquering a mountain or achieving success on a major summit. I'm not trying to top out on anything! Nevertheless, there is a very good possibility that I'm going to lose my life by slipping off a simple trail which trekkers use every day.

I wonder what the meaning of this is. It would have been so easy to walk down the river to Jomsom and have a fine dinner and a good sleep before flying back to Kathmandu in the morning. Why did I decide to chance hiking in a storm when I could have stayed in the lama's house where it was at least safe and warm?

Again I caress the wet mud and stone of the cliff with my left hand to maintain a safe proximity to the wall. Then I move one more step forward, shift weight and drag the left foot forward. Repeat. The minutes of traversing through the pitch black night turns to an hour.

Gira calls through the darkness: "Take rest now."

I stop and simply stand along the wall. There is no place to sit. The wind is blowing harder now and the temperature is dropping fast. Fortunately, the snow has yet to arrive.

Then I recall the strange event of the early afternoon when the recorder seemed to turn itself on and I heard the words of Tom Frost: *If you're climbing for the right reasons and you're ready to listen, you'll hear your inner voice. The one can cost you your life, the other can save you.*

Suddenly, like a jagged flash of lightning across a dark summer sky, the realization hits me that the recording this afternoon was not a coincidence. Perhaps the tape which so miraculously started playing as I trekked up the desolate riverbed contained more than just a theory about climbing mountains safely.

Perhaps it was offering me a clue to the goal I've been trying to achieve for so long; the message which only an inner voice can deliver.

Until now, I've been looking for solutions to questions which have no answers. *Why did Chris choose to move toward high-risk sports? Why was he ascending an icefall at the moment it collapsed? Why do people climb mountains? Why do some lose their lives and others live on?*

What mistaken and arrogant notion prompted me to think that at the top of Pisang Peak I would find the answers to these questions? I was indeed engaged in the Faustian bargain which Victoria accused me of in Bangkok. Why should I discover the meaning of the basic questions about existence which have baffled human beings throughout the ages simply by climbing a mountain? Did I expect to find a stone tablet with an explanation of the mysteries of life and death in five easy lessons lying on the snow-covered summit?

Climb mountains for the wrong reasons and all you get is confusion! Ask the wrong questions and you get the wrong answers!

More devastating, however, has been my assumption that the inner voice is only a warning bell about climbing mountains, a spokesman for ambition, for temporary safety and welfare rather than the message of an inner knowledge which can lead to comprehension and acceptance of what all who I have met on my journey have told me. *If you really loved your son, then you still do even if he's not here anymore. That kind of love can be sustaining and meaningful as long as you live,* Victoria told me. *We have to understand how much we've been blessed by knowing the kinds of people these fine young men of ours really were. And only when we get to that stage can we really derive any kind of joy from our lives without them. And I think that if my Raymond or your Chris were to speak to us now, that is what they would want,* Guy Cachat told me in Chamonix.

Abruptly, I return to the present when Gira calls out to move forward again. As we proceed, a strange serenity replaces the fear and doubt I was experiencing on this trek. Suddenly, I know we're going to get off this cliff safely. We just have to keep going, feeling our way up the trail and then slowly, step by step, continue until the path descends once more to the riverbed.

In another few minutes, we see the lights of the airport village. Gira calls out: "Jomsom, Jomsom! See light!"

"Yes, I can see the lights but we're not there yet," I respond. Too many nights of waiting for fully lit helicopters in Vietnam have taught me that lights shining through darkness can be miles away, even though they appear to be close. We keep stumbling along in the dark. We can't do anything else. Finally we make out the dim stone houses of Jomsom in front of us. Though it's tempered by exhaustion, I am feeling joyful to finally reach our destination. We find a small inn and, after paying Gira his porter fees, I enter a cold room and light the candle left on the night table. Then I roll out the sleeping bag onto the hard bed and take a few Motrin pills, wanting nothing more than to drift off. For several minutes, I try to sleep. But thoughts about this whole trip are beginning to rush through my head like a spring brushfire.

At last the mystery is unveiling. It took a muddy

cliff above the river on a blue-black night to expose the truth I've been looking for during the past year. The time has come to stop searching and start listening.

Acceptance. Appreciation. Love that transcends even death. These are the words of the inner voice that now speaks to me with a stunning clarity and precision.

I know now there is no blame to be placed on the son who climbed the mountain nor even the father who might have inspired in him a love for the dance of danger or passed on the gene for living on the edge. The inner voice which is now speaking to me through the cold and windy night is clear and unequivocal: *If you really loved the person who is now gone, don't confuse yourself by trying to find out why it happened or who should be blamed. Nor will reaching the summit of Pisang Peak or any other mountain give you the answer. And if your son went a mountain too far by soloing an El Capitan before he was ready or leading a pitch on a frozen waterfall in warming weather, allow yourself to feel pride in his aspirations and deeds. Indulge in a bit of self-congratulation that you were the father of someone who, like Thoreau, conducted his life so that in the end he would not have to say when it came time to die, that he had not lived.*

As for the Rinpoche, I know now he was right after all. Chris is not gone. Whether he has taken on the physical body of a reincarnated young boy is not the important issue. The real truth, the one that can be kicked and felt and smelled, is not so much that there is a rebirth of a particular person, but rather the perpetuation of the more pervasive truth that love extends beyond the temporary absence or even the death of those we love. The Rinpoche's words come back again: *Your son is not lost. Death is only another stage in the endless cycle of our lives. When you learn that, you will understand the meaning of what happened.*

As the small candle on the night stand flickers from the pane-rattling breeze rushing down the narrow street outside, the questions I have asked so often since I first learned that my son died are beginning to mold themselves into answers. Comprehension is slowly evolving from the endless confusion of the past year. The pain is disappearing now and sleep arrives along with the satisfaction of knowing that in the morning, if all goes well, I'll be able to catch a flight back to Kathmandu and, a few days later, head for home via one last stop in Canada where Chris's and my final farewell took place less than a year ago...A farewell I have now begun to understand was only a passing moment in time.

18
chapter

Reunion

Living out the qualities of someone no longer with us,
who has inspired us with the kind of person they were,
is a worthy endeavor.

Reverend Frank Hall, Minister
Unitarian Church, Westport, Connecticut

It's early December when I arrive at Vancouver's steel and glass airport in British Columbia where Chris and I began our last reunion less than a year ago. It was here in this western Canadian city that he and his brother, Justin, and I met to begin a week of travel and whale-watching. The weather has turned cold now and the distant mountain peaks of Vancouver Island are covered with snow. Now the act of shuffling slowly out to the sidewalk, where the three of us laughed and hugged each other such a short time ago, is a painful yet necessary step in closing the circle and ending my journey.

A taxi deposits me at the colorful Granville Island market in the heart of Vancouver where we went that first day in early September to stock up on smoked salmon, cheese, dried apricots, candy bars and a bottle of wine. The tourists are gone now and only the local population is left to purchase the fresh vegetables, apples, fish, meats and wide varieties of other foods. Crafts, too, are sold in colorful kiosks throughout the waterfront area.

That day, when my two sons met me at the airport in Vancouver after my flight from New York, was a happy one for all of us. The prospect of spending a week with the two boys, plus the fact that my Civil War play, *Battle Cry of Freedom*, which I had just finished casting in New York, would soon begin a tour of the United States, had me in fine spirits as we all jumped into Chris's old pickup and headed for the market before catching the ferry to Victoria where we planned to spend our first night.

Chris, too, was excited. He had managed to convince the Forestry Department that he could do his job for them by working six months a year in Portland, Oregon. As soon as the paperwork went through, he would begin this new position with the inherent freedom that the arrangement implied. Justin, too, was feeling good about his first full-time job as a program director with the YMCA in a small town in North Carolina. We joked and enjoyed each other's company on the short ferry ride to Vancouver Island and as we drove to the beautiful city of Victoria, we were blissfully unaware that three months later our joy-filled world would crash.

Particularly for Chris and me, the six days together consisted of one long conversation. For hours, we discussed every subject imaginable: politics, religion, careers, women, sports and anything else that came to mind. If there was one thing totally new and even exciting for me, it was how much we were in agreement. Justin would sometimes join us, but his interests are more centered on people, though he did say later he was envious of the intense talk that was constantly taking place around him. It had been a long time since Chris and I had time and opportunity to be with each other. Yet, during that week, as we sat in bars, restaurants, on the oak benches of the ferry or stood at the aft deck of the whale-watching boat, we verbalized our thoughts with the candor and confidence of old friends who had rediscovered each other. In fact, it seemed that we were both new people. The earlier dissension of his teenaged years, the previous competition between father and son were gone. Chris no longer seemed to dismiss my unsolicited advice while I was genuinely impressed with his analysis of people, politics and even his own career. An acceptance of each other's views, even a striking similarity of opinions, had taken place.

It reminded me of the final scene in Turgenev's *Fathers and Sons* in which the Russian author writes of the young son, Arkady, who has finally come home to accept the responsibilities of running the family estate and discover how close he and his father have become. "We must draw close to one another now, and learn to know each other thoroughly, mustn't we?" Arkady's father says as he invites the once rebellious son to stay and help with the farm. "Of course," the son answers in a surprising reversal from his former disdain of his father's life. Turgenev illustrates his conviction that reconciliation and reunion between father and son is in accordance with the mainstream of humanity. It is the ultimate act of acceptance and harmony.

Much has happened in the interval since Chris and I met that last time. As I stroll through the marketplace, I try once more to capture the joy of that first afternoon when we three were all together. A slight wind is skipping off the water. A woman with long dark hair nods briefly when I order a box of smoked salmon. It is the same fish

Chris, Justin and I bought that day before catching the ferry. We decided to have a "taste" and consequently the salmon was eaten before the boat blew its whistle and churned out of the harbor across the straits of Georgia toward the genteel city of Victoria.

As I wait for my order, I remember that first evening when the three of us had dinner on a small quay overlooking the Inner Harbor. Sailboats were coming in from the sea to dock for the night , while behind us, the slanted towers of the famous Empress Hotel were silhouetted against the cool night.

"Are you excited about your new job, Chris?" I asked.

"Sort of," he replied. "The problem is that I'm not sure this is really what I should be doing."

"It's tough for your generation," I responded. "You have so many choices. When I finished college, they still had the military draft in effect. Every young guy had to go into the service. So, we went into the Army for two years...and by then most of us knew what we didn't want to do and what we wanted to do."

Chris laughed: "Maybe that's what I should do, join the Army."

"Actually, when you think about it, you two belong to one of the few generations in American history without a war to fight in. You don't really have to do anything. Your choices are unlimited and that has got to be confusing."

"So that's why we climb. It's a substitute experience," Justin said.

"Good point," I replied. "Climbing has a lot of the same attributes as war. Skill, danger, hardship. Win. Lose. Maybe the next time we think of declaring war against a country, we should just challenge them to a climbing contest."

That night, the three of us stayed in a small hotel near the harbor where Chris told us of a climb he had undertaken on El Capitan in Yosemite National Park a month earlier.

He had met a girl by the name of Heidi Wirtz from Crested Butte, Colorado who was looking for a climbing companion. Chris agreed to go with her and so they started up the first pitch early, before the sun had fully spread its light across the rock wall. They climbed steadily until about two in the afternoon when suddenly dark clouds began to gather on the horizon. There was little they could do but keep going. In another hour, a hail storm hit with full force. Chris and Heidi ducked into a small ledge where there was just enough room to move around so they could wait out the bad weather. The storm did not abate, however, and for the next two days they were stuck on the ledge. They talked, they tried to sleep and while they waited, they read poetry to each other.

"I reached into my bivy sack and found a book of poetry called *Turtle Island* by the Pulitzer Prize winning poet, Gary Snyder," Chris said. "Mom sent me the book a couple of weeks earlier. Anyway, Heidi read a poem called 'Bedrock.'"

Snowmelt pond, warm granite
we make camp
no thought of finding more
and leave our minds to the wind.

"That pretty much summed up our situation," Chris said.

"It must have been pretty boring," Justin said.

The following morning, wanting to play tennis, we trudged up to Beacon Hill park where one-hundred-year-old hybrid rhododendrons and thousands of other flowers decorate the Fountain Lake area. Chris and Justin played a fiercely competitive match, which I watched with pride. Perhaps that should have rung a warning bell. Some say the gods have a way of expressing their jealousy with unusual cruelty when a man is too prideful of his sons.

The prophet Abraham learned that lesson when God ordered him, in a difficult test of devotion, to, "Take your son, your only son Isaac, whom you love, and go to the land of Moriah and offer him there as a burnt offering." Soon I, too, would have to make such a sacrifice, although unlike the case of Abraham, to whom an angel appeared at the last minute, telling him to spare the boy, I would experience no last-minute reprieve.

That afternoon, we left Victoria and started up the rugged coastline of Vancouver Island where Chris had made reservations on the whale-watching boat. As we drove out of Victoria in the old pickup, with Justin squeezed in the middle of the seat, Chris handed me the reprint of an article he had written for *Bike Magazine* which had been published that summer.

"They paid me a hundred and fifty dollars for it," he said proudly.

The article was titled, "Avoid the 'Made in China' Label." Chris had written about the prospect of buying inexpensive Chinese goods. In the piece, Chris noted his experience at almost buying a titanium mountain bike until he examined it carefully and realized it was a cheaply manufactured Chinese import with a lot of flaws. After describing his initial feeling of outrage, he wrote: "But then I started wondering why the Chinese factory workers who built the frames should care. Do any of them get to own and ride their own bikes? Do they earn any more money welding expensive bike frames than they would at the factory across the street making those 99-cent flip-flops? No, they probably wouldn't, which seems to explain their apparent apathy, and who could blame them?"

The article reflected not only his outrage at China's human rights record, but also his disgust with that country's annexation of Tibet, of which he was so painfully aware because of his year with the Tibetan community in Nepal.

"I suspect that if all this is going to change, it will be economics that do it," I said, referring to Chris's article.

"Yeah, politics is an anachronism," he replied. "The political process is nothing more than a rubber stamp for what's happening in the money markets."

"Imagine what would happen if we eliminated all the state legislatures in the country," I stated.

"Nothing. It wouldn't affect anyone or anything," he said.

"You're probably right," I answered. "Although a lot of well-paid lobbyists would be out of work."

After a long drive along the rugged coastline of Vancouver Island, we arrived at a small tourist lodge near the Johnstone Straits where several pods of whales live year round, gobbling up salmon and surfacing regularly for air to the delight of visitors like us.

The next morning, we boarded the whale-watching boat in high spirits. For several hours we saw nothing, though the captain was constantly on his radio communicating with other boats who were also looking for the black and white whales. Chris and I sat on a bench at the front of the boat while Justin watched for whales next to the captain on the observation deck.

"What kind of apartment would you like to have when you move to Portland?" I asked.

"None at all. I'd like to have a van and live in that," Chris responded.

"That could be pretty uncomfortable," I answered.

"I know that. But what I'd like to do is live a totally minimalist kind of life. You know, no frills. No unnecessary possessions. Owning things, buying things...it's all such a waste of time and energy."

At this point, I reminded him that he was probably still upset about losing all his possessions which had been stored in a barn that burned to the ground several years earlier.

"That taught me a lesson," Chris answered. "I lost everything I really valued. My books. A lot of stuff I wrote in college. I also had a Tibetan painting which I had spent months painting. The *thanka* was just burned up along with everything else. After that, I decided I wouldn't place value on material things anymore. In fact, I wouldn't even own anything that wasn't absolutely necessary for survival."

"That's understandable, Chris, but it will be hard to live that way, particularly if you get married and have a family."

Chris looked out across the water for a moment and then nodded. "I know. But for now, I want to live as simply as I can."

The conversation ended as the captain announced the presence of whales not far from our location. In a few minutes, the leviathans were leaping out of the water next to the boat. As we crowded to the starboard side to watch, the captain turned up his underwater sonar radio so the wild cries of the highly communicative mammals could be heard as they raced through the water.

"Fantastic!" Chris called to Justin, as we all watched the long-awaited spectacle.

As evening darkness begins to slide across the Vancouver skyline, I continue to wander around the marketplace. The river has turned a silky black now and the small taxi boats are no longer plying their way back and forth between the island and the mainland. Watching the silent aqueous mass flow unperturbed toward the sea, I'm reminded of the Zen teaching that suggests we should develop a state of mind like the river. People throw all sorts of things into the water, but it remains untroubled, flowing peacefully to its destination, absorbing the garbage and flotsam without comment, intent only on attaining its goal.

I'm not so sure it was a good idea coming here alone, with no one with whom I can talk. Yet the isolation forces me to ponder and form some kind of evaluation of my journey. What have I discovered? Has it been worthwhile, attending funerals in Chamonix, spending star-filled nights camping on a rock ledge in Yosemite, undertaking arduous climbs up and down the windswept Himalayan mountains, near-death mishaps on Pisang Peak and the Aiguille du Midi? Has there been a resolution to the endless thinking and talking and brushing away of tears in order to learn and understand the meaning of all that has taken place? What happens now that my own journey to understand my son has ended? Chris's own words analyzing his solo of El Capitan come back:

> I had indeed taught myself volumes about the art of climbing big walls. What I hadn't predicted, however, were the most important lessons climbing alone would

bring: Learning to listen, learning patience and having confidence in one's own strengths and abilities.

If Chris had learned so much from his climbing and his journeys to Nepal and the French Alps, what have I learned from mine? Where do I go from here? I think back on the long and dangerous trek in the dark night above the Kali Gandaki and realize that was the moment of truth. The moment when I knew Chris would always be a spiritual presence in my life and when I understood the dance of the father-son molecules, continuously pushing us onward to the next mountain. That was when I finally understood how similar our rhythms have been as each of us moved along the winding, twisting river of our individual lives. Then, ultimately, I experienced that flash of sudden understanding of what the inner voice had been telling me throughout the trip: Learn to maintain your love for that person who is gone in a pure and unrestricted way, without the need for his physical presence. Chris is a part of me and my life, whether alive or dead, and always will be. I know that now.

The shops are beginning to close down. Young girls and old men, middle-aged women and boys hurry to put away their unsold goods and pull down the canvas curtains of their small booths so they can go home for the day.

I take a seat at a small bar next to the river and look out over the sparkling city on the far side. My journey is over. In the morning, I'll fly back to New York. The long Civil War novel, the one that was postponed for a year so I could make this trip, is waiting to be finished. The dentist needs to be paid and another appointment made. The car insurance will be due. My daughter Alexandra is coming for the holidays with her husband and their two little girls. I wonder what I should get for Justin's Christmas present.

A waiter stops to ask if I want something and on a sudden impulse I order a martini, something strong that will have some kick to it. Then, I take a pen from my pocket and begin to write a message on a series of paper napkins without really knowing what I have in mind. The words begin to take shape on the soft tissue:

Dear Chris,

This trip is just about finished now. I've taken a long journey in order to understand what happened to you. In the beginning, I was really angry about what happened, your climbing that ice wall and getting caught in an avalanche. I blamed you and I blamed myself. Losing you seemed so pointless, so wasteful. So I decided to take up climbing to see if I could understand why you were taken away.

I even tried to climb Pisang Peak, which stopped you twice when you were almost at the top. The same thing happened to me, Chris. I couldn't get through the wind and snow of that last *couloir* below the summit.

It was really disappointing. Losing never came easy to either one of us, did it? Then something happened on the way back from Lubra that changed everything and enabled me to understand all this. I learned that if I can preserve my memory of your presence and maintain my love for you, then you're not really gone. To some people, that may sound obvious or even simplistic, but it's a very difficult sensibility for a grieving parent to achieve, a very distant destination to which a bereaved father or mother must travel. My journey, in your shadow, has helped me to achieve that sensibility and arrive at that destination.

You see, I had to learn that what you did everyone must do in order to have a meaningful life. You went a mountain too far. That's always dangerous. But, Chris, I think we all have to do that in our own way. I'm not saying each of us must actually climb a mountain or solo a rock wall. What I'm talking about we can do at home in our own room, in an office or a church, anywhere really. The important lesson you've taught me and a lot of other people who knew you is that we each have to search for what our mountain is and then, as you would say, "Go for it."

I met a Buddhist Rinpoche in Nepal who suggested that you've been reincarnated into another life. I'd like to believe that and I hope it's true. What matters to me and what I do know for sure is that your determination to live life to its fullest is a philosophy that will continually be reincarnated and will go on living a long time for me and a lot of other people who knew you

Anyway, I miss you a lot and I'm thankful for what I've learned from you this year. The hardest task for me has been to appreciate how lucky I've been to know you. Now, I'm trying to maintain my love for you even though you're not here anymore. That's the toughest climb of all. Well, Chris, it's time to go now. I've still got a good bit of living to do, but whatever happens, I want you to know that I'm going to try to keep right on going for that next mountain, just the way you did.

By my second martini, the letter is finished. I don't sign it. Instead, I slowly pick up the napkins and crumble them in my fist. Then I walk outside and over to the edge of the river and throw underhand so the balled paper rises slightly before drifting down toward the dark water. Like a delicate butterfly alighting on a flower, it lands softly and, for a second, rides on top of the glistening current. In a few more seconds, the letter disappears downstream.

I turn and walk across the asphalt street where I can hail a cab. It occurs to me that the mushrooms I've been seeking throughout the night of this long journey have sprouted and are growing in the backyard now. But growth is an ongoing process. The next mountain is waiting to be climbed.

In fact, there's not just one, but several. There's the difficult path of mindfulness the Rinpoche talked about, the necessity of being compassionate and caring. There is also the need to remember what Guy Cachat told me in Chamonix about getting rid of sorrow and anger and instead learning to be grateful for having known Chris. Each of these are like distant mountains filled with unseen crevices and steep pitches and swept by sudden storms and avalanches. Everyone of them is dangerous and filled with hardship, and well...too far.

The sky is dark now and a chill breeze is sweeping the marketplace as I raise my arm toward an oncoming taxi. It shudders to a stop and soon we're speeding through the empty streets toward a hotel for the night. The plane leaves early in the morning and by the next afternoon I'll be back where I started from. Perhaps it will snow before Christmas in New York and the magic of the holiday season will remind me of the days when Chris and I wandered with such happiness through Central Park and the teeming, life-affirming streets of the city. I might even get out my old ice skates and take a few turns around the rink at Rockefeller Center. If I do, I'll be thinking about a small boy by the name of Chris who used to bump into other skaters, knocking them down, because they were all skating the wrong way.

Epilogue

Christopher Purnell's ashes will be placed at the Sakya Monastery in Nepal where he studied and lived during his junior year of college.

Glossary

ANCHOR: Point at which a rope is fixed to the rock.

ARRET: Narrow ridge, frequently covered in snow.

ASCENDERS: Metal clamps which slide up a rope but not down, allowing a climber to walk up a vertical wall or ascend a single rope; another terms for JUMARS.

ATC (AIR TRAFFIC CONTROL): Small device attached to the harness that allows the climber to pass a rope through a small aluminum loop in a controlled manner. While rappelling, the climber can break or slow his descent by pulling his rope against the ATC to prevent the rope from slipping through the loop.

ATRIER: Nylon webbing attached to ASCENDERS (JUMARS) which allows a climber to step up or down as in the use of a ladder.

BELAY: To secure a climber who is above you by controlling the rope. "ON BELAY" is a signal from the 'BELAYER' that a climber is safe to continue climbing.

CAM: Short for CAMMING DEVICE, which can be inserted into a rock crack and easily removed through a spring action release built into the handle. When hooked to the climber's rope, it provides an anchor to protect the climber from falling.

CARABINERS: Loop of metal with a gate on it, like a removable chain link, which is used to attach equipment.

CRAMPONS: Clamp-on, spiked soles which fit onto climbing boots to provide traction in snow and ice.

HARNESS: Clothing worn around the torso to which climbing equipment is attached.

JUMARS: See ASCENDERS

PITON: Spike or wedge driven into rock or an ice surface to serve as a climber's support.

PLACEMENT: Piton or other device inserted into a rock crack and hooked up to the belay rope to prevent the climber from falling.

"PRO": Slang term for climbers' protection, i.e. pitons, cams, etc.

RAPPEL: To descend a cliff or wall by sliding down a rope.

RATING: Number denoting the technical difficulty of a climb.

SLING: Loop of nylon tape which can easily be attached between an anchor and the climber's rope.

TRAVERSE: Climbing horizontally.